This book is dedicated to my biggest influence
and inspiration, my mother Alicia.

Hugo Huerta Marin

PORTRAIT OF AN ARTIST

Conversations
with Trailblazing Creative Women

PRESTEL
Munich · London · New York

INTRODUCTION

For thousands of years, the portrait has served to depict the idols of ancient civilizations—kings, deities, emperors, and heroes—down to dictators, rabble-rousers, colonizers, and those who wielded their power for more dangerous ends. It has been the territory of the sculptor, the painter, and the photographer. Yet the concept of portraiture has evolved its intricate character over time.

I have always been interested in this concept and in how artists have depicted history through portraiture; in the elitism and formality that is historically associated with the portrait, and the question of who should be captured in it. I have always wondered what ancient faces would have looked like in life—what we are today is quite different from what we were a thousand years ago.

Growing up in Mexico City, in a Catholic and conservative society where women are often treated as inferior to men, I was raised by a mother who showed me a different reality, and who—alongside other powerful women leading my way—helped to expand my consciousness. Art is no exception; there are countless female artists whom I look up to and who represent an endless source of inspiration to me. Their work shakes the structures of established belief systems and questions the norms we are conditioned to accept.

Years later, when I moved to New York, I was introduced to the performance artist Marina Abramović and soon afterward I began working with her. After this event, the world as I had understood it no longer existed. Marina broadened my horizons on a personal and intellectual level and made my world immeasurably bigger. One late summer night when we were working in upstate New York, I had a strong desire to take her portrait. I wanted to capture her essence through a lens, but also through her words, in the most candid way possible. The conversational side of that study was more successful than I had ever dared to hope. Out of this experience came the idea of creating portraits of the many other pioneering female artists who have reshaped the creative industries in a significant way.

8

And so I did …

Over the course of seven years and countless journeys, I asked Marina Abramović, Cate Blanchett, Annie Lennox, Miuccia Prada, Anjelica Huston, Carrie Mae Weems, Diane von Fürstenberg, Yoko Ono, Tracey Emin, Catherine Deneuve, Shirin Neshat, Ann Demeulemeester, Tania Bruguera, Rei Kawakubo, Kiki Smith, ORLAN, Julianne Moore, Inez van Lamsweerde, Charlotte Gainsbourg, FKA twigs, Uma Thurman, Isabelle Huppert, Jenny Holzer, Debbie Harry and Agnès Varda if I could take their portraits. I asked to meet them in their homes, studios, theaters, galleries, or places where they felt comfortable, in an attempt to get to know them better. I wanted to ask each of them questions about their oeuvre, but also to pose them a series of the same specific questions in order to get a sense of the differences and similarities between their experiences.

There are traces of every woman I have portrayed in me as an artist, and each of these encounters has left me with an intellectual, emotional, spiritual, and psychological inheritance that I will forever carry with me. At its core, this book is about artists. Artists who broke the mold. Artists who changed the game. Artists who smashed something down in order to build something up. Artists who fractured the boundaries of what art can be. Artists who challenged the status quo. Artists who questioned the thoughts, attitudes, and desires determined by society's dictates. Artists who are representative of a larger community. Artists who opened the path for other artists. Artists whose voices will resonate throughout the future generations. This book is about art, beauty, desire, pain, success, repetition, exposure, fame, shame, death, sex, repulsion, attraction, rebellion, spirituality, race, heritage, gender, and religion. Most of all, this book is a portrait of some of the pioneering artists who I believe helped shape the world as we see it today.

MA

MARINA ABRAMOVIĆ
NEW YORK, 2014

NA

RI

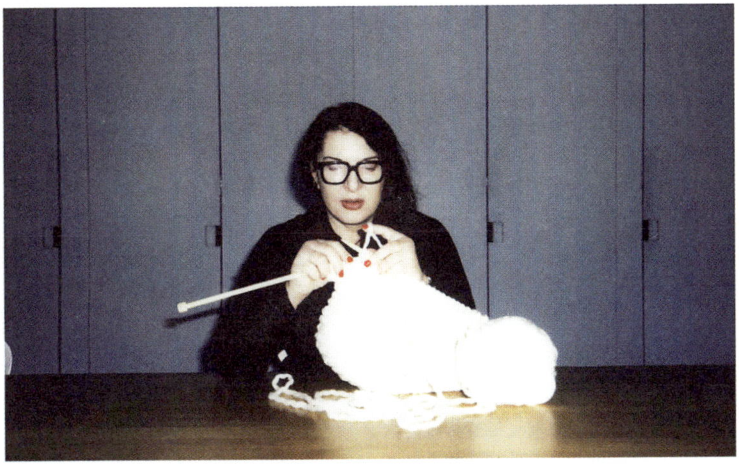

Born in 1946 in Belgrade, Marina Abramović is without question one of the most influential artists of our time. Since the beginning of her career, she has pioneered performance art. Exploring her physical and mental limits, she has withstood pain, exhaustion, and danger in her quest for emotional and spiritual transformation. She was awarded the Golden Lion for Best Artist at the 1997 Venice Biennale. In 2010, Marina had her first major U.S. retrospective and simultaneously performed for over seven hundred hours in *The Artist is Present* at the Museum of Modern Art in New York. She also founded the Marina Abramović Institute (MAI), a platform for immaterial and long-durational work, to create new possibilities for collaboration among thinkers of all fields.

How can I begin to describe Marina? She loves white walls, she collects crystals, and she is fond of buying trees for her house in upstate New York. Perhaps the best way to describe her is through a piece of advice she gave to me once. One time when we were both in Brazil, I was hesitant about participating in an Ayahuasca ceremony. I asked her if she thought I should do it, as I knew that her own experience with Ayahuasca hadn't been pleasant, and instead was Kafkaesque. She replied: "Nobody's life has changed by somebody else's experience." I guess that says it all. Perhaps the best way to describe Marina is that she exposes herself to life.

HUGO HUERTA MARIN:
You are a pioneer of performance art and you brought it into the mainstream. What do you think is the future of performance?

MARINA ABRAMOVIČ:
Performance is one of the most transformative forms of art. It never dies, even if at times it seems it has completely disappeared from art practice. It appears again in very unusual ways,

and in all its splendor. If you look at its history, it's difficult to determine where performance as a medium began. How far back do we look? Do we start with the Surrealists? Dada? The Futurists, or Fluxus and the Happenings? Do we talk about the theater and [Jerzy] Grotowski or Tadeusz Kantor? Do we think about [Joseph] Beuys or Nam June Paik? There are many points of reference where performance has come and gone, but the peak of performance came in the early seventies as a form of conceptual art called Body art. It originated with Vito Acconci's idea that "the body is the place where things happen." That became the sole idea of Body art.

However, in the late seventies, performance eventually lost its force when the act of performing took its toll on artists. They began to prefer working in secluded studios over constantly being in front of the public, which took a lot of energy out of them. This, along with pressure from the art market to produce work that could sell, moved performance artists to explore new mediums such as painting, sculpture, mixed media, videos, and so on. It was interesting to see how these works became figurative, and how certain elements of performance art were still evident in them. Artists like [Sandro] Chia and Francesco Clemente, along with others from that generation, painted literal images that could be looked at as a score of a performance. During the eighties, when many people died in the AIDS outbreak, it seemed as if the entire art population, along with performance art, disappeared. At that time, artists were working mostly with video. After that, performance art began to be a part of the nightclub scene—what you witnessed in all those clubs in London, Paris,

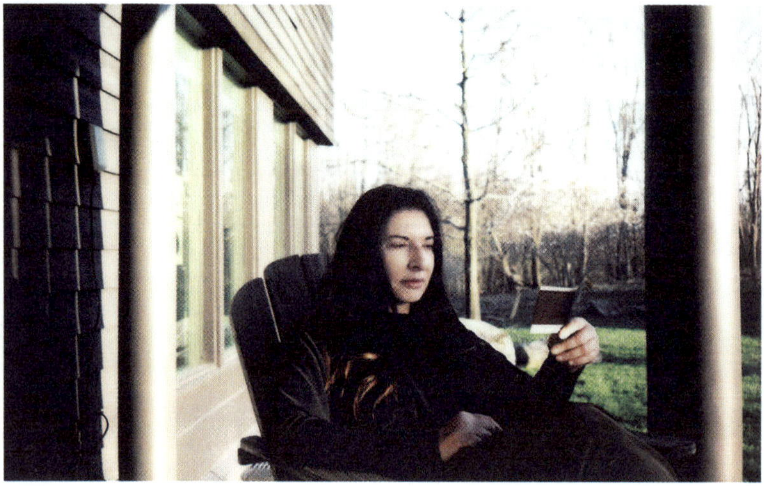

PERFORMANCE IS ONE OF THE MOST TRANSFORMATIVE FORMS OF ART. IT NEVER DIES, EVEN IF AT TIMES IT SEEMS IT HAS COMPLETELY DISAPPEARED FROM ART PRACTICE. IT APPEARS AGAIN IN VERY UNUSUAL WAYS, AND IN ALL ITS SPLENDOR

and Berlin was performance at its full force. One of the leading performance artists from that period — and in my opinion, the most talented — was Leigh Bowery. Bowery invented a completely new style of performance art by incorporating theater, dance, and video back into the performance. Then, Tino Sehgal arrived on the scene. He was a choreographer and a dancer, and he created an entirely new set of rules for performance art that involved very large audiences. He was able to work continuously throughout the different time periods of performance art.

I believe performance art is like a phoenix, dying and being reborn from its own ashes over and over again. Every generation has had a different attitude toward performance art and how it should have pushed the limits more. In my opinion, in the future it will firstly need to deal with the idea of immateriality as a result of the present incredible movement in technology and media. Moreover, I believe that performance art will move toward sound. The noise movement is quite important because to me, it seems greater in its immateriality and deals directly with emotions. I don't know where performance will go. I don't even know what I'm doing right now, or what it should be called. Sometimes we don't have labels for the new things we do, and so we need to take the time to understand what kind of label we should give it. OK, that was a long answer (*laughs*).

HHM: That was a great answer. You have talked about the sacrifices that "the cause" implies. What is the biggest sacrifice you have made for your art?

MA: The biggest sacrifice I have made is to learn how to make art and still be very conscious of my own energy, and realizing that I can't have a normal life, a normal family, or normal things like everyone else does such as children and a fireplace, or knitting sweaters for my grandsons. This is something that I can't have; you just can't have it all. But at the same time, I don't see this as a sacrifice because I always wanted to make art more than anything else.

HHM: Who owns the performance? Is it the artist? Museums? Oral history? Art history?

MA: First of all, I think this question should be directed at any art piece. Performance is like any other work of art. Artists produce the work, but sometimes they can be very selfish in that they don't like to give their work away. For example, they will work on a painting but will never "finish" it because they don't want to separate themselves from their own work. In my opinion, that's not the right attitude. I think that once a work is completed, it doesn't belong to the artist anymore: It belongs to everybody else. An artist must be democratic. Art has its own life that is detached from the creator. Of course, you can say that if a collector or museum buys the work, it therefore belongs to them, but good art is transcendental, and it belongs to everybody.

HHM: Why is pain so important for the artist?

MA: I think pain is important for everybody. Human beings have two general fears in life: the fear of dying and the fear of pain. Artists from every culture and civilization in history have dealt and deal with this in different ways. Pain is the door to perception; it is the door to consciousness. We are so afraid to confront it, but once we do, we are able to understand it, and when we can understand it, we can control it and no longer fear it. When we don't have fear, we are liberated and feel confident within ourselves. We are all inevitably going to die, but if we don't feel fear, we can die with a smile on our faces.

HHM: Do you fear death?

MA: I'd be lying if I said I didn't. At the same time, I have worked hard on overcoming this fear, and I think about it almost every day. At this very moment, sitting here at the Sean Kelly Gallery and giving this interview, I would have to say that I do not fear death. However, if I were in an airplane during turbulence or bad

TO ME, THE MOST RADICAL PERFORMANCE IS ALWAYS THE LAST ONE

weather, I would definitely fear death, because it's an instinct that cannot be controlled. But I've come to terms with it. We are closer to death every single day, and that is very important to remember. That way, we can appreciate life more.

HHM: What has been your most radical performance?

MA: Performance is not easy; I must train my entire body for it. For the performance *The Artist is Present*, to the outside world, I was only sitting in a chair. But that required extensive preparation. I needed to train my body like a NASA program. For an entire year, I didn't eat lunch once, so I wouldn't produce acids in my stomach. Normally, through conditioning, the body learns that it will be fed around lunchtime, and therefore produces acids. If you don't eat lunch, your blood sugar level goes down, and as a result, you can get sick. I spent an entire year drinking water only at night in order to suppress my urge to pee during the day. You must train your body to finish the work. To me, the most radical performance is always the last one. I mean, I'm currently doing *The Generator* and I'm not even performing. Instead, I'm sitting with you and doing an interview. It is radical, you know? If you think about it,

you are here in a commercial gallery where you have to see something, hear something, or buy something. But instead, you can't hear, you can't see, and you can't buy. It's kind of insane, but at the same time, it pushes the limits.
In my world, nothing is impossible. You must relate to yourself and the pure experience: this is important. I don't know if I can go any more radical after this piece. But you never know what might happen (*laughs*). This is what brings you back to your true self.

HHM: In your work, why is the process more important than the result?

MA: Because the result comes anyway. The process is more important because it is a journey wherein you change and don't necessarily see the result right away. The more difficult the journey, the more strength and energy it requires from you, and the more you appreciate it. The journey is to make the change, not the destination.

HHM: Is documentation part of a performance?

MA: Absolutely. In the early seventies, I created art without documenting anything because of the radical belief among artists that documentation was not part of performance art. But later, I changed my mind and realized that, while performance is indeed an art form, documentation is the only reminder in history, apart from the people present in the piece, and it can leave a trace of something that happened in the past. Even the pharaohs demanded documentation and had it engraved on the pyramids. Why shouldn't artists or performance art have the same right?

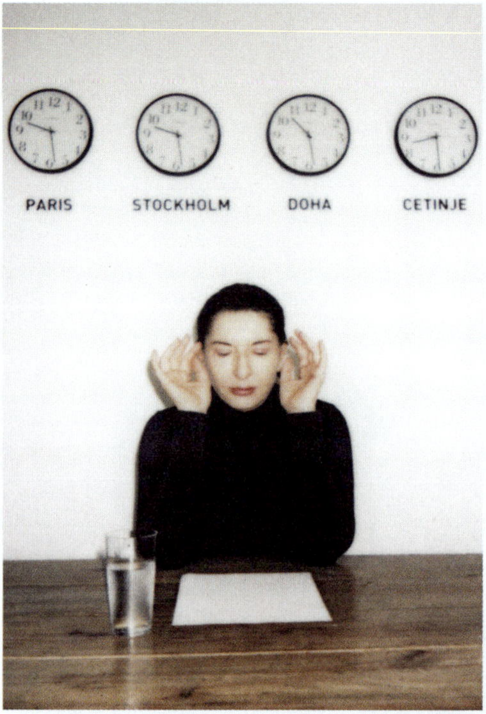
PARIS
STOCKHOLM
DOHA
CETINJE

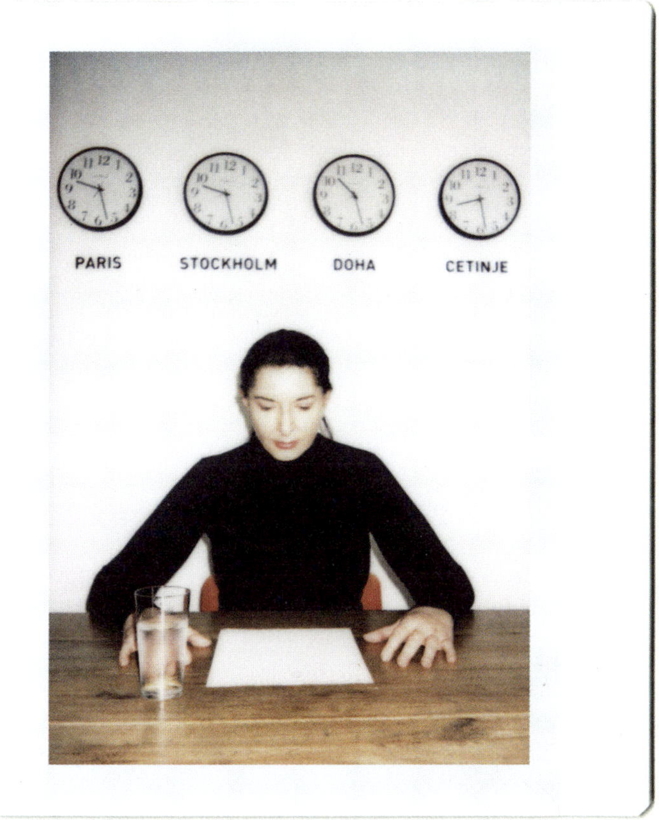
PARIS
STOCKHOLM
DOHA
CETINJE

HHM: You seem to perfectly understand Franz Kafka's statement: "Remain quiet, still and solitary. The world will freely roll in ecstasy at your feet."

MA: I do. That quote is so important because it's true, and it's actually for this reason that *Nightsea Crossing* was created. If you believe that you are just sitting motionless on this chair right now, you are wrong. In reality, you are moving — the earth is spinning and rotating around the sun, as are all the other planets in the solar system. The sun is moving inside the galaxy, and the galaxy, in turn, is moving inside the universe. There is so much movement happening already that if you move within it, you are actually missing the essence of being in one place. Because once you are there, in that moment, all will be revealed to you — that's the effect.

HHM: Artists and philosophers argue that there is a lack of spiritual approach in contemporary art. Do you agree?

MA: I think that good art always has a spiritual component, but there is also a lack of good art to begin with. Every century has had about three or four great artists, and the others just follow in their footsteps. Every great artist, from every generation, from every century, who has created great art and has sent a message that transcended time, has used a spiritual element in their work. Otherwise, the art would not have an impact and would not transcend. The juxtaposition of good work with the spiritual element is essential: It gives you the depth that you need to understand, and future generations can reuse it again and again.

IT IS VERY IMPORTANT THAT ARTISTS CREATE WITHOUT COMPROMISE, WITH HONESTY, AND DO THE BEST THEY POSSIBLY CAN

HHM: Do you think that art should raise philosophical questions?

MA: Art should not just raise philosophical questions, but should raise every possible question. Even if a question doesn't have an answer, it should be asked anyway, because the right questions already contain the answers in themselves. But there are still a few questions that we don't have the answer to: Where does life come from? Why are we on this planet? What is this all for? Who are we? Every generation of artists is constantly trying to answer these questions through their work, with more or less success, but in the end, we still don't have a definitive answer to any of these questions: We are absolutely in the dark.

HHM: Will there be a form of legacy left for the young performance artists of the future?

MA: I don't know. It's not for me to say, nor is it up to them to decide. But it is very important that artists create without compromise, with honesty, and do the best they possibly can. One important thing to remember is to be humble because we don't know what the future will bring. But if I've left some form of legacy behind, that means my entire life was worth it.

HHM: The concept of beauty is crucial in the history of Western art, and it has been reflected in your work. What is your concept of beauty?

MA: My concept of beauty is definitely not conventional: for example, that the color of a painting needs to match your couch or carpet. My idea of beauty can be disturbing. Beauty can be ugly. Beauty can be found in things that are not symmetrical. Beauty can be decomposition: worms eating flesh. Beauty doesn't have a definition. What is important is what moves you, and sometimes people have a different approach to that. It can simply be a ray of sunlight coming through the dusty window, and you see particles of dust floating in the light. It can be incredibly beautiful, but it's just dust.

HHM: You have travelled extensively. Is there a place you can call home?

MA: No, I don't have a home. I don't have a studio either. I hate studios and believe they are bad for the artist. I think they make artists lazy and redundant. I like to go out and do research. I love to go to places away from civilization where they don't have Coca-Cola or electricity. Those are my favorites! I'm interested in nature, in different cultures, in people who have something to tell us that we don't already know. I expose myself to life and get my ideas that way. I think the planet is my home. If you've travelled as much as I have, you know that once you settle down in a steady place, you become claustrophobic. I would love to go to space and see how the earth looks from there. I believe that nomadic life is the only way to explore and stay curious. I can sleep under a table. I can sleep anywhere. I have traveled around India in third-class trains where I had to sleep standing up, and I loved it. The only place you can truly call home — and one you know better than any other, yet don't know completely — is your own body.

HHM: Is there a place you haven't been to but would like to visit?

MA: There are two places I have always been interested in: Mecca, which you are forbidden to enter if you are not Muslim, and Athos in Greece, which you can only visit if you are a man.

HHM: Why Mecca?

MA: To me, Mecca is such an interesting place because it is absolutely powerful, a "place of power." If you see images of that odd, black structure [the Kaaba], there is constant movement around it, a permanent tornado of human activity, which I find fascinating. The energy never leaves the space, and it is always regenerating itself. Some myths say that inside there is a meteorite, or the remains of an alien spaceship, or knowledge.

HHM: You have said that you don't think of yourself as a feminist. Why?

MA: I think there is a new movement: a new feminism. In my opinion, the word "feminist" has been overused and has resulted in misunderstandings. There are other aspects of the feminine that I find much more interesting. I've been working with shamanism and with Tibetan Buddhism, and when you reach a state of enlightenment, or a state of clarity of the mind, it's interesting how the body becomes more feminine rather than masculine. The change in that energy pattern is very important for men, because their masculine energy sometimes results in hardness and violence. On the other hand, there is more of a balance between nature and spirit in feminine energy, and we are likely to achieve a more spiritual state of mind. So, to develop this feminine side, men must embrace high spirituality. I'm only interested in feminism in the strong connection that femininity has with nature: for instance, the way Planet Earth is perceived as female, and how it is considered a mother. I believe this gives our souls much more clarity. But feminism and how it relates to the idea of division between the sexes — I'm not interested in that. I believe it is important to understand the male aspect and the female aspect in relation to spirituality, as both men and women possess feminine and masculine energies.

HHM: Do you believe in art, or do you believe in artists?

MA: Neither. I believe in human beings, no matter the profession. Human beings have so much potential. I don't care if you are an artist, a shoemaker, or a street cleaner. What's important is understanding who you are.

HHM: What are your thoughts on the rise of the artist as celebrity?

MA: It is a side effect; it comes as a result of your work. It's important not be attached to it, but rather to be aware that it comes and goes. You should take the best of it and create a platform so you can be heard. As a result, your work can have a deeper influence on people. As a celebrity, you have power, but that power can be very dangerous and can destroy you. The negative aspect is that the people who were initially fond of you and your work begin to hate you because you've become a rock star — when in reality, they were the ones who put you in that position (*laughs*). For instance, you might end up being criticized for working with a fashion designer. I find this negativity interesting; I believe they want to see you suffer and struggle. I couldn't pay my electricity bill until I was fifty, but now I can.

HHM: At what point in your career did you feel like you were a successful artist?

MA: The moment when I was featured in *Sex and the City*. With my permission, an actress portrayed me on the show. It was at that moment that I knew I would become part of the mass culture. The day after the show aired, I went to an expensive vegetable store near my house in Amsterdam. They had delicious strawberries, but they were so expensive. I almost never went there — because I never had any money in those days — and the sales lady, who knew me from before, looked at me and said: "Oh! Please take these strawberries for free. We saw you on *Sex and the City*!" And I remember thinking, "Wow! This really works!" (*laughs*).

HHM: (*laughs*) Do you worry about being overexposed?

MA: Yes. It's really hard, especially now when there is so much work to do. Being exposed also has to do with the energy you are projecting. There are moments when I'm fine and I have energy, but there are other moments when I am really low on energy, empty. That can be dangerous because the work suffers as a result. That reminds me of something my old teacher once told me; that we should learn "holy selfishness," which is a very good term. I asked him what it meant and he replied: "You have to withdraw from everything in order to rebuild your energy." You can shine like the sun, but if you don't have that kind of energy, you are like a black hole sucking everything in, and that can be lethal.

HHM: What inspires you the most?

MA: Nature. It is definitely something that we have to spend more time with, by going to unpopulated landscapes, waterfalls, rock formations, mountains, volcanoes. Oh! I love volcanoes. I could just sit and watch them while they erupt for hours. You can understand things from life by just sitting and watching. You can have thousands of sensations just by looking at the night skies.

HHM: Do you have any recurring dreams?

MA: Not anymore. I used to have a strange one: There were people inside a house in the forest, and I had just gotten back from a very long trip. I arrived at the house to find a big celebration, and everyone was happy. It seemed like a permanent party where I recognized every single person — but only in the dream and not in reality. It was a recurring dream, but one detail that changed is that I would arrive at the house from a different place each time. Eventually, I stopped dreaming it for a long time, but then I had the dream once more. This time, however, when I arrived at the house, everyone had grey hair and looked very old. After that, I never had the dream again.

HHM: What are your thoughts on the big international art exhibitions such as documenta or the Venice Biennale?

MA: The big group exhibitions worked in the seventies, but I don't think they work anymore. In my opinion, everybody is tired of the big biennales, big art fairs, big exhibitions. I think people are looking for something different, and I am trying to figure out what that could be. In my opinion, one of the most important exhibitions has always been documenta as opposed to any biennale. Biennales happen every two years, and documenta happens every five. Five years is a good period of time within which something can happen and when artists can create new work. Two years is definitely not enough. Artists need time, just as a good wine needs time to mature.

HHM: What is the most honest thing you can say about yourself?

MA: I'm not fake. I'm kind of a real thing (*laughs*). When I'm tired, I am tired. When I'm desperate, I'm desperate. When I am sad, I'm sad. I don't pretend to be somebody else. I am who I am.

C

A T

E

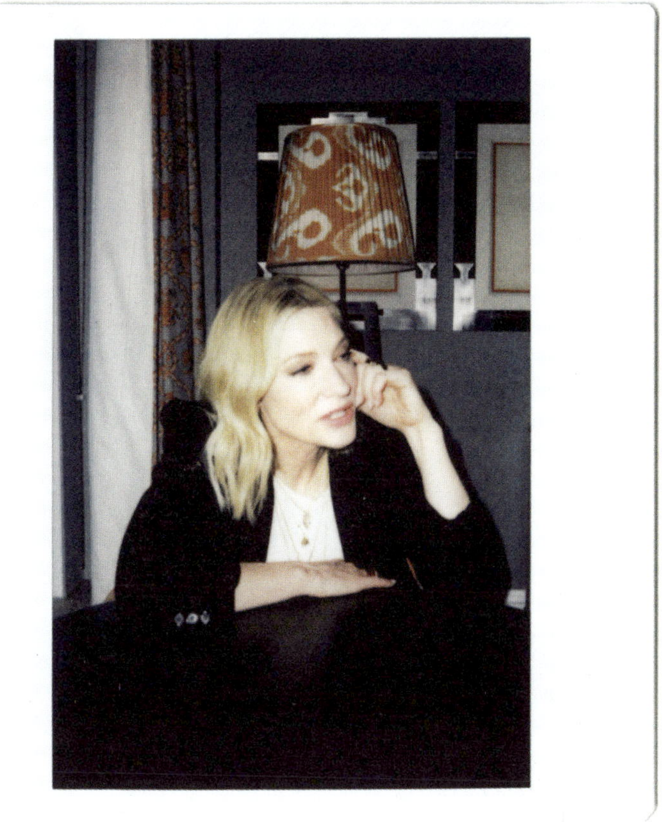

CATE BLANCHETT

NEW YORK, 2018

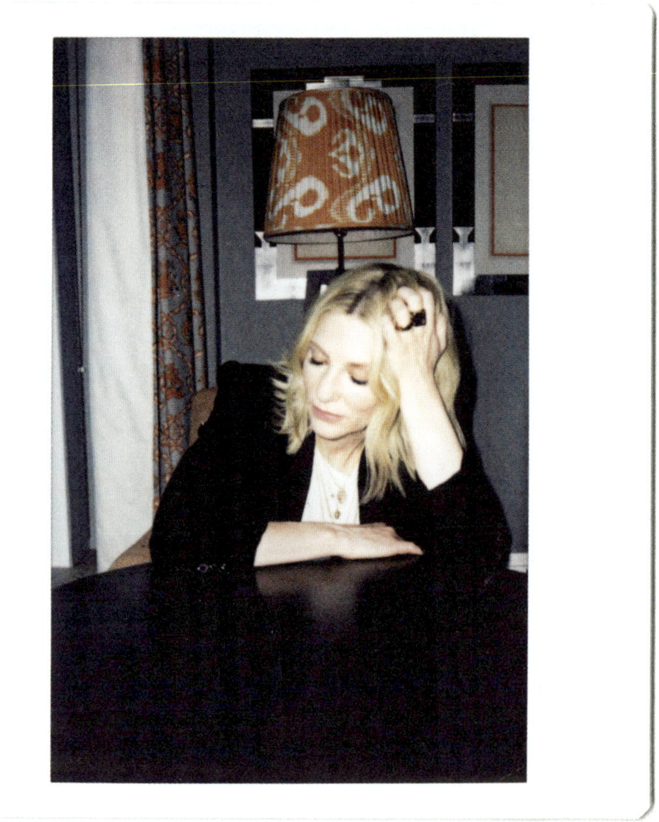

Cate Blanchett is an Australian actor, producer, humanitarian, and dedicated member of the arts community. She also holds Honorary Doctorates of Letters from the University of New South Wales, the University of Sydney, and Macquarie University. Cate Blanchett is equally accomplished and celebrated on the stage, having led the Sydney Theatre Company as co-Artistic Director and CEO for six years alongside Andrew Upton. Her countless extraordinary film performances have garnered her three BAFTAs, two Academy Awards, and three Golden Globes.

It was shortly after 4 p.m. on a hot May afternoon and I was waiting for Cate Blanchett to arrive at the Whitby Hotel in New York. I am not usually star-struck, but hearing Cate's Marlene Dietrichesque voice in the hallway made my hands sweat for a second. She was lovely, sharp, and forthcoming. She also turned out to be the sort of person who spices up conversations with so many intellectual references that it was sometimes challenging to keep up, yet there was nothing arrogant about the way she discussed artists, writers, playwrights, and directors she likes. She is a rare and unique artist whose talent and convictions enrich both screen and stage. She has played Katharine Hepburn. She has played Bob Dylan. She has played both a homeless man and the Queen of England. In person, Cate still retains an ethereal quality that is rare in this current fast-fame-obsessed era.

CATE BLANCHETT:
I was looking into that building before (*points out the window*). Is there grass in there? It reminds me of an installation I saw where there was a whole garden inside a room. You stood in this contained expanse … the experience was tranquil and beautiful but somehow full of anxiety.

HUGO HUERTA MARIN:
It is abandoned. It is visually powerful.

CB: I love that. You don't see much abandoned in Manhattan anymore. Every inch is already taken, claimed.

HHM: I am curious to know more about some of your influences.

CB: OK. How do we do this?

HHM: I wanted to know what makes a good script or an interesting project for you?

CB: Well, it depends. If you're talking about film, I have read some incredible screenplays that have made worthwhile films. But for me, ultimately, it's the quality of conversation. Whom are you going to be in dialogue with? Whom are you responding to? Who is looking down the lens? Who completes the atmosphere? Whom you are performing opposite is particularly important on stage because theatre deals so much with those moments of suspension between people. That's why I love dance—it's the moment when someone, something, lifts off. In film, it's the moment when someone is presented with a choice and you watch them winding it up before they land and make a decision. The bare bones of the story are really important to me. The character is totally immaterial and secondary, so it has never been an issue for me—the size of a role or whatever. In the end, if the story is interesting and the other people whom I am around are interesting to work with—and I have been lucky enough to work with some very interesting people—then I'm hooked.

HHM: In all of film history, who do you wish would have directed you?

CB: Ingmar Bergman, I would have to say.

HHM: I once read that David Lynch's cinematic style is inspired by Francis Bacon's paintings. How do you think art influences film?

CB: I can see that … It's a distillation of influences, isn't it? We are talking about the moving image, but a still frame of a movie can be an extraordinary painting. I mean, look at Richard Prince. But, there is a cross-referencing between the moving image and the still image. Personally, I never know where the moment of connection or inspiration is going to come from. Frequently, it comes from visual imagery, or sometimes from listening to John Cage, [Franz] Schubert, or Laurie Anderson, the sound of a storm — something that will set your brain and your heart racing. I remember talking independently to Katie Mitchell, who is a wonderful theatre director, and to Liv Ullmann, who each introduced me to a Danish painter called [Vilhelm] Hammershøi. They talked about his influences on them, the way he would set up a frame, and how he rarely painted figures from the front. Instead, he would paint rooms with doorways through which you'd see other doorways, and then you'd see a space with a lightwell and a person on top. It was all about how and where you placed the person within that frame.

HHM: That's interesting. I once read that Caravaggio invented Hollywood lighting while incorporating shadows into his paintings.

CB: Quite possibly. His sense of directional but emotional light was, is, extraordinary. Shadows are wildly exciting places. I am really interested in theater in found spaces, but also in what people conceive to be conservative theater, which happens in a proscenium arch because a proscenium arch is a framing device. So I find it fascinating what someone being *Upstage Left* as opposed to *Downstage Right* means, and what *Center Stage* means. I've learned a lot about the intersection between theater and film through working in the proscenium arch.

HHM: Would that be the main intersection between working in theater and film?

CB: Well, in the proscenium arch, you have a big, huge framing device in which you move bodies in space, and people often say, "Oh! You know you have to make yourself much smaller when you work in film, theater is so exaggerated." But the thing is, I find that working in both mediums has been very instructive. I feel I can use a wide shot much more effectively, having worked in the theater. You know, that was the thing about Bruce Beresford's *Tender Mercies*—it is all shot in wide shots and therefore the actors have to use their bodies in more expressive ways. Then, when he comes in to a close-up, they quite simply don't have to move as much. But also, the intimacy of the close-up is useful in the theater. You still want to have that same level of vibration when you are in a two-thousand-seater auditorium because you have to play for the people in the front row and the people in row XXX up in the balcony.

HHM: I read that you once said there was something shaman-like about being an actor.

CB: Oh, yes, quite possibly.

HHM: That it can produce a great amount of superstition in terms of how you connect to it. It reminded me of something I learned in Brazil about acting: how the Brazilian concept of acting is deeply connected to shamanism, healing, and incorporation.

CB: It is an ancient art form. I went to Delphi with my children and when you go to the amphitheater there, you stand on the stage in that huge outdoor auditorium and you can whisper and still be heard. The acoustic is so profound that actors in ancient Greece could bring an audience down to a sort of micro level and channel the energy in that space, from body to body. I think the reason a lot of people are fearful of the theater is that you are really implicated as an audience member: You are asked to bring something to the evening, and you are exposed in a way. As an actor on stage, you are channeling the energy you receive from the audience, and I think you are much more disconnected or dislocated from your audience when you are working in film—it's a much more private and intimate, isolated experience. I'm not saying one is more important or more profound than the other, but I definitely feel that there is a very acute awareness of your audience when you are on stage. That is what I love about going into these old theaters in the West End. Because

ACTORS HAVE ALWAYS BEEN PARIAHS, AND IN SOME WAYS — CERTAINLY IN THE FILM INDUSTRY — THEY HAVE BECOME GODS

of the cost of the real estate, what goes inside those spaces can be a little bit creatively safe but still — the paint on the walls, the history of the souls and the stories that have been told there. I think you can't help but channel that history.

HHM: I find what you just said about ancient Greece very interesting. It reminded me of the Mayan pyramids in Chichen Itza — a handclap in front of the stairs of the Kukulcan Temple produces an echo that sounds just like the Quetzal bird. It all seems to have a strong connection with performance and shamanism.

CB: Yes! I also think it's interesting when new theaters are built. Strangely, the acoustic quality is often really poor. I mean, I went to drama school but I've always thought that it's really important as an actor to have control and to channel the flexibility of one's voice, so you can play with that acoustic. But in theaters that have been built recently, the visuals are considered, but the quality of the acoustic is not.

I don't know if you saw Simon McBurney's piece *The Encounter*?

HHM: I haven't.

CB: It's traveling around, if you ever get to see it. It's a complete auditory experience, and in a theater, which is really interesting.

HHM: In your opinion, what role does an actor play in society?

CB: Today? The question presupposes that there is one type of actor. I am as interested in the history of commedia dell'arte as I am in the notion of method, or hyper-realism, or the grand traditions. There are many different types of actors, and not everyone gets into performance for the same reasons or with the same ambition, but in the end, for me, actors are communicating a story. These stories are often related to the health or state of society. I think that's why actors are often attacked, because they have to open a portal. It goes back to your question about shamanism, because what happens in the theater is that you are channeling a collective unconscious. I think, as an actor, you have access to that because you expose yourself, and you absorb people in an exposed way when you tell them a story. I mean, actors have always been pariahs, and in some ways—certainly in the film industry—they have become gods. I wonder though if you are also asking about celebrity, which is tangential to acting.

HHM: It is an interesting position to have. There is also a very fine line between this and the question of the function

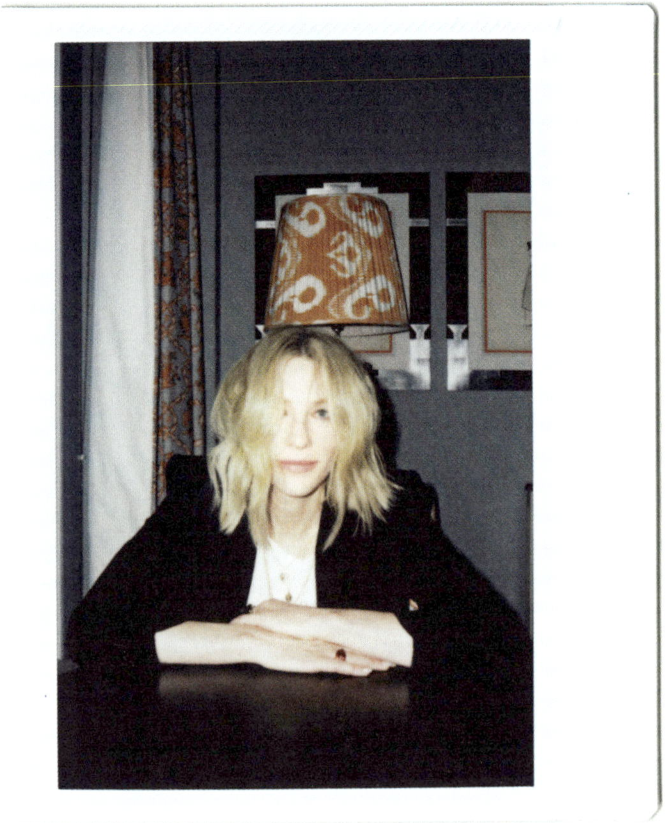

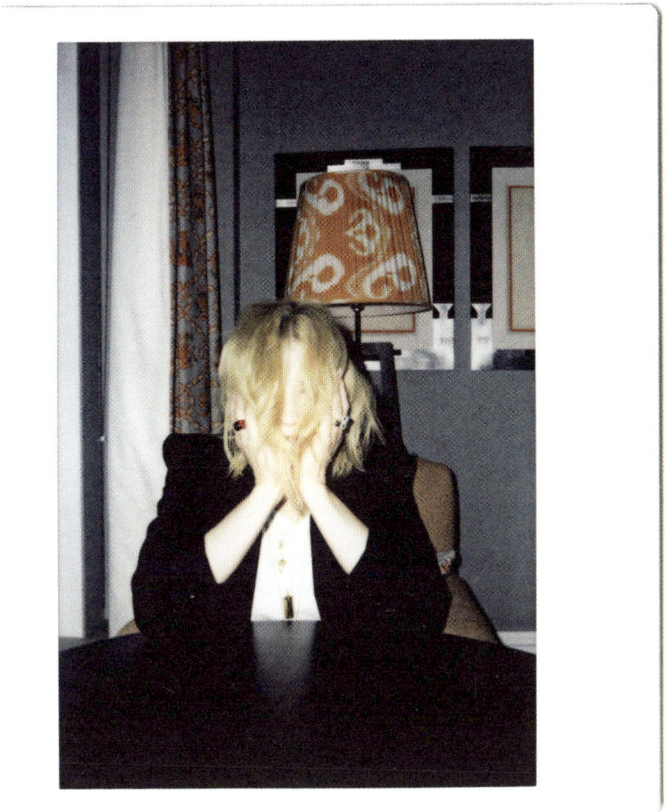

of art, and how artists often portray societies and the time they live in.

CB: Yes.

HHM: And how the most interesting art often challenges the boundaries of what art can be. Can we talk about the genesis of the piece you made in collaboration with artist Julian Rosefeldt, *Manifesto*?

CB: Well, we met through Thomas Ostermeier, who is the artistic director of the Schaubühne theater in Berlin. One fantastic weekend, when all the galleries were open, I was there and I encountered Julian's work. We got to talking and we stayed in contact, and we agreed to find a way to work together. Eventually he said he had settled on the manifesto idea. I had read artists' manifestos while studying fine art at university, but I hadn't read them for a long time. Julian said he wanted to explore the idea of the manifesto and investigate where the manifesto sits today—in a sort of opposed idealistic world (*laughs*). But what was fascinating to me and what I loved about it was that I knew the work was going to be absorbed and viewed in a completely different context: in a non-literal space, in a museum, a gallery context. I think the thing that frustrates me about the film industry is how literal it is. What I love about the theater is doubling, meaning you can play a bear and you can play a woman with no legs in the same play and be the same actor—you just change your body, your energy production, your costume, and if it is done well, the audience accepts it. That sort of non-literalism doesn't really happen very often in film. So I was very excited about exploring this idea and reaching an audience who were in a different relationship to the work.

HHM: Many of these manifestos were written by world-famous artists, but at the time they were written, these artists were often young, angry individuals. It seems to me that the whole piece has a sense of resistance.

CB: That's what I found interesting about the process. I thought I sort of understood them—as you are saying, there is a lot of anger and a lot of self-assertion. At the time that these manifestos were written, the artists didn't know they might become so-called masters or heads of movements. They were just part of the establishment of ideas that the artist often rejected or worked against later in their career. They were assertions of their individuality, they wanted to smash something down in order to build something up. They had a similar kind of rhythmic energetic attack that makes them all kind of "the one voice," which was really interesting to me. I don't know if you saw it in a gallery …

HHM: At the Park Avenue Armory.

CB: Oh! Which is a great space. I'd love to perform live in that space.

HHM: Watching it in that huge space rather than in an average movie theater had a very different impact.

CB: Yes, I think that is one of the spaces that worked best because the work completely took it over. The screens were very large, and the wonderful thing about it was that people could go in for two minutes or two hours, and they could choose the order and how they visited or revisited, or absorbed or discarded, the work. It was turned into a film for funding reasons, and some people might have enjoyed that. But for me, it's a less successful rendition of the work, because it makes you form more literal meanings, simply because it's a film and so the mind searches for a narrative.

HHM: Absolutely. Also, the relationship between the text and the reality of the situation. It was almost as if you were speaking in Chinese and yet the audience could understand what was happening in every scenario.

CB: That was part of the process. Julian came up with a lot of different scenarios and we were trying to marry the right scenarios to the right manifestos, because some of them lent themselves more to a monologue, while others lent themselves more to a conversation, or an interior voice.

HHM: It is fascinating to see how you morph from a primetime news anchor to a Russian choreographer to a schoolteacher, and from Marx and Dada to Futurism and Fluxus. What was the process of building these characters like?

CB: It was like doing stand-up in terms of the spontaneity. I mean, we talked, we met, we emailed one another, we talked on the phone, and then we met with Morag Ross, the makeup artist, who happens to be one of my closest

IT'S IMPORTANT TO WORK FROM A PLACE OF HAVING NO SENSE OF CONSEQUENCE

friends. We had an afternoon with Morag, Massimo [Gattabrusi], who did the hair, and Bina [Daigeler], who was doing the costumes, and we said, "OK, so what are the characters going to look like?" And then Julian suggested that all of them could have different accents. And I said, "Oh! Okay, why don't we make this one Scottish, this one from the North, this one from somewhere in Eastern Europe," and so on. There was no rehearsal.

HHM: Wow.

CB: I got up and did it, for better or worse. And that is what I mean about exposure. I thought, "I just have to do it. We don't have enough time to do it twice." I remember the scene of the funeral, where we were losing the light, and we just did one take and that was it. That was the level of risk, but also knowing it was … I don't know. I think it's important to work from a place of having no sense of consequence.

HHM: I was very impressed to see the attention to detail in every aspect of this piece. In every performance, costume design, the locations …

CB: That's 100 percent Julian. The locations are amazing, aren't they?

HHM: It brought to mind my talk with artist Kiki Smith. She said that her concept of beauty was in the attention to detail. What is your concept of beauty?

CB: I subscribe to a more Eastern concept of beauty. Something is not beautiful unless it has a flaw in it. As a woman working in the film industry, there is always the conversation about the level of luminosity or attractiveness one has, or how sympathetic a female character is. I think all those conversations are really uncreative. I don't want to patronize an audience and tell them how to think or feel about the character that one is creating. You can find beauty everywhere, even in moments of grief because people are so completely exposed, or in people who are incredibly stressed—you suddenly see through the facade to a rawness.

HHM: Do you consider yourself a political artist?

CB: No, I don't consider art to be political. I think the way art is disseminated and dissected, viewed, and processed can ultimately be political. I think art is a provocation—a provocation to have dangerous conversations. Of course I have political beliefs, but I think it is dangerous for artists to speak only to people who think like them. I have often lived in places where there have been few people who share my worldviews or politics. You know, that is my one and only problem with Berlin. Oh, my God! There are so many Australians there making art (*laughs*).

IN THE FILM INDUSTRY WE HAVE "RESIDUALS." BUT IN TERMS OF CREATIVE OWNERSHIP, I AM A BIG BELIEVER IN GIVING IT AWAY

HHM: (*laughs*) I can think of some of your performances when you have played a different gender, like Bob Dylan.

CB: Well, that was Todd Haynes' idea. He is so fascinating.

HHM: Throughout history, artists have been into role-playing. Frida Kahlo often dressed like a man. And Marcel Duchamp and Mike Kelley also cross-dressed. There are a lot of artists who switched back and forth, but that is often reserved for fine art. It is not very common to see that in Hollywood. In pop culture, I believe people expect socially acceptable behavior.

CB: You don't get asked to do that very often. It's like Todd Solondz, when he divided one character into seven different actors. I love it when film goes to unconventional places. But there was an enormous amount of pressure on Todd to make a linear narrative out of Dylan's life and creative urges and to remove certain parts and make it more accessible.

That's why, as a filmmaker, your relationship with your producer is really important, and that's why festivals are really important, because that's often where this work is allowed to breathe. You know, we saw this amazing, amazing film—we just gave a special Palme d'Or at Cannes to Jean-Luc Godard for *Le Livre d'image*, because it really shifted our gaze. It was at times almost unbearable and unwatchable, but it haunted us. I think increasingly, when cinematic artists are pushing the boundaries of cinema, one thinks, does this belong in a museum? The challenge and the opportunity in cinema is that it is a much more democratic place—people's televisions are much more democratic places—and that's why it's so great that in certain countries, there are art channels where you can encounter a work in your living room that you perhaps wouldn't necessarily go to see.

HHM: Going back to the subject of performance, the director has input regarding the performance ...

CB: Absolutely. It is a conversation.

HHM: Who owns the performance at the end? Is it the actor? The director? The audience? The oral history? The film history?

CB: It's interesting. If there is ownership, it resides in memory. You know, it's really interesting having children and then wanting to take them to the theater, but also show them films that my husband and I were profoundly influenced by in our childhood and then in our teenage years—films I haven't seen for twenty years or longer. I'd watch a film with my children and my memory of the performance, the story, is different to the film itself. For instance, I was watching *Psycho* again the other day, and I had forgotten whole tracts of that film. Somehow, it had set spores off in my memory and the performance was entirely different to how I remembered it. So, I'd absorbed the influence. I think as soon as you perform something, you have to give it away. But, that said, conversations about authorship are vital, because with the commodification of visual art in particular, where does the copyright exist when an artist's market value goes up? It's really complicated because if a work is sold and resold and resold again, shouldn't the artist benefit from that? In the film industry we have "residuals." But in terms of creative ownership, I am a big believer in giving it away.

HHM: I agree, art should be for everyone.

AN

N

ANNIE LENNOX
LONDON, 2017

IE

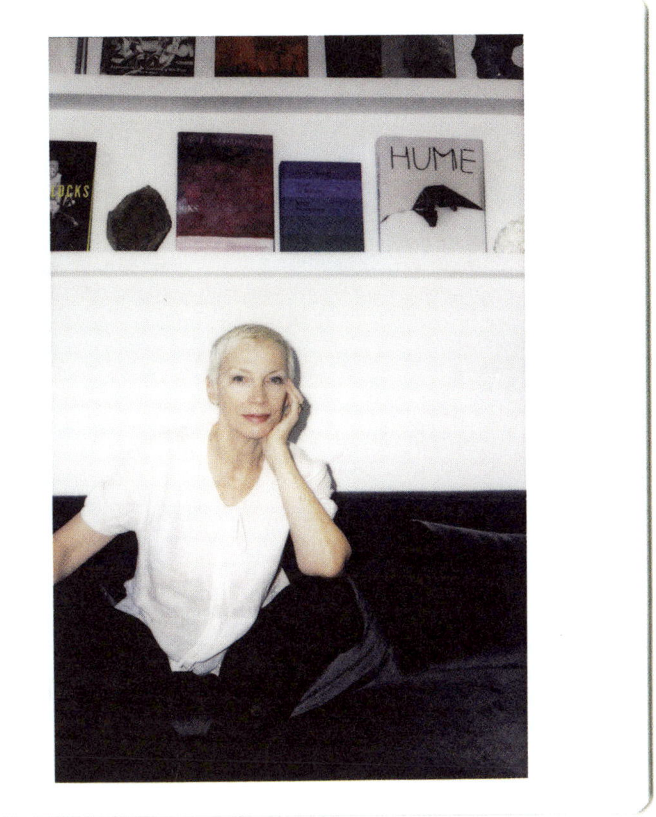
HUME

Singer, songwriter, performer, and human rights activist Annie Lennox rose to fame in partnership with Dave Stewart as Eurythmics in the early 1980s. After a decade of global success, she branched off to become a notable artist in her own right. Over the decades, Annie has received numerous accolades in recognition of her contribution to the music business, including eight BRIT Awards, four Grammys, a Golden Globe, and an Academy Award. Her leadership on humanitarian issues has been recognized with doctorates and fellowships from the world's leading academic institutions.

Annie arrived whistling to our meeting in Notting Hill, and this small yet candid gesture immediately broke the walls between us. She was warm, smart, and passionate, and retains the glow and striking looks of her pop heyday. With her androgynous beauty, Annie was pop's ultimate feminist icon. Her musical career was full of unconventional moves and statements. Now she is using her voice to campaign for the fight against HIV/AIDS. Annie is a modern rebel, combining extraordinary insight with a visionary approach.

HUGO HUERTA MARIN:
What is the biggest challenge you have encountered while making a new music project?

ANNIE LENNOX:
The simple answer to that is just "Beginning." Music is invisible. You can't see it, you can't touch it, you can't taste it. It is different to using actual material, as your work has everything to do with ideas. The medium of music can be external, because you may need to use an instrument to inspire you—it could be a guitar, it could be a keyboard of some kind—but it has to start with this fledgling idea, and I think that idea needs to be really strong, like a seedling. It has to have some essence.

Once you've got the seedling of the idea, the challenge is to move forward from that concept: Where are we going now? What does this mean? Some people might write a whole bunch of lines and verses, and that could be the bare bones of the song—and that is a good start. Then, you can maybe create the music on top of that structure, or it might come in a different way, where the music and the vibe come first. I don't think there is a particular formula, although I know that there are hundreds of young songwriters who are working in their studios and are turning out lots and lots of songs, and trying to apply certain kinds of approaches and certain sorts of structures; and it is infinite, isn't it? At the end of the day, music is infinite.

HHM: Talking of beginnings, what was your relationship with London like in the seventies when you were first starting out?

AL: Tough. Really tough. I came here because I'd auditioned for the Royal Academy of Music and I was given a place. That became my passport out from my provincial hometown in Scotland. I always sang. Even when I was tiny, I was just singing all the time. It was very natural to me. When I was about seven, my school asked if I would like to take a test and if I passed I could apply for piano lessons. I passed the test and started having two piano lessons a week. It cost four pounds a term back then. I come from a working-class background. My father worked in the shipyards and we didn't have much money to go around, so every penny counted, even if it sounds like a small amount nowadays. Anyway, when I was eleven I started to learn classical

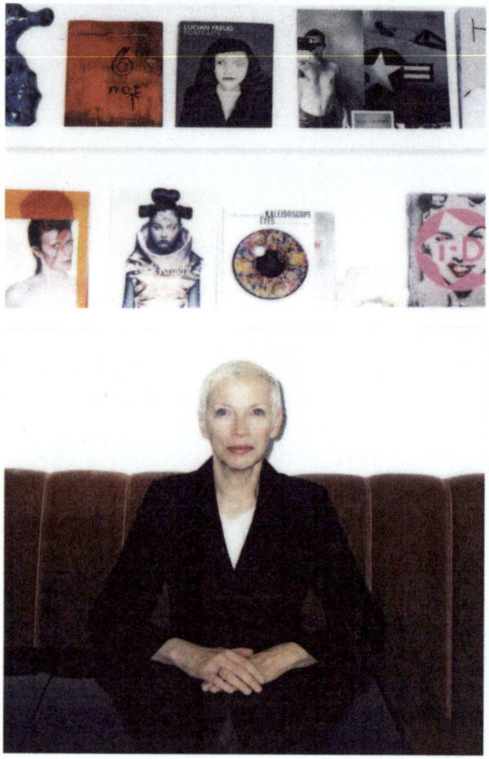
LUCIAN FREUD
KALEIDOSCOPE EYES

flute, which I loved, and when I was seventeen I was offered a place at the Royal Academy of Music in London. I wasn't thinking about being a singer or a songwriter at all. I stayed at the Academy for three years and was a complete failure as a student. It just wasn't working, so I was trying to see what the alternative could be, but I had no idea. For a few years, I felt very disquieted. I kept moving from place to place—bedsit to bedsit.

HHM: What has your relationship with London been like lately?

AL: Well … it is better than it was. As a young girl, I felt like a lost outsider. I was looking for a place to belong, and it didn't happen. It was a really lonely place and quite melancholic. I had a constant feeling of isolation and loneliness, and I still feel that. I don't know … In the past, I was the one looking through the window and always thinking I could never afford to go in, but now I don't really want to be a part of that. There are still circles within circles everywhere, where people belong, and as much as I love the diversity of London and that you can have a place for all the different cultures, I think it is hard to feel that you belong unless you belong to a community.

HHM: Is London still at the cutting edge of music these days?

AL: I don't know where the cutting edge of music actually is, because to be quite honest with you, I think activism and advocacy have eclipsed my music making. I'm not so interested in the cutting edge of music anymore; I'm interested in other things.

HHM: At the beginning of your career you constantly used visual imagery to make a statement. Wearing men's suits, cutting your hair and dyeing it orange, or using eighteenth-century costumes ...

AL: Video first arrived as a brand-new phenomenon. Now, everybody knows what video is, it's ... generic. At the time, though, it was so innovative. It was like adding a whole other range of color to your palette. Dave [Stewart] and I—in Eurythmics—just absolutely fell in love with it because it was another extension, and another form, of our expression. Some videos can be interpreted in many different ways—you could make so many different videos for one song.

HHM: Did you have any creative input in those videos?

AL: Totally. We had the concepts. When it started, when it really started, we made a couple of videos before "Sweet Dreams." Dave had bought a tiny little camera and he came to me with the idea for the "Sweet Dreams" video, which I think is a classic piece of Pop art. He said, "OK. There is going to be a desk, like in a corporate office, and we're going to have gold discs on the walls. A cow is going to come in." I said, "OK ... cool. We have a cow. Fantastic!" I mean, you have to imagine this little tiny studio in the heart of Soho. The cow was taken down in a lift with a cow handler. And the moment the door opened and this cow came out, it was like being on another planet because, you know, when you take an animal of that size into the human landscape and put it into a room ...

OVER THE YEARS I'VE COME TO REALIZE THAT WHATEVER YOU SAY, NOBODY SEES IT LIKE YOU DO

it was insane! There was a point when we were filming, where Dave was tapping in unison to the track on an old-fashioned prototype computer made out of wood—I was sitting on a long boardroom table, and the cow was free to walk around. Then, the cow—as a cow can be—was really curious, and I could see from the corner of my eye, while I was lip synching, this massive head coming closer and closer to Dave. The cow almost touched him, its eyes were fixed on Dave, and Dave just turned his eyes toward it and they looked at each other; it was so cool (*laughs*). It's this kind of completely unpredictable thing you can capture on film that makes it so thrilling, magical, even.

HHM: Back then, several journalists, feminists, and members of the LGBTQ community gave different meanings to your work …

AL: Well, over the years I've come to realize that whatever you say, whatever you express, whenever you put your head above the parapet to communicate with the big world out there, where there are billions of people with their own perceptions, understandings, reference points, cultural experiences, and inner evaluations—nobody sees it like you do. To be honest with you, I still feel that nobody's really got it—whatever it is we try to say. Isn't that funny? But I have told myself it doesn't matter whether they got it or didn't get it, or they just got a little bit of it, or they didn't get it at all—it's just how it is. At the same time, it is very interesting when something happens and when people do actually get it, and they coalesce and come together to form a movement. It is very powerful, whether you agree or not.

HHM: I believe a message—whether people get it or not—is resonant even today. I was at a nightclub in London last week, and "Sweet Dreams" started playing. Drag queens singing in unison and dancing with great confidence. It was as though an anthem was playing. So powerful …

AL: Curiously, I feel "Sweet Dreams" is more of a mantra than a song … You can choose to apply any meaning to it and it just works. I'm thrilled when people connect with it—whichever way they choose. Funnily enough, at the time, for me, the words were self-deprecating and far from celebratory. It was a wry comment on the human condition. I'm always delighted to hear that people find it liberating or celebratory, but there was always a particular twist in there …

HHM: If we're talking about a message, do you think music should also raise social and political questions?

AL: Well, I think it can, but I don't think there is a "should" in it. Certain particular anthems have deeply touched me—one of them being Peter

Gabriel's song "Biko" about the South African political activist Steven Biko, who was murdered in a prison cell during the Anti-Apartheid struggle. He was a fugitive, risking his life for a cause, moving from place to place across Southern Africa. It's very painful because this man lost his freedom, lost his life, lost so much of the joy of his own personal right to live, for his belief in a higher cause. Real heroes are these ones … So, we go back to the original point, which is: Should music also raise social and political questions? Well, songs that stand for causes are noble songs—they bring people together, they are extraordinary—but there are fewer and fewer of them, and they are hard to write. I mean, Bob Marley always had a sense of social injustice and that social injustice continues to this day; John Lennon, too. And they are both dead. It's strange how the people who come forward with these messages very often have short lives.

HHM: I was curious to ask you about Nelson Mandela. Can you share your experience of meeting and working with him?

AL: Yes, absolutely. I have to preface this because there is a lot of history behind it. But I remember that after the first time I heard about Apartheid in South Africa, I vowed never to set foot in the country, because I was so appalled by the racist system. It was, and still is, terrible to me. But my more personal story with Mandela really began in 1988, when Eurythmics took part in an amazing concert to celebrate his seventieth birthday at Wembley Stadium in London. It brought all these brilliant international musicians together and was broadcast to millions of people around the globe. Mandela had been incarcerated in Robben Island for about eighteen years around that time, and nobody really knew what he looked like at that point. Yet this "invisible" man was the symbol of the Anti-Apartheid Movement. I think that if you hadn't heard of Mandela back then, you definitely knew who he was after that event.

Years later, in November 2003, Dave Stewart was asked to put a concert together to launch Mandela's HIV/AIDS foundation, 46664. Mandela had retired from the presidency of South Africa and become a powerful elder statesman. On the day before the concert, all the artists were invited to join with him in Robben Island. Standing in front of his former prison cell, Mandela delivered a speech to all the assembled artists and international press. He told us how the HIV/AIDS pandemic was decimating the entire continent of Africa. At that point in time South Africa had the highest rates of infection in the world. Mandela said: "There is a genocide taking place in my country." One in three pregnant women were HIV positive with no access to treatment. And I can tell you that to this day, that ratio hasn't changed. In the years to follow, Mandela and the 46664 campaign invited artists to take part in a series of different concerts to raise awareness and funds, so I took part in almost every event and became passionately committed to advocating and campaigning on this issue, which really lacked the voice of women. Generally speaking, people around the world were not aware of what was happening. Subsequently, I went to South Africa, Uganda, and Malawi, with small film crews, making short clips about the pandemic, which directly highlighted how women and children were being affected by AIDS. I just couldn't believe the extent of it. It was just unbelievable how governments could block access to treatment for entire populations that were dropping like flies. It was a complete wake-up call. The South African president at the time, [Thabo Mvuyelwa] Mbeki, had taken a denialist stance, refusing to even acknowledge that the virus was the cause of AIDS. It was totally insane. People were going with traditional healers, or fake quack doctors, who sold them snake oil and told them they were going to be cured. And of course, people just kept dying in their hundreds of thousands, because they couldn't get treatment.

HHM: It is remarkable how these music concerts opened the door for bigger conversations worldwide, but we don't see that anymore. I believe artists are constantly portraying the time in which they are living, one way or another. Do you think contemporary music symbolizes the emptiness of a modern society?

AL: Well, over the years I've witnessed how the corporate world gradually took over the music industry. We were always signed to major labels and we always had contention between us. We wanted the distribution power of big record labels, but we didn't want them to control our work—trying to push us into certain directions. The music industry in general has always had a notoriously dark side, with lots of dodgy individuals ripping off and exploiting artists while making massive fortunes for themselves. And now, it's evolved to a whole other level.

ANNIE LENNOX

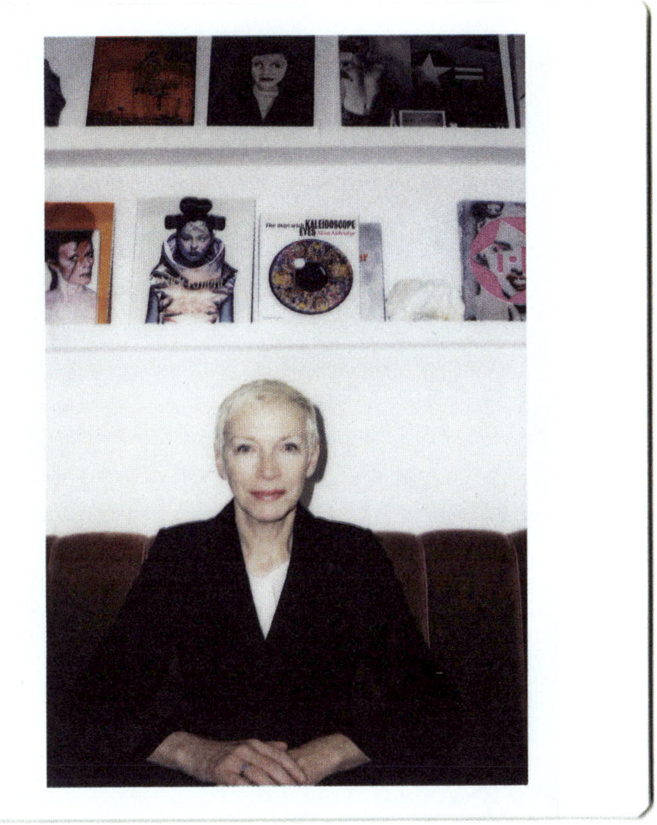
KALEIDOSCOPE
EYES

THE WHOLE GAME OF BEING A CELEBRITY AND BEING IN THE TOP MAGAZINES CAN BE A VERY FAUSTIAN PACT

Now everything is about branding and massive global corporate industries. The appeal of music is so powerful … Commerce and art are strange bedfellows, but the connection is so strong that I don't think you can fight it. It is what it is, and you are just living your existence with your own values.

HHM: Do you think that making money has changed the way you make music?

AL: Well, when we finally made some money, our budgets for our videos went up … not to say necessarily that the higher the budget, the better the video. But there was definitely more opportunity to facilitate our ideas and in the best way possible. At a certain point, I think there is a momentum that comes with making music, making videos, being part of the system, touring, giving interviews, appearances on television, and all of that. I mean, I lived that life for decades and so now, I've kind of stepped out of it. I don't like the values associated with it. I also think the whole game of being a celebrity and being in the top magazines can be a very Faustian pact.

HHM: Do you think things have changed in the music business for female artists?

AL: Here's the thing. When I first had the notion that I wanted to be a singer, songwriter, performer, recording artist, the role models that I looked up to at the time were Carole King and Joni Mitchell. They were, for me, the two women that I could say were doing it. And I thought if they could do it, maybe I could do it as well … and then more came along … Chrissie Hynde — incredible, just incredible! There was also Debbie Harry. You know, they were my contemporaries, but still — it was rare. There were lots of women who were amazing singers, but they didn't happen to be songwriters as well. So, actually, at that time, to be so rare was an advantage. Now, I think there are plenty of singers and songwriters. The music industry looks to have maybe one or two massive new artists every few years and they take over and become the latest thing. So, there's not a lot of space for the thousands of aspiring female singer-songwriters. That is a fact. I think that is really cruel and scary for them.

HHM: We have seen some iconic performances of yours, like the one at the Freddie Mercury Tribute Concert with David Bowie. Do you have a special performance you keep fondly in your memory?

AL: Yeah, well … definitely that one. I am very critical of everything I do, of myself and of my work, and I think a lot of artists are harsh on themselves. You almost need to be, because at least then, you know you have done the best you could. I remember the rehearsals.

I remember a lot about the preparation for that performance. Basically, on the day of the concert, I noticed that all the artists who were around—most of them were men, and it had a certain male energy around it. I wanted that performance with Bowie to be absolutely extraordinary. So, I didn't mingle with anybody. I sat for hour after hour in my dressing room. I didn't let anybody see me, and eventually, as the hours passed, I just gradually put my makeup on and became this other creature. It's like having an alter ego, because yes, it is you physically but you are like an actor—you enter into the character. And it being in the context of Freddie's death, and that it was an advocacy platform for HIV/AIDS, I decided—at least for me anyway—that my character would be Death. It was all intuitive. I didn't work it out to the specific word, but I just felt like that was what it symbolized. And then, there was Bowie, who was just the quintessential, most beautiful individual. He didn't know I was going to do it, because we just had a very relaxed rehearsal. He suggested I should wear a frock, and I agreed. He then told me to ask Antony Price to make it, so I called him up and he agreed to do it. I told him I didn't want it to be a pretty frock—it needed to be dark, black, and enormous. I wanted something resembling an armor on top, in silver. I also thought of wearing a mask and resembling a death warrior. When he was performing, I got close to him without touching him. But when I did, he stood his ground—he kind of got around me. Embodying this thing—this weird creature—I had the courage to get really close to him; he played along, and we kept singing. There was also the energy of that huge audience—it was extraordinary.

I can look at that moment, and for me, it was like a peak moment, a peak performance. And another memorable performance was at the Grammys in 1984 (*laughs*). Eurythmics were nominated for a Grammy. I had an idea of what I wanted to do, because people were always wondering, "Is she a man? Is she a woman?" So, I decided: "I'm gonna be a man … I'm just gonna give them what they want." So I got dressed in a suit and I never told anybody, apart from Dave. We did all our rehearsals, and all was cool. But then, when we had to take our places—which is always a scary moment before the curtains go up—Ken Ehrlich, who has been the director of the Grammys for ever and ever, was panicking. He kept looking around and pacing back and forth, saying, "Where is Annie?!" He couldn't see me, and I was standing there right in front of him, dressed as a man. He started to freak out, and I just said: "I'm here, Ken," and he got down on his knees! He couldn't believe it, but he couldn't do anything about it. There was nothing to do, and nobody could stop it. It was breaking boundaries back in those days, and the audience was like, "What the fuck?!" And that was strong!

HHM: (*laughs*) Fantastic stories. It is really interesting the way you described these characters, and I am curious to know more about your references. For instance, what is your concept of beauty?

AL: I see beauty everywhere, but at the same time, I also see the opposite, and that is quite hard to deal with. I am the kind of person who is sensitive and keeps looking at everything—like

THERE IS A LOT OF DARKNESS AND MELANCHOLIA, BUT THERE IS A LOT OF BEAUTY AS WELL. I FEEL WE LIVE IN A POLARIZED WORLD

those blossoms there, for example—we are looking at some fresh, white cherry blossoms. In London, they are exploding—after having had months and months of darkness, it can get really tough, and you are just desperate to see something happen, something that can emerge from this troglodyte existence. Actually, the big celebration is in the trees, and the flowers and the plants that emerge; they are bright yellow or fantastic pale pink or pure white. There is beauty everywhere, but there is also the other side—the yin and the yang. If you listen to Eurythmics songs or to my songs, they contain both elements. There is a lot of darkness and melancholia, but there is a lot of beauty as well. I feel we live in a polarized world.

HHM: Beauty can also be disturbing.

AL: That's right. If you think about it, Gilbert and George took—and this sounds kind of repugnant—but they took excrement and they used it in a visual art context, wherein the subject makes the viewer feel personally revolted, but turning it into an art form, making the two things coexist. I find it very challenging, because it makes you think of how this is a natural bodily function—something we normally never really discuss, never want to talk about, don't want to look at because it's disgusting, yet it comes from our bodies—and the artists have confronted us with it. This is why art can be so powerful.

HHM: What are your thoughts on the rise of the artist as celebrity?

AL: I cannot stand the word "celebrity." I mean, everything is morphed now—we've got people who are famous just for being famous. I guess we just have to accept that, but I still have an old-school way of thinking in that you do something of merit—of value—and then, as a by-product, your work becomes the thing you are known for. But we are way beyond that side effect, and it disturbs me because it is a vacuous currency, and it is toxic.

HHM: Do you worry about being overexposed?

AL: I don't, because I don't think I am. I have always kept quite a low profile, and that has been my methodology.

HHM: What inspires you the most?

AL: Inspiration can come from so many different things. I think what inspires me most is having a connection with people. There is nothing like it.

HHM: What is the most honest thing you can say about yourself?

AL: I try to live as an authentic person. I try be kind, I try to be honest and I try to be decent … I try.

MI

U

MIUCCIA PRADA

MILAN, 2018

CC

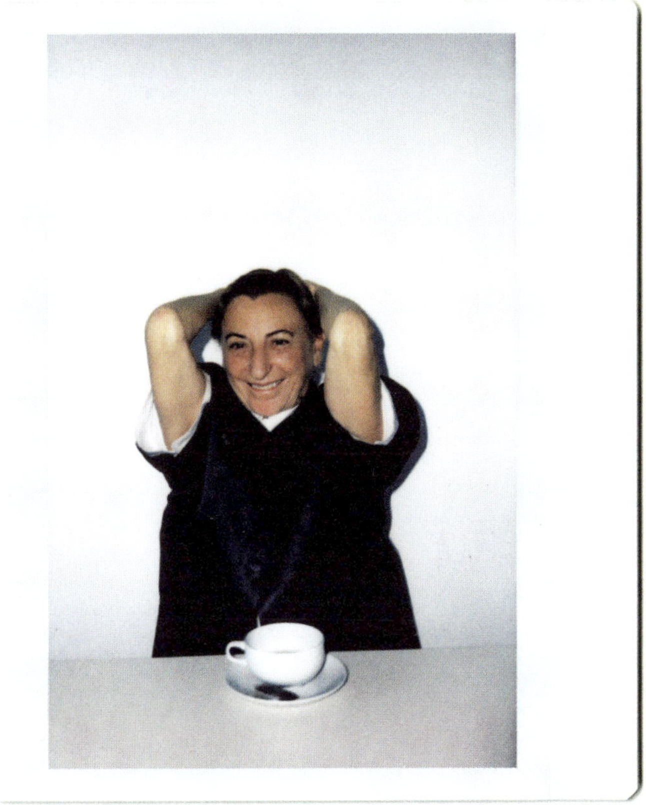

IA

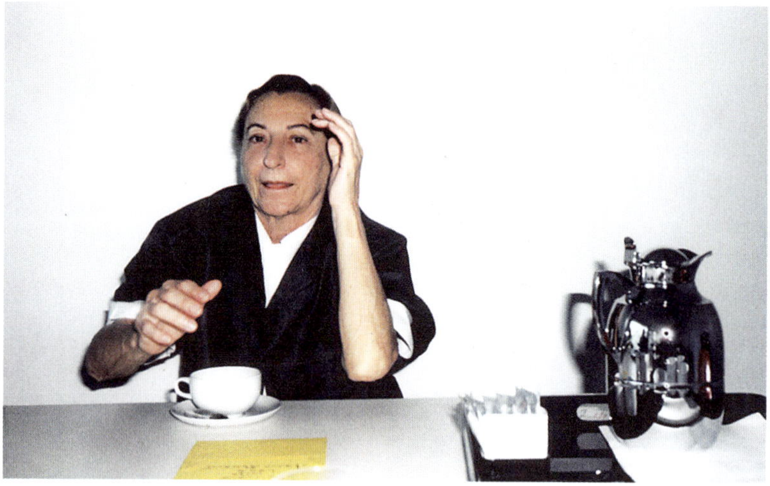

Miuccia Prada—or Mrs. Prada, as she is known—is a pioneering fashion designer, businesswoman, curator, film producer, and renegade, and ultimately, a revolutionary. Her work has always taken an intellectual approach and revealed her talent for upending the rules with aplomb. After earning a degree in political science from Milan University, she began designing accessories for the exclusive family business founded by her grandfather Mario Prada in 1913. At the end of the 1970s, she met her husband, Patrizio Bertelli, and together they became the driving force of the development and international expansion of the fashion house. Their passion for contemporary art led them to create the Fondazione Prada—which they co-chair—with the aim of exploring "the most radical intellectual challenges in contemporary art and culture."

We met on a sunny day in Milan at the Prada S.p.A. headquarters on via Vergamo. Near the entrance, I could see the famous slide created by the artist Carsten Höller, which travels from the interior of her third-floor office to the ground floor below. She was charming from the moment we shook hands. For someone so dedicated to nurture resistance, I was delighted to realize that this fashion designer extraordinaire is, above all else, kind.

HUGO HUERTA MARIN:
Let's start at the beginning. Before joining the family business, you received a PhD in political science. Do you think politics influenced the way you started designing?

MIUCCIA PRADA:
One of the things that I was involved in before joining the company was politics. I had joined the women's rights movement and was part of the Unione Donne Italiane [Italian Women's Union]. I was raised to be political, and in the

end, politics are really what I carry with me deep down. In a subtle way I try to bring them to my work.

HHM: You were also trained as a mime. How did this training influence your work?

MP: I do not think it did particularly. It was just a result of the curiosity I had when I was young—to know what was going on, what was new, what was interesting, what was exciting. The Piccolo Teatro was very influential and it was during a time when ideas were changing, new theater, new … everything. The people and the ideas that circulated influenced me more than the training. The only thing that might have influenced me was the discipline. You needed a lot of discipline to be there—one day of training could consist of just learning how to move your hand back and forth.

HHM: It seems to me that you have an anti-establishment position in fashion. Would you say there is a sense of resistance in your work?

MP: Yes. Resistance is a word that I like a lot. What it means is very complex. I share thoughts with artists because they provide resistance.

HHM: To me, it is interesting to think about clothes as a political tool.

MP: Is fashion political for you?

HHM: Yes, it can be. I can think of Gestapo uniforms …

MP: I was thinking of Louis XIV dressing himself to control politics in the [Roberto] Rossellini movie [*The Rise of Louis XIV*] …

HHM: Exactly.

MP: Fantastic film.

HHM: I can also think of the punk movement. How can a piece of clothing be political?

MP: You can try to look political in your clothes. But of course, in a very soft way, you should dress according to your thoughts; I always say that you should not dress as a sexy bombshell to conquer a rich man, only if that is how you feel. It should not have a purpose. What has a lot to do with politics is your mind, not what you choose to wear. Who cares? I always say that you can wear whatever you want, because it is a free choice. I do not think there is a politically correct dress code—there were times I went to demonstrations wearing Saint Laurent and vice versa. In the end, any gestures can be political. Politics are much more than clothing.

HHM: Yes. But I also think there have been a few moments in history when the language of a culture was shifted by clothes. Do you think fashion can still be that revolutionary?

MP: I think that is a reaction. What I am trying to say is that some people complain that nothing new happens in fashion anymore, but fashion reflects what is happening in society. At the time of the miniskirt, there was the women's revolution, people reacting politically, intellectually, and also in terms of clothes. Clothes were part of the protest, but the origins of those protests go deeper.

HHM: What are your thoughts on the concept of uniforms?

MP: I have always loved uniforms because they can set you free from having to care about and choose what to wear. I was preoccupied with the concept a few years ago. Even if I've never made them for my shows, I love them because in them you can hide who you are. You are free, liberated. I always say that clothes can help you, mainly when you are in a good mood (*laughs*). When you are in pain or suffering, or when you are sick—when tragedy hits—you could care less about fashion.

HHM: How has Prada changed as fashion houses have expanded? Is there a moment when you think a big house becomes too big?

MP: No, I never thought that. I enjoy the idea of expanding because I have always thought that the idea of making clothes for a small group of chic and sophisticated people is limiting. That is too easy for me, and being confronted with the big world outside is

WHEN IT COMES TO FASHION, YOU HAVE TO REALLY CONFRONT YOURSELF

so much more exciting and challenging. I am very interested in that because it is difficult. Now, with so-called globalization, in theory, you should know about everything, everywhere. You try to catch part of something or all of it, because you are obliged by your job to do so. I also very often say, whenever I have conversations with artists at the Fondazione [Prada], that I am very proud of my job because it is the only thing that obliges me to be in touch with reality. Art is more theoretical—you can say and do whatever you want. When it comes to fashion, you have to really confront yourself. Sometimes you believe something is fantastic, but no one wants it. Other times, people want something you hate. These confrontations are really interesting because you learn something.

HHM: It's interesting to think about it even from a cultural point of view—how in some places, designers are restricted in the way they design clothes: You can't show the legs in some countries, bodies are smaller in China and bigger in Eastern Europe, you can't show nipples in America, and so on.

MP: In fact, political correctness can also be a limitation on creativity, but it is very interesting, because if the group you are designing for is small, you can do whatever you want. Now, there are so many different audiences and instinctively, you just go with it, because it is a form of respect. Some people would say that we are taking away freedom, but I think you should respect the views of others. It is a big issue, but again, an interesting one.

HHM: I am also curious to know how a fashion house can understand the concept of luxury, particularly when it comes to the Eastern and the Western market.

MP: I must say that the concept of luxury is very similar everywhere (*laughs*).

HHM: You have said, "Fashion never opened itself to the 'ugly.'" Do you think things have changed over the years? That we are witnessing more of an aperture to the strange and the bizarre?

MP: When I started my job, there was a kind of taboo about that. I found it wrong, because everywhere in film, in art, in theater, there was the nasty and the ugly. And that was the most interesting part. But in fashion? Only beauty, bourgeoisie, perfection. As a fashion designer, I always wanted to break those rules and introduce "real life" into fashion. The task is not yet done, because so far, fashion still tends to expose classic beauty. For me, exploring beyond that concept was simply natural. What is the exact meaning of beauty?

HHM: Also, Prada's cultural recognition extends beyond fashion.

MP: Yes, I believe so. I ascribe relevance to different things. My ideas are political, and that means I struggle for whatever they stand for—for culture, for understanding, for equality, and so on. And the instrument I have is fashion, and I also have the Fondazione. I actually had to develop that because fashion was not enough of an instrument (*laughs*). I always used to say that to be a fashion designer was the worst. I was ashamed for a very long time. But later, I decided that it was the instrument I had, so I tried to practice what I believed through my company. In fact, we always try to expand to culture, architecture, movies—we try to move, to give more substance, to give more food for thought. For instance, there is Miu Miu's *Women's Tales*, a continuous collaboration with female directors to whom we give a platform to produce and showcase their ideas on feminity and vanity. It is a place for conversations about these subjects. In general, I would say that I like beauty, and I am very interested in the aesthetics of art, architecture, design, or whatever it is, but I am much more interested in ideas.

HHM: The Fondazione has such an interesting and specific style. It was designed by OMA under the direction of Rem Koolhaas. What drove you to this collaboration?

MP: Basically, it was a way to have a dialogue with clever people and to translate my ideas. It is a way of knowing, of understanding, of learning to enlarge all the possibilities to solve a problem.

HHM: I also find the short film collaborations so interesting. Why did you decide to work with [Roman] Polanski, Wes Anderson, and all these filmmakers?

MP: I think that if you want to get to know somebody, you should work with that person. Just knowing them socially isn't enough. I did it because I am interested in their work, in what they have to say. I am interested in discussion, and introducing all of that to my own work, to my life. Of course, these are also choices based on respect, affinity, admiration …

HHM: You have also made technological collaborations, like the one you made with the artist James Jean. For me, that collaboration was ahead of its time and opened doors for different disciplines in fashion.

MP: Well, I didn't think about it because for me, these are just instruments for ideas. I'm thinking of what [Alejandro González] Iñárritu did at the Fondazione. He was using technology, but he was introducing his ideas and concepts through it and showing how his ideas could be realized. It was also a moment for a great discussion about the role of virtual reality in movies and in real life. I remember him commenting on the paradox that to make people more aware of reality it seems you have to make a fake film … Also, there is something on which I am fixated now, while we are talking about movies: We are starting a serious film program at the Fondazione. In Italy, the tradition of going to movie theaters is diminishing and arthouse programming is very small, but we are trying to make it happen … We will continue to do so and to promote it as much as we can.

HHM: And when it comes to independent projects like the *Prada Marfa* store, do you support these kinds of projects?

MP: They didn't need support. They just wanted a few bags and few shoes, and of course, I gave them to them. Coincidentally, they are doing one of the next big exhibitions at the Fondazione. They are very clever—they have great ideas and they are very good artists. We are all very excited about it.

HHM: Speaking of the Fondazione, I am curious to know how you started collecting art.

MP: It's a funny story because basically, I was educated through literature, movies, and theater—I was never much interested in art. At one point, I met some friends of my husband in Tuscany. They were artists, and afterwards they came to visit our spaces in Milan. Back then, sculpture was a more difficult topic than painting, and having seen our bare industrial spaces, they said, "Oh! you should do an exhibition about sculpture." My husband and

I agreed, and we decided to do it. We basically started studying and visiting artists, talking to them and just learning … We spent ten years studying and meeting artists.

HHM: It is a very eclectic collection. Even this Carsten Höller in the middle of your office. How do you decide what to collect?

MP: Basically, my husband and I collect separately. He understands the absolute beauty of a piece of art, and is more educated in that sense, and I am more interested in the ideas and the concepts behind it. In the end, for both of us, it was a learning process, so we started buying art from the fifties, the sixties, and so on. A learning process rather than collecting—I could care less about collecting. Actually, I don't like to be seen as a collector at all. At the moment, I am buying very little, because I don't know what I am interested in exactly—just pieces that I love, or pieces we need for an exhibition at the Fondazione.

HHM: So, would you say your concept of beauty is more intellectual?

MP: Yes, I would say so.

HHM: Sometimes the line between art and fashion is very fine …

MP: For me it is huge.

HHM: But then, what happens when you have a show at a museum like the Metropolitan Museum of Art in New York?

I STILL BELIEVE ART IS ART, AND EVEN IF THERE IS A LOT OF MARKETING AROUND IT, WHEN A GREAT ARTIST DOES SOMETHING, IT IS DONE FOR THE IDEA. WHATEVER A DESIGNER DOES—EVEN IF IT IS REALLY BEAUTIFUL—IS DONE TO BE SOLD, SO THERE IS A HUGE DIFFERENCE

MP: The Met is something else. If you want to know about the relationship between art and fashion, it has always been a delicate point for me, because at the beginning, I wanted to keep the two things separate—even if in my mind, they were not separate at all. But I didn't want people to think I was somehow taking advantage. I wanted to be good on my own, so I always refused to collaborate with artists when it came to my job—even if everybody does it now, and sometimes it might even sound stupid not do it. I don't like to use people or use art to be more appealing. I still believe art is art, and even if there is a lot of marketing around it, when a great artist does something, it is done for the idea. Whatever a designer does—even if it is really beautiful—is done to be sold, so there is a huge difference. In general, I don't like it; there is also no real reason why I don't do it—probably because everyone else is doing it, and I want to do the opposite (*laughs*). I always want to be different from others, but of course, collaborations are great in theory. What do you think about collaborations?

HHM: I think collaborations are fantastic, and good art—like good design—shows. When a collaboration is authentic, you can see it; otherwise, it's just following something that already exists.

MP: Yes, that is true.

HHM: Good art would never feel like a trend.

MP: So true. But don't think of me as an artist. I can tell I am creative and so on, but …

HHM: I think you are.

MP: Sometimes. Is that a compliment? (*laughs*).

HHM: Perhaps it is just what it is. Some people are doctors, others are shoemakers, others are artists.

MP: That is a good way of saying it. But now, everyone wants to be called an artist (*laughs*). But I am joking, I understand.

HHM: At what point in your career did you feel that you were a successful designer?

MP: More or less never (*laughs*). I always see problems and what I need to improve on, and also my career was always difficult, especially at the beginning. I was doing what I liked, but I was too strange for the classic—there was something that disturbed them—and not necessarily avant-garde enough for the avant-garde. I was always in a grey area.

HHM: Do you worry about being overexposed?

MP: It's a difficult balance because my work is about exposure by definition, but personally I feel the opposite.

HHM: What inspires you the most?

MP: Everything and nothing … It depends. Right now I am fixated on the concept of resistance, and the lives of people. That interests me a lot.

HHM: What is the most honest thing you can say about yourself?

MP: I have no idea … (*laughs*).

AN

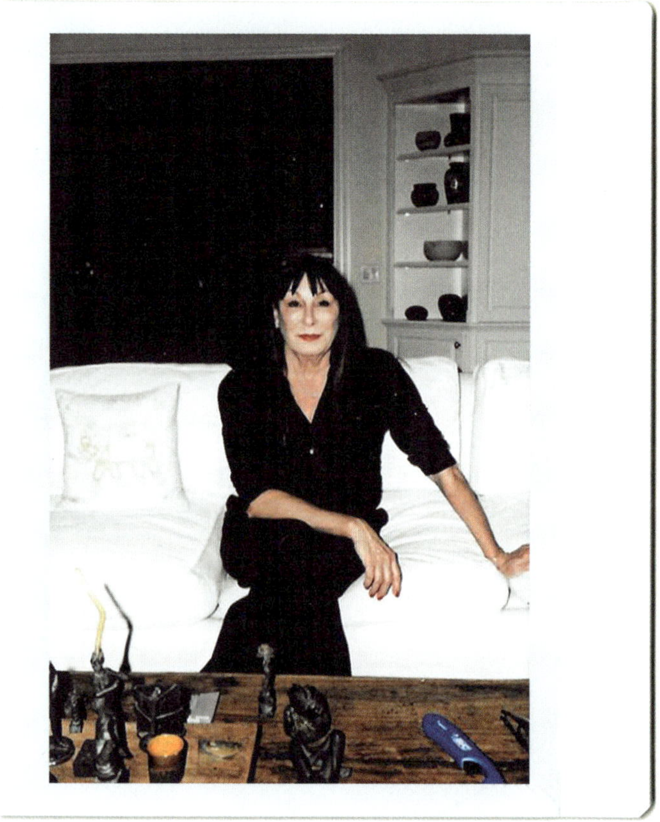

JE

LI

ANJELICA HUSTON

LOS ANGELES, 2018

CA

Anjelica Huston is an actor and director who continues her family's legacy in film, which began with her grandfather, Walter Huston, and continued with her father, John Huston. Throughout her career, she has received several awards for her work, including two Independent Spirit Awards, the Los Angeles and New York Film Critics Circle Awards, and an Academy Award for Best Supporting Actress. Her directorial debut was an unflinching adaptation of Dorothy Allison's bestselling novel *Bastard Out of Carolina*, which garnered her critical acclaim.

In her house in the Pacific Palisades in Los Angeles a scrappy Jack Russell terrier called Oscar followed me through the door right into the living room. "He falls for handsome men, you know," Anjelica said. When I asked her if Oscar was gay, Anjelica replied, eyes sparkling, "Oh, he is deeply gay." We both laughed. Somehow this scene seemed to me to be pure Huston, a way to quietly keep my attention with the promise of something just a little scandalous. Tall and striking, with black hair and features that suggest a Greek sculpture, Anjelica Huston is an eloquent and passionate commentator on her life, her work, and the experiences that enlightened it.

HUGO HUERTA MARIN:
Where did your interest in film start?

ANJELICA HUSTON:
My interest in film started at a very early age, when I was exposed to my father's [John Huston's] films. I grew up in the West of Ireland and lived in County Galway, and there were very few cinemas in Ireland at that point in time. There was a cinema in the main town of Galway, which was about an hour away in the old days ... There was a projector in our house in the countryside, and there was a rotation of

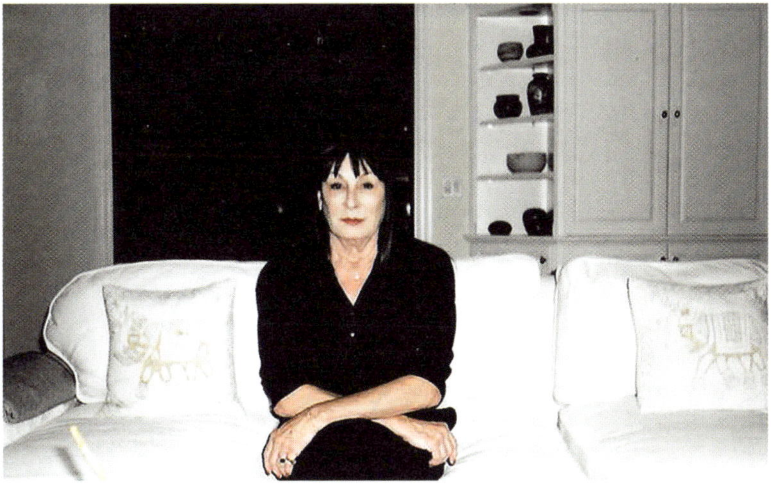

maybe four of my father's films that we watched over and over and over again, and I knew them very well. The films were: *The Treasure of the Sierra Madre*, *The African Queen*, *Moulin Rouge*, and one or two of his war documentaries, *Let There Be Light* and *The Battle of San Pietro*. The first time I ever watched a film of another kind was when I went to a party at the local Pony Club in Galway, and watched a Disney film. Of course, we didn't have television in those days either, and certainly not in the West of Ireland. I watched a film called *The Living Desert*, which has to do with the usual theme of animals and the desert, with everybody waiting for the rains and finally the rain comes and it's a big hallelujah. I loved the film; I thought it was really great, but the film that had the most impact on me as a child—apart from my father's films, which I kind of took for granted, as one would take one's parents for granted—was a film called *Gidget*, which came to Galway, and oh, my God! There was a moment when the heroine looks down the front of her blouse and says, "I'm a full-grown woman"—I thought it was fantastic.

HHM: Your filmography features a hit list of risky choices. What makes a good script or an interesting project?

AH: If there was a good answer to that question, I think there would be a lot of better films out there (*laughs*). But, I think a good script should be four-dimensional. It should give you an idea of who the characters are in depth. That doesn't necessarily mean overwriting, it just means that you have to have a strong sense of character, and I think … drama. For me, it also has to be emotional. It doesn't matter if it is well written, just as long as it is emotional, or as long as it grabs you. It doesn't have to be intellectual. I much prefer to go on a dream or on a ride, rather than having to work things out in my head. And so, in a way, it is hard for me to watch certain films—films that have a lot of mathematical sense, films that are technical or kind of sci-fi, are just hard for me to follow.

HHM: One of the many iconic moments in your career was your role as the Grand High Witch in *The Witches*.

AH: Oh, yes.

HHM: I once read you believed witches are goddesses gone wrong …

AH: Yeah, they are. They are fallen angels.

HHM: My favorite myth as child was the one of Medusa. The idea of a goddess-turned-monster with snakes instead of hair, who turned people into stone, was fantastic. Do you think these roles highlight women's empowerment?

AH: I don't know about women's empowerment. Certainly, female anger … And I think that perhaps there is a connection between the two of them. I've noticed that women feel at their strongest when they are at their angriest. It is the state in which they are the least appealing to men, so I think there is an aspect of a woman feeling angry, unattractive, and kind of brutal that they quite enjoy, because it doesn't have to do with being appealing to men, or having to follow the standards of romantic love.

HHM: In that sense, I am curious to know what could trigger such anger when one is incarnating this type of character. I find it interesting how actors play with events from the past and present, as well as the ways they might draw from their own experiences while performing.

AH: Acting is very alchemical. Sometimes you can lose yourself in it; you can go very deep—and people do. Sometimes, it depends how aware you are and where you are looking, because if you are looking, signs are everywhere …

HHM: What role do you think an actor plays in society?

AH: I think to reflect what is going on, and to show life at its best, at its worst, and at its most mediocre. I think reflecting conditions is one thing, but I also think fantasy is great—to take people to another place. One of the most powerful things I've ever seen—and I told Sacha Baron Cohen about it the other night when I saw him at a *Vanity Fair* party—was that I had a friend in Venice [Beach] whom I used to walk with. I'd see him in the morning, and we would walk together. One day he didn't show up on the boardwalk—I hadn't seen him in quite a while and I heard he had Lou Gehrig's disease. This was around Oscar time, and I had tapes from all the nominated movies, including *Borat*, and by the time I was able to go over and see Michael, he was paralyzed up to the neck and could barely eat by himself anymore—it was very bad. I played *Borat* for him and watched him watch

I THINK REFLECTING CONDITIONS IS ONE THING, BUT I ALSO THINK FANTASY IS GREAT—TO TAKE PEOPLE TO ANOTHER PLACE

it, and in that space of time, Michael transformed … His back arched, his lips peeled back from his teeth, and he laughed like hell. For an hour and a half, Sacha Baron Cohen was able to distract him from his condition …

HHM: Fantastic.

AH: It was a miracle.

HHM: You have worked with some of the greatest filmmakers of our generation, and you have directed some very interesting film projects. What do you find interesting about directing?

AH: Finding the nucleus of the story, the drama of the story, the honesty of the situation. What would happen if? How would you feel if? And a lot of the time, this is the stuff you can't work out in advance. Sometimes, you have to let it work on you, and that is scary, because you don't know where it is going. So, you just have to trust it is gonna happen, and sometimes it doesn't happen. But I think you need to be prepared, be prepared …

HHM: One of the modern-day filmmakers I like the most is Wes Anderson. What drew you to him in the first place, and what do you find interesting about his work?

AH: My agent drove me to him initially. He said, "You have to watch his films," because I hadn't watched any before he asked me to be in *The Royal Tenenbaums*. So I went and saw *Bottle Rocket* and I really liked it. I liked that he has a kind of gentle irony. I thought he was wonderful with actors, and that his work was unexpected. I thought he really had a great sense of invention, and I hadn't seen any movies that looked quite like his. Then, I met him in New York. We had breakfast together and I immediately liked him. He was very proper, straight-laced, and concise, particularly coming from a Texan—I didn't understand that connection well (*laughs*).

I thought the script for *The Royal Tenenbaums* was so good and so precise, but I felt there was one thing missing from it. I told him what I thought, and it was the kind of thing where, you know, I was asking him to give me a final scene. But, for me, it was an important scene because Etheline [Tenenbaum] forgives Royal [Tenenbaum], and I was able to sell the idea to Wes, and he wasn't defensive about it—and that's one of the things I really like about him. He isn't thinking, "Oh, the actress wants another scene." He actually listens to you and asks for your counsel about what you think might work, or if you have an idea about this or that. He is always good in that way, listening to your feelings about what you need for a part, or something that you think might alter the atmosphere. Like in *The Life Aquatic with Steve Zissou*,

Zissou and Eleanor [Zissou] split—they are separated—and he goes to see her. I said to Wes, "I want a lover in the room. I don't want him to come and see me all sad and alone." So, he gave me a toy boy (*laughs*).

HHM: (*laughs*) A different story.

AH: Oh! She is doing ballet, she has a cutie in the room, you know, it is a different story. Also, his aesthetic—he has a great sense of color, and great fashion sense. He is an artist.

HHM: Speaking of a different artistic realm … I read you met John Steinbeck and Jean-Paul Sartre as a child. How was your experience of growing up surrounded by this remarkable group of writers and artists?

AH: I think I was incredibly lucky. John Steinbeck was a fabulous man—you couldn't have a better guest in your house. He was funny. He played Santa Claus at Christmas time and even wrote a story about it. He was wonderful with my father, and was extremely direct. He always talked to me as an equal even when I was young. He gave me a gold medal of the Madonna of Guadalupe as a present, and wrote me a letter about how a girl named Trampoline had given it to him. I only understood later why she was called Trampoline—she had been up and down a lot (*laughs*). He was a wonderful, straightforward, intelligent, great man. He was fabulous. I always liked artists best …

HHM: Did some of them influence you more than others?

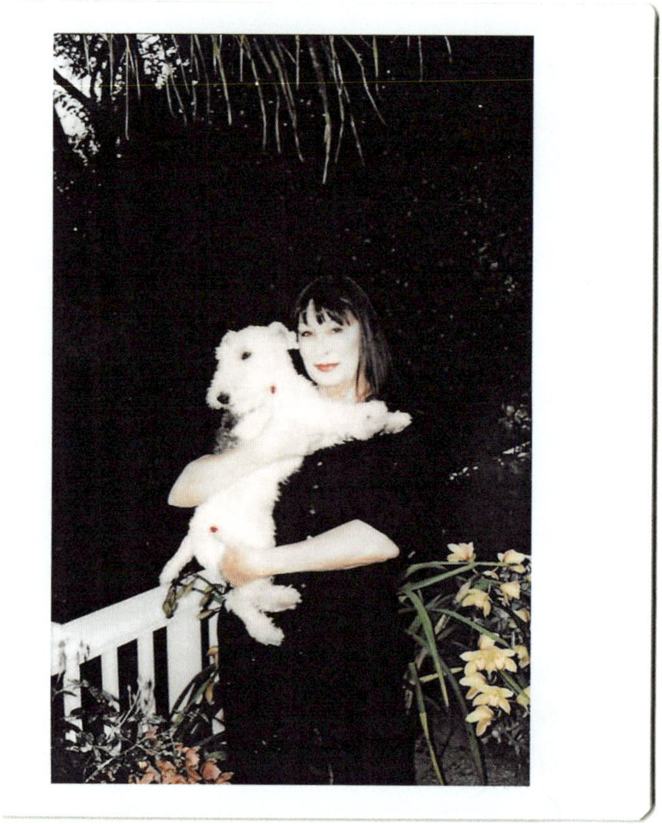

AH: I don't know about that. I know that I am very influenced by Edith Wharton, Jane Austen, and Lillian Ross. I love Willa Cather, and I have a passion for Dawn Powell and Dorothy Parker. I mostly love female novelists from the eighteenth and nineteenth centuries.

HHM: That is an interesting selection of writers. Joan Didion said ...

AH: Now, there is another great writer.

HHM: She said that somehow, writing always had an element of performance in it. Do you relate to this concept?

AH: Yes, I do. You have to make it interesting for the reader, and it has to do with the way words look together in a sentence—how words look on a page. It is a very subtle thing, but some just work together, while others need to be switched around to make a sentence beautiful. I do think there is a sense of performance and presentation to writing.

HHM: What is the most valuable book in your library?

AH: I have a book that was hand-painted. It was a gift from my great-aunt, Margaret, who was an opera singer and by all accounts, a big character. She had a conservatory in Santa Barbara and was a powerful woman. This beautiful hand-painted book was given to her by one of her students. It's such a fantastic testimony to my great-aunt. And then, I have a book of photographs that my husband made for me when we were first married. In a fire, I'd take both of those books.

HHM: I would like to ask you about another big subject in your career. What is your relationship to fashion?

AH: Lately, I don't know. I used to have a really good relationship with fashion: I loved it, and it loved me. But there comes a time when you grow up, you know. Fashion has gotten younger and younger, up until this moment, where no girls under eighteen are featured in *Vogue*—as if that's gonna work … I think fashion is for the people who look best in it. At a certain point in your life—unless you make fashion your end goal or your main interest, in which case you dress in extremes, or have a real attitude toward fashion, like Iris Apfel or Diana Vreeland—you no longer want to dedicate your life to it. I feel I sort of did that, at a time when it was really great and really fun. I worked with fantastic photographers. We were naughty and we were allowed to be naughty, and nobody talked about …

HHM: Political correctness?

AH: The lexicon had not yet been invented, so yes, things were a bit dangerous and yes, that was part of the allure. Then, fashion went silly in a way, and became something else … I like to say fashion became "girls in their mother's dresses and their father's shoes." But fashion is all over the place now. I don't know if it even knows where it wants to be anymore.

HHM: Back then, you were photographed by Richard Avedon, Irving Penn, Guy Bourdin, Helmut Newton, David Bailey, Herb Ritts …

I'VE ALWAYS LIKED TO BE AN INTERPRETER. I THINK WHAT I LOVE ABOUT BEING AN ACTRESS IS THAT I CAN TAKE AN IDEA AND RUN WITH IT

AH: Bob Richardson. Maybe the greatest of them all.

HHM: It seems to me that you had an interesting symbiotic relationship with photographers, both as a muse and as a great subject.

AH: Thank you. I like to think so too (*laughs*). I've always liked to be an interpreter. I think what I love about being an actress is that I can take an idea and run with it. I love being directed. I love when somebody has a good idea and I can play with it—that is what I also loved about modeling. I remember I'd heard for years how difficult and hard Helmut Newton was.

HHM: He had quite a reputation …

AH: He was fantastic. I was doing the Paris collections with David Bailey and Guy Bourdin, and when we finished, and Fashion Week was over, I went back to my apartment at three o'clock in the morning and received a call from *Vogue*. They needed a picture for the lead page, and they asked me if I could come to the Place du Palais-Bourbon and do a picture with Helmut Newton right away. I was so excited. I got into a taxi and got to the corner of the square, which was where *Vogue* was, and there was Helmut. He was all set up. It was just him, he didn't even have an assistant with him … perhaps one, which by today's standards sounds ridiculous. I changed into the dress, came out, and mine was the first photograph in the series of Polaroids where the girls' eyes went red. I loved it. He was so enthusiastic and electric … "Go back! Walk forward and do this! Do that!" I was in heaven! (*laughs*). We parted as good friends. We did this thing, dawn came, and that was that, and then he booked me a lot. I loved working with him. It was odd because he also loved working with my husband—not then, as I think he met him later in the eighties, but Bob [Graham] was one of his favorite subjects.

HHM: Andy Warhol also made portraits of you. How did that happen?

AH: Well, when I first came to New York, I was staying at the apartment of my best and oldest friend, Joan Juliet Buck, who at the time was working for a fashion magazine as a junior editor. She kind of took me around New York and introduced me to her friends. A lot of people were hanging around Max's Kansas City, and I think that was when I first met Warhol. He liked exotics, and, you know, we were very young, pretty, and I came from an interesting family, so I think he was happy to have us around. Then, we went out to the Factory and there were a lot of fascinating people around. He had a very interesting coterie: Bob Colacello, the model Viva, Gerard Malanga … It was a very rich time in terms of art and what was going on in the places people congregated. It was also the first time I ever met any

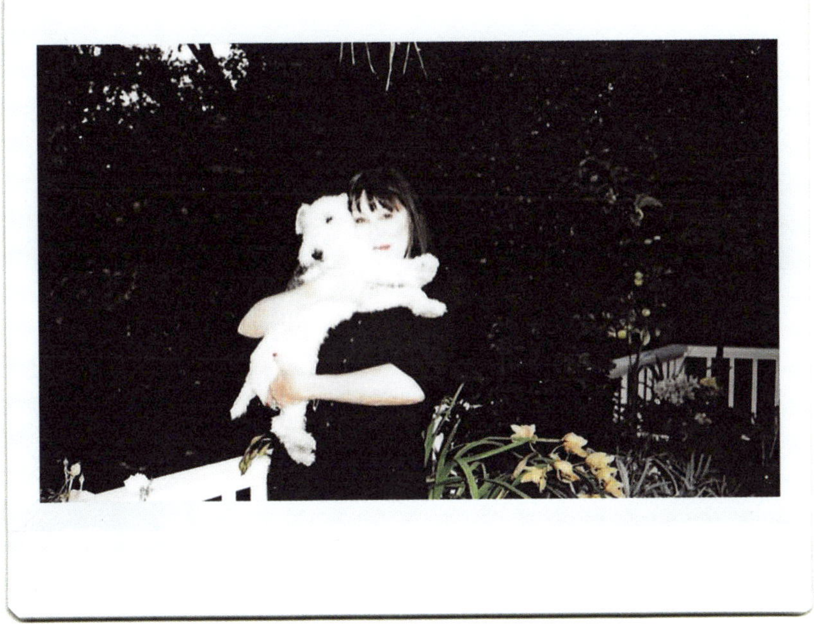

transgender people. I was attracted to them and kind of fascinated by them. People like Candy Darling, Holly [Woodlawn], and Jackie Curtis. They were such interesting people to me—I was still kind of innocent and new to this particular side of New York. I found it all very interesting.

HHM: I believe those social scenes, such as CBGB, Max's [Kansas City], and Studio 54, helped mold New York City as we see it today.

AH: Definitely. I think these were the primal years for fashion and rock and roll, there is no question about it. Although I think I went to Studio 54 twice; I was not totally happy there …

HHM: Why?

AH: Too many people hit on my boyfriend (*laughs*).

HHM: (*laughs*) Beauty is a key element in the history of film and fashion. What is your concept of beauty?

AH: It is kind of a difficult question to answer, because the more I see myself age on film, the less I like to look at myself in it. Although, when I see other people aging on film, it is not an uncomfortable thing.

HHM: You have always been strongly connected to the art world. Where did your interest in art start?

AH: At my father's and mother's knee. My mother had amazing taste. She took my father's direction and went looking for a house in Ireland to raise my brother Tony and me. She found this house in County Galway, and she commandeered the decoration. She was also an interpretive artist because she was a ballet dancer and was therefore very disciplined. She understood basic things like … I don't know, one of the things I remember her saying about decorating rooms was that the floor should always be an earthy color and the walls should always be a sky color.

HHM: That sounds right.

AH: It sounds right if you think about it. That was also a concern of my husband's in terms of architecture, scale, and how people fit into their environment.

HHM: At what point in your career did you feel like you were a successful actress?

AH: I think after I won the Academy Award.

HHM: Do you worry about being overexposed?

AH: Never! (*laughs*).

HHM: What inspires you the most?

AH: Love and appreciation.

CA

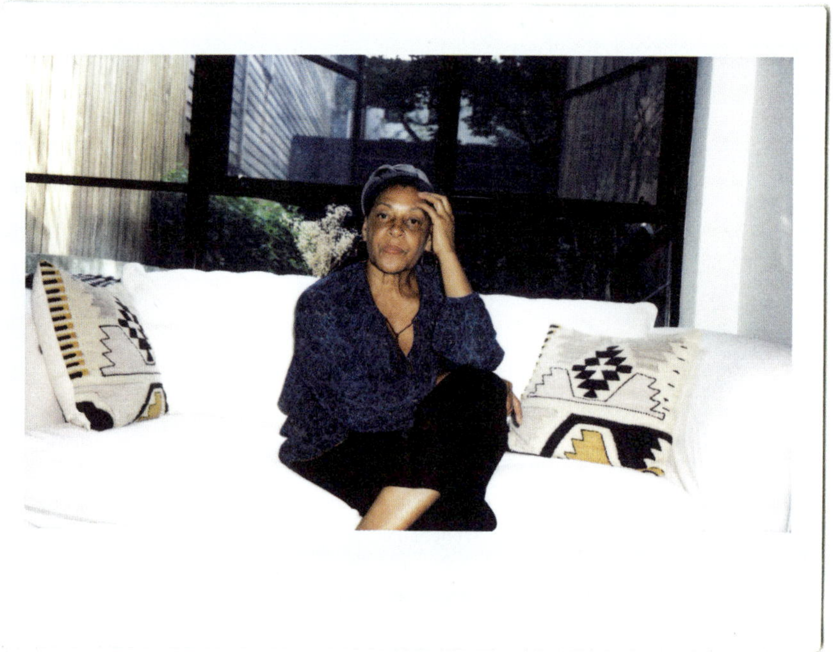

CARRIE MAE WEEMS

BROOKLYN, 2018

R

RIE

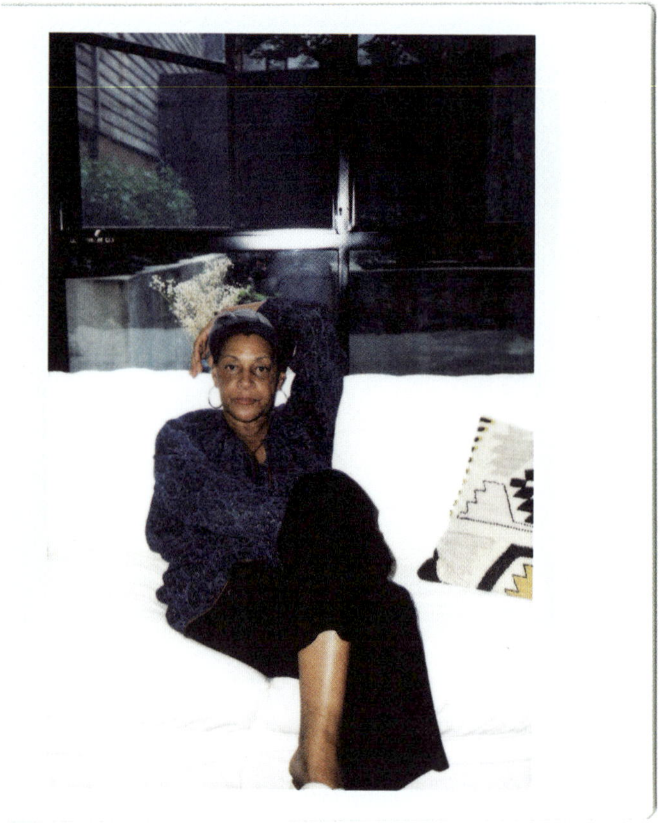

Through image and text, film and performance, and her many connections with individuals across a multitude of disciplines, Carrie Mae Weems has created a complex body of work that centers on her overarching commitment to helping us better understand our present moment by examining our collective past. Carrie has received several awards, grants, and fellowships, including the MacArthur "Genius" grant. She is represented in public and private collections around the world, including the Metropolitan Museum of Art, the Museum of Modern Art in New York, Tate Modern, and the Museum of Contemporary Art in Los Angeles.

I met Carrie in a sound studio in downtown Brooklyn while she was recording her voice for an upcoming project. The room seemed to be ideal for this type of conversation as she filled the space with her eloquent and profound voice. In person, Carrie has a magnetism that's almost planetary and her references move from theoretical and sociopolitical to anecdotal. She is an artist who has made her career creating spaces for contemplation in the place of absence. She is a gifted storyteller who works fluently with text and image, creating new narratives that insist on the worth of Black and brown bodies in art and in life.

HUGO HUERTA MARIN:
Can we talk about the genesis of your seminal work the *Kitchen Table* series?

CARRIE MAE WEEMS:
Well, I was teaching photography in New England at Hampshire College, and I was working with young students—young men and women—and it was a very particular time: A lot of work was being generated, a lot of theoretical ideas were being discussed around the objectification of women, and how women were presented in film, TV, popular culture, society …

And I noticed that all my female students were taking these photographs where they were never quite squarely facing the camera—they were always sort of hiding behind their hair or their hands or an object, whereas all the men were always squared to the camera. I was thinking about the ways in which young women are thinking about themselves. I was thinking about theoretical theory, feminist theory—which was really powerful and dominant at that moment—and I was also thinking about how very few African American women have been described in any of these texts. You know, Laura Mulvey's seminal texts on the gaze had so little to do with the way Black women have been theorized. There was very little theory around Black women and Black bodies in general. It was in that context that I made *Kitchen Table*. I started with one image one night when this wonderful man—who happened to be a neighbor—came over. I was looking at this man under this light and thought: "What a fabulous moment." So, I invited him back and I made this photograph of him titled, *Jim, if you choose to accept, the mission is to land on your own two feet.*

I started questioning the idea of the role of Black men and agency, and began thinking about that set, that room, that environment, that light—where I could build a set of photographs that would, for me, answer a number of the theoretical questions that had been circulating. I thought about the ways the gaze could be focused, could be challenged, could be re-contextualized to bring in Black bodies themselves, you know? I started in that way and it was a wonderful endeavor. It was as though all the lightbulbs were turned on and I had a sense of clarity … So, I would go to the space and make photographs, then immediately

YOU CAN'T LOOK AT BLACK BODIES AND NOT THINK OF RACE— AT LEAST NOT IN AMERICA

go to my dark room, process the film, look at the film, come back home, go back to the same set-up again, photograph it again, go back to the lab … It was a very intensive period of photographing and re-photographing. I was very clear on what I wanted the images to look like, and whom I wanted to bring into the orbit along with me.

HHM: It sounds as though the work deals more with individuality than race.

CMW: Oh, absolutely. But you can't look at Black bodies and not think of race—at least not in America. The project is not about race, and in that way, it has been wonderful because the work has been embraced internationally. Whether I show the work in Spain, South Africa, Paris, Germany, Hong Kong—wherever I show it, people respond pretty much the same way. People are really interested in the stories of women they relate to. The situations they relate to.

HHM: It has the sense of documentary photography but it is actually constructed as a vehicle for questioning ideas. In that sense,

I wanted to ask you, what invisible things do you think photographs make visible?

CMW: Just about every emotion there is, every condition there is, and it is made available through the articulation of a form captured. All those emotions are there. It is one of the great things about the tool—about the medium of photography. It has the extraordinary ability to describe and to imply.

HHM: What is the function of photography for you?

CMW: Well, I've used photography as my launch pad and it has taken me into the world—not that I am a documentary photographer—but I am deeply interested in looking at things, people, architecture, social situations, cultural phenomena … I am deeply curious about the world. I have always been looking at it. Photography allows me to move through it as a kind of participant-observer.

HHM: It's interesting that you don't consider yourself a documentary photographer.

CMW: I was always interested in documentary but I really didn't like photographing people without their permission, and I don't like being photographed without my permission. But I love and respect the tradition of documentary; it has done extraordinary things. We have been able to see the world in a very interesting way, so this tension between the constructed image and the found moment is the tension that exists within *Kitchen Table*, and it also has a weird proximity to time—you don't really know when it was made. It could have been made yesterday, or fifty years ago. It has this open conceptual quality that allows it to continue to be vital. Young women and young men are still coming to that work, looking at that work, thinking about that work, engaging with it, and I think that is really special.

HHM: I agree. I remember the first time I saw the *Kitchen Table* series in 2014 at the Guggenheim, and the impact it had on me, knowing that it was the museum's first survey of an African American female artist …

CMW: No. First African American artist—ever. That is important.

HHM: Certainly. How did the exhibition affect your career?

CMW: I am not really sure, because I have been working for a really long time, have been busy for a really long time, have been outspoken for a really long time, and have always been asked to do a lot of different things. It feels like I am still in the same place in a lot of ways, you know? I mean, another reality is that it didn't really change the market for my work. You would have expected it to, but it didn't. So, how did it change my career? I don't really know … I think maybe in some ways, winning the MacArthur was probably more important in that way … On the other hand, the Guggenheim exhibition was a complex installation project because they split it in several ways and it broke the continuity of the exhibition,

THE IDEA OF DIGGING THROUGH HISTORIES IS A DEEP PART OF MY LIFE, MY THINKING, AND MY INTERESTS

and there were problems because of that. This is just my own critical thinking about the show. The thing that was most interesting about it was building a sophisticated program around the show, where I invited over 180 artists to join me over the course of a week to explore the dynamics of what artists are doing in the field: artists, dancers, writers, poets, singers ... That shit was fabulous! What artists bring to the table and how they use their platforms is extremely interesting to me.

HHM: I am certain this brought a lot of attention to the Black artistic community.

CMW: Of course. Showing at the Guggenheim — one of New York's most premier institutions — was no small thing. The feedback was amazing, and the pride of the community was extraordinary. You know, people would just approach me in a grateful way. That is not what I expected, but there was a sense that a culture was being represented, and that was important.

HHM: Do you consider yourself a political artist?

CMW: No, I don't. But I consider myself a political person.

HHM: In your series titled *From Here I Saw What Happened and I Cried*, there is a strong connection to the trauma of history. When did you first become interested in the concept of memory?

CMW: Probably very early on. I started my life thinking I was going to be a scientist. I thought I was going to be an archeologist or an anthropologist. The idea of digging through histories is a deep part of my life, my thinking, and my interests. Of course, the investigation of my own family is history, which is returning again in my work. In these ideas about playing within memories and associations and history—because it is memory in relationship to history, not memory for its own sake—I am interested in the exploration of what is known about the past and how that gets passed on.

HHM: The historical past and the historical present.

CMW: That's right.

HHM: What does the viewer bring to these photographs?

CMW: I don't know, but hopefully, some level of understanding, because I think there is always a negotiation between yourself and the viewer and the object. I am interested in engaged conversations, whether that happens between you and me, me and the object, you and the object, or the triangulation of that. So, I am open to the mind of the viewer, the interpretation of the viewer, and sometimes, of course, the viewer tells me more about the work than I already knew, which is also really wonderful.

HHM: Often, the work made by Black or Latin artists is considered to be exclusively about skin color or cultural background, unlike work that's made by white artists, which is assumed to be universal at its core.

CMW: Right.

HHM: In that respect, how do you think things have changed in the last few decades?

CMW: Not much. In fact, I think it is intensifying in a certain way because of the position museums and cultural institutions are in now. You see, we all now know something that I have been talking about for forty years—that we will be undergoing a profound demographic shift in this country and that it is going to mean something, and in a few years, this reality will be true. None of these institutions have big collections made by brown people, none of them … Brown people or women, for that matter. Primarily, they are institutions that were built by white men or by women for white men, but that is why they were built. Now there is a kind of shift in the thinking, but the thinking isn't really complex, the thinking is reactionary. So, it is sort of like, "Oh, OK. We've got to show some Black people, we've got to show some brown people, and we've got to show some women." All the granting institutions

NONE OF THESE INSTITUTIONS HAVE BIG COLLECTIONS MADE BY BROWN PEOPLE, NONE OF THEM [...] NOW THERE IS A KIND OF SHIFT IN THE THINKING, BUT THE THINKING ISN'T REALLY COMPLEX, THE THINKING IS REACTIONARY

are saying: "If you don't have Black representation, we can't fund you." "If you don't have any African Americans, Latin Americans, or Asians in your program, we can't fund you." These are billions of dollars we are talking about for thousands of institutions. Historically, the white institutions have been trying to figure out how to negotiate this rapidly changing world that we are in, and how to engage brown artists. The question is more, "Can we get you in?" And not, "What is the structure of your contribution?"

HHM: Absolutely.

CMW: Right? I am very interested in the ways in which someone like Okwui [Enwezor] comes along in the context of the Venice Biennale. It's not necessarily the greatest Biennale of all time but it's certainly a significant one, and one that never existed before. These incredible minds are finally being heard, relaying on some other sorts of parameters for consideration, and then there are the young curators coming to the race saying, "Oh, yes!" There is a whole new pathway to be explored concerning the relationships between modernism and invention, and the Black and brown bodies in the world; the abstraction, the sort of post-colonial thinking that is more than simply an articulation of the colonial experience. In some ways, there is a shift, but it is coming from and for the wrong reasons.

HHM: It is not part of a dialogue; it is a requirement.

CMW: It is a requirement. But what you do with that requirement is what matters.

HHM: Yes. It reminds me of what the Cuban artist Tania Bruguera told me about Latin American writing. She said that despite there being more visibility for Latin American art, we still face many stereotypes. Therefore, it is important to remember the Latin American critics as part of the equation, as they explain the artistic process from a Latin American perspective.

CMW: Right.

HHM: To fully understand the complexity of certain realities and present them to other groups that are not aware of them.

CMW: We live in a time where everyone is allowed to talk about anything that is presented in this world, and I see this as a really important moment to negotiate and navigate with the art professionals to talk about the work that is changing the face of the world. We need to demand that they know about the work and talk about it beyond race or cultural background.

HHM: In your series *All the Boys*, you talk about the system, power, race, and police brutality. Was it your intention to bring awareness to the ways in which African Americans were and are depicted?

CMW: Yes … Sort of … I worked with the idea of the hoodie—the idea that the way people dress can get them killed, that it is a cultural signifier, and I think it is a fascinating thing. But *All the Boys* came from a larger project called *Grace Notes*, which was really looking at—regardless of all things—how one not only maintains the scope of one's humanity in the face of deadly forces that are pressing against one, but also maintains the core of oneself. The core of our humanity. I was more interested in the response of the Black body toward these forces of resistance, and it was in this context that I began to understand the extraordinary sense of grace; this amazing sense of compassion.

HHM: What is your concept of beauty?

CMW: Well … You. I find the world amazing, so it is not confined to anything. It's simply a condition. Beauty is a condition of living.

HHM: What are your thoughts on the rise of the artist as celebrity?

CMW: Oh, well, it is all about money. Cultural production, money … What else is there? There is nothing left, there is no industry. So, you have robots, technology, and, you know, a few personalities.

HHM: At what point in your career did you feel that you were a successful artist?

CMW: One day, I went to Neiman Marcus to buy something, and I gave the woman my credit card and she said, "Oh, you are Carrie Mae Weems. I can give you a discount!" I thought I had arrived (*laughs*).

HHM: (*laughs*) Do you worry about being overexposed?

CMW: In a weird way, yes. It has not really changed how I act in the world, but I do think about it.

HHM: Do you have any recurring dreams?

CMW: Not anymore. But one recurring dream I had was that I always tried to get back home, so I could work in the fields with my family, but I couldn't.

HHM: What are your thoughts on the big international art fairs like documenta or the Venice Biennale?

CMW: I am sort of turned off by the art fairs and by the economy that is related to the arts. It is just so obscene, and I think we are in for a rude awakening. I think paying attention to what young artists are doing right now is so much more exciting than what is going on in most of the institutions, and certainly in fairs that are disappointing. Although, I have to admit I was very excited by Okwui's fair in Venice.

I think it set a precedent, and even though it was presented in a context that makes me gag for the most part, I understood what he was doing, and I was very happy for it. It was very important to see. I think these are really critical projects that brown people can do, because brown people have a context for doing them: We are bilingual in a very interesting way. Every day, I walk into this very complex world of whiteness. I can play with it and dance in it and do all kind of stuff in it, and then I go home and I can do that there too, but they are very separate worlds. Many times, when I go to major cultural events in New York City, you know, there are hundreds of people, and I am often the only Black person in the room. And that is a problem.

HHM: What is the most honest thing you can say about yourself?

CMW: I am terrified. And I make work out of my deep terror.

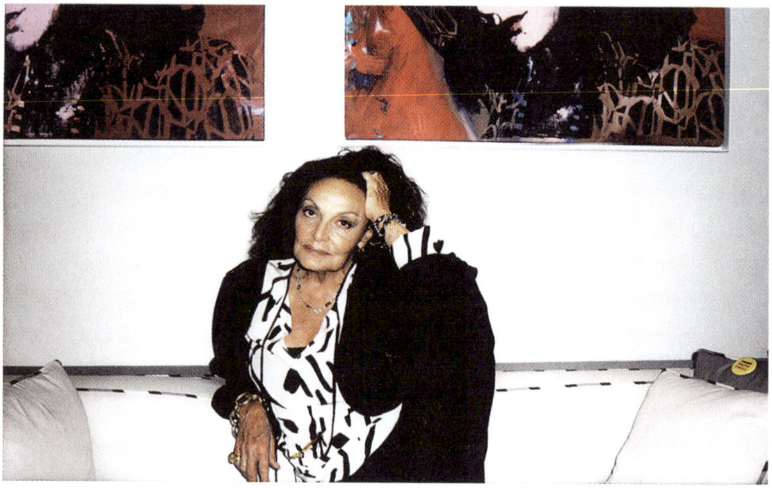

NE

D IA

DIANE VON FÜRSTENBERG

NEW YORK, 2017

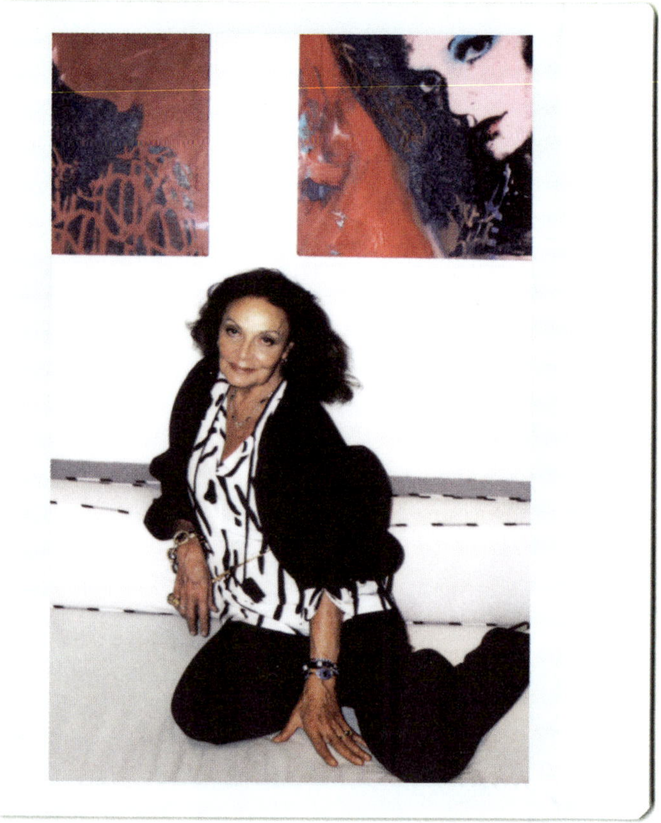

Diane von Fürstenberg is a fashion designer, a philanthropist, and the founder of her eponymous company. In 1974, she created the iconic wrap dress, which became a symbol of empowerment for women all over the world. DVF is now a global luxury fashion brand celebrated for its powerful connection to generations of women.

It was a sunny New York summer's day and I am not exactly sure how I ended up riding with Diane around Manhattan. She suggested we continue our conversation in the car, and one minute later, we were inside her Bentley outside of her corporate headquarters in the Meatpacking District. During the period of time I spent with her, I witnessed her speaking four different languages with different members of her team, writing a speech for an event she was hosting that evening, and shaking hands with all the people who approached her on our way out. I was captivated by the fearless woman talking about the fashion industry and her nights out at Studio 54. Diane is a fashion designer by profession, but she's also an activist, an avid feminist, and, needless to say, a living icon.

HUGO HUERTA MARIN:
The concept of beauty is vital to the fashion industry. What is your concept of beauty?

DIANE VON FÜRSTENBERG:
The first thing that comes up for me when talking about beauty is nature. I never cease to fall in love with nature; with stones, with the sea, with the colors, with the textures. Nature is the most incredible artist.

HHM: That's interesting. For me, influence sometimes comes from South and Latin American cultures. Do you ever get inspiration from pre-Columbian cultures?

DVF: Yes, of course. I just suck it in. But inspiration comes mostly from nature—from bark. Bark is the most beautiful thing!

HHM: There seems to be a dialogue between women and your designs. Is your work a celebration of femininity?

DVF: And freedom.

HHM: Patti Smith once said that most of her poems were written to women because women are the most inspiring. She asked: "Who are most artists? Men. Who do they get inspired by? Women."

DVF: Listen, until we go into artificial intelligence—which is almost around the corner—the woman has been the womb; mother. Everything has come out of the woman until now … So, yes, I do think women serve as inspiration.

HHM: What do you think is the difference between how men and women design clothes?

DVF: Christian Lacroix once said to me: "Men design costumes; women design clothes." For instance, jersey. Usually, men don't design with jersey because it doesn't look as glamorous as satin. Women like jersey because they know how it feels. Women are more practical. But I don't think you can generalize. I think it is sexist to do so.

HHM: On the other hand, when you think about [John] Galliano or Thierry Mugler's designs in the nineties …

MY IDEAS ALWAYS COME FROM LIFE. I CELEBRATE LIFE. I LOVE LIFE

DVF: Absolutely.

HHM: What was your relationship to New York at the time you created your iconic wrap dress?

DVF: I arrived in 1970. I was a young princess and I had married a prince … Did you read my book?

HHM: I did.

DVF: I was pregnant and I had little dresses in my suitcase. I arrived in New York and New York was so different from what I was expecting because I thought it was going to be modern and it wasn't. Instead, it was dangerous, it was cheap … and because it was cheap, there were a lot of artists around. It was a hub of art. [Robert] Rauschenberg, [Andy] Warhol, this and that … everyone was in New York because it was cheap—even Chelsea. It was an amazing thing; there was sexual freedom and it was before the AIDS pandemic. I mean, I was young at the best time in the world.

HHM: Would you say your ideas come from a similar place?

I BECAME A DESIGNER ALMOST BY ACCIDENT, MOSTLY BECAUSE I WANTED TO BE INDEPENDENT [...] BUT WHAT MADE ME WANT TO DESIGN WAS WOMEN. IT IS STILL ALL ABOUT THE WOMAN

DVF: My ideas always come from life. I celebrate life. I love life.

HHM: What is your relationship to New York nowadays?

DVF: I think New York is like Venice, where art and commerce meet.

HHM: At what point do designers decide the tone of what is coming in fashion?

DVF: You know, I became a designer almost by accident, mostly because I wanted to be independent. I worked with a man who had a printing factory and I learned all the processes. But what made me want to design was women. It is still all about the woman.

HHM: You don't follow trends …

DVF: For me, fashion is a symphony. I mean, I created a dress in 1972 that is still around today. So, if we are talking about trends … How can you decide what is coming next? Obviously, designers get inspired by the street, by people, by behavior, and then, suddenly, it becomes an ongoing thing—it comes from the moment. Why do trends and clothes suddenly look like the clothes of the homeless or refugees?

HHM: Does having your designs shown at the Metropolitan Museum of Art's Costume Institute or the Smithsonian give them a different meaning?

DVF: For the first time, MoMA is doing an exhibition on fashion called *Items: Is Fashion Modern*? They are showing items from Hermès, the iconic Levi's, and of course, they are showing my first dress—the wrap dress. It is a leopard wrap dress that was made forty-five years ago. That to me is wonderful because it means it is timeless.

HHM: You are also considered an icon in the fashion industry. Has this affected the brand in one way or another?

DVF: You know, when I first started, I never thought about a brand. Suddenly, I had huge success. I was so young and I became the brand. You become bigger than yourself and therefore, you inspire others. The minute you start inspiring others is great because it is not about ego or titles anymore. Instead, it's about "If you can do it, I believe I can do it too." And that is my mission in life.

HHM: To resonate?

DIANE VON FÜRSTENBERG

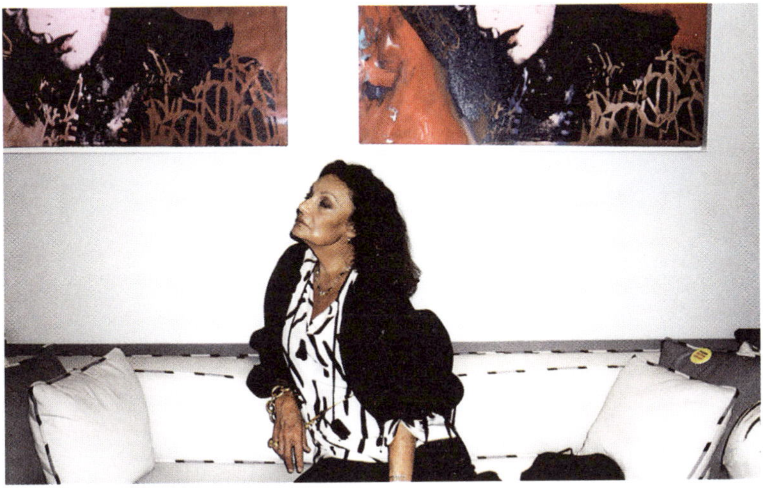

DVF: To inspire freedom. To celebrate freedom.

HHM: You understand fabrics, colors, prints, and shapes in a masterful way. When did you first become interested in fabrics and prints?

DVF: When I started to work with a man who had a printing factory in Como—the center of silk. Then, I learned about illustration and how to take illustrations and put them on repeat … At the beginning, I didn't know anything about it at all but then I became more and more involved. Nowadays, it has become my signature; it's what I do best.

HHM: Do you think that today, fashion is driven by commercialization rather than intellectually interesting design?

DVF: Fashion is not art. Fashion is design and what differentiates it from art is that it has a utilitarian meaning, and that is important. What is the utility of fashion? Obviously, it's to cover the body but it's also to make a woman look beautiful.

HHM: Having said that, what role do you think sex plays in fashion?

DVF: I think a very important one. Whenever I have fittings, when these young designers design clothes, I always ask, "Who gets laid in that?" That is one filter for me.

HHM: We've seen young designers design bolder collections for the more classic and established fashion brands. What do you think of shock as a strategy?

DVF: Shock? I think anything you do as a strategy sounds terrible. It has got to be real. To use shock as a strategy is disgusting.

HHM: With regards to a different artistic realm, I read you had opened a small publishing house and had a literary salon in Paris. What role does literature play in your life?

DVF: Huge. I love books more than anything else. I never thought I would work in fashion; I always thought I would be in literature. When I was a very young girl, I asked my teacher, "What can you do for a living if you like books?" And she said, "You could be a librarian." The librarian at my school had very bad breath, and that was the end of that (*laughs*).

HHM: (*laughs*) You have also been strongly connected to the art world—from your relationships with artists, to being photographed by Warhol, Terry Richardson, and Chuck Close …

DVF: I just love art, plain and simple. When it moves me, it moves me. You know, art is all about emotion. It is something like nature; you just stand in awe.

HHM: Do you think pain is important for an artist?

DVF: I think art—good art—often comes from pain. I mean, look at Egon Schiele. He died when he was twenty-eight. He was miserable, his work was all about pain, and it is still resonant today—one hundred years later. His pain, then, had a purpose.

HHM: Francis Bacon, Frida Kahlo …

DVF: Absolutely. On the other hand, [Pablo] Picasso didn't paint from pain, [Henri] Matisse didn't work from pain. But who wants to read a book about happiness? It's so boring.

HHM: Do you think female artists are more inward-looking?

DVF: It is very unfair to talk about art and women because for so long, women were not allowed to be artists and the same happened in architecture, literature, science, and so on … Women are artists of life, which is why I love Marina's [Abramović] work so much, you know, because her art is about—Ah! It is about life! It is about courage and it is about daring.

HHM: Speaking of art imitating life, I recently visited a Warhol retrospective in Mexico City. I couldn't stop watching the video featuring the Empire State Building in a leading role. Do you think he started the obsession with icons and brands we see nowadays?

DVF: I don't think he started it; I just think he was a visionary. I actually produced a documentary on him. His obsession with icons came from the fact that he was raised in a Russian Orthodox environment and was a great believer. He attended church with his mother and when you go to an Orthodox church that often,

WOMEN ARE ARTISTS OF LIFE, WHICH IS WHY I LOVE MARINA'S [ABRAMOVIĆ] WORK SO MUCH, YOU KNOW, BECAUSE HER ART IS ABOUT—AH! IT IS ABOUT LIFE! IT IS ABOUT COURAGE AND IT IS ABOUT DARING

you quickly realize it is all about the icons. So, that concept started in his childhood. Then, he came to New York as an illustrator and became fascinated with Coca-Cola, Campbell's soups, Jackie Onassis, and Elvis Presley, and he created art in ways no one ever had before. People didn't take him seriously at the beginning. He made movies with no scripts, which were actually the beginning of reality TV, and he took Polaroids and was recording all the time. I mean, he did social media before anyone. Nowadays, he would have gone crazy …

HHM: How was your relationship with him?

DVF: I was a friend. He painted me twice, once in the seventies and then in the eighties. He put me on the cover of *Interview* twice. People are always speculating about our friendship but the truth is that Andy Warhol was a voyeur—he was not very expressive, he was always using his little recorder or taking pictures. He would suck you up like a vampire …

HHM: I was curious to know if the lips in your logo came from that *Interview* cover?

DVF: You know, we just got rid of it; it is no longer there. But that's OK, it will come back later. They were actually never meant to be a logo. It was just that I once hired a young English designer and he made a T-shirt out of them. And yes, they originally came from the cover of *Interview* magazine. We only used the lips from that cover but they stayed with us for fifteen or twenty years. Then, last year, we changed everything. At the beginning, I thought, "Oh my God, this is terrible!" But then, looking back, I said, "Thank God!" You know, you have to move ahead.

HHM: What are your thoughts on the rise of the artist as celebrity?

DVF: I mean, right now, it's such a big deal. I think it is boring.

HHM: Where do you go to be alone?

DVF: I love being alone … for anything and everything. That is how I find my center and do not get lost.

HHM: Do you worry about being overexposed?

DVF: You know what? I don't.

HHM: What is the most honest thing you can say about yourself?

DVF: I practice the truth.

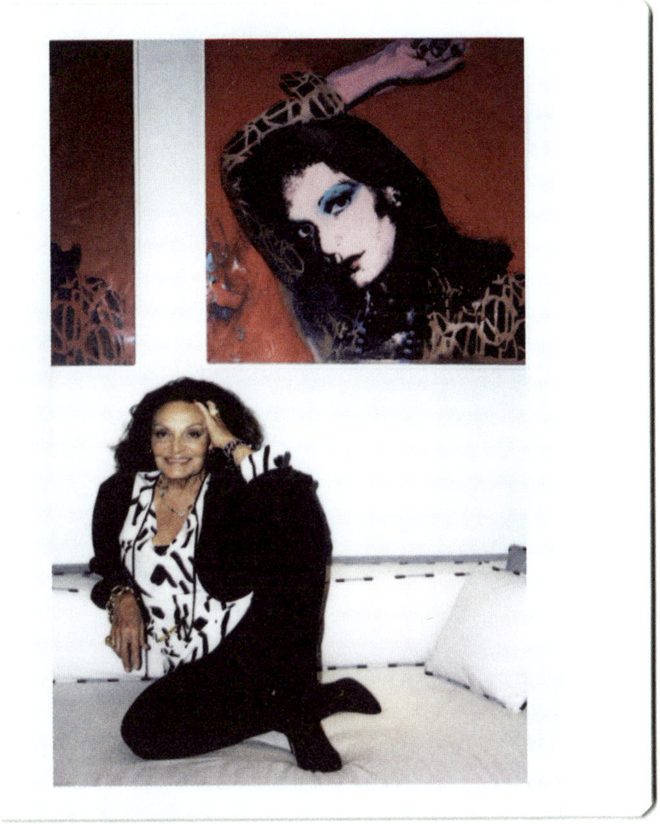

Y

O

KO

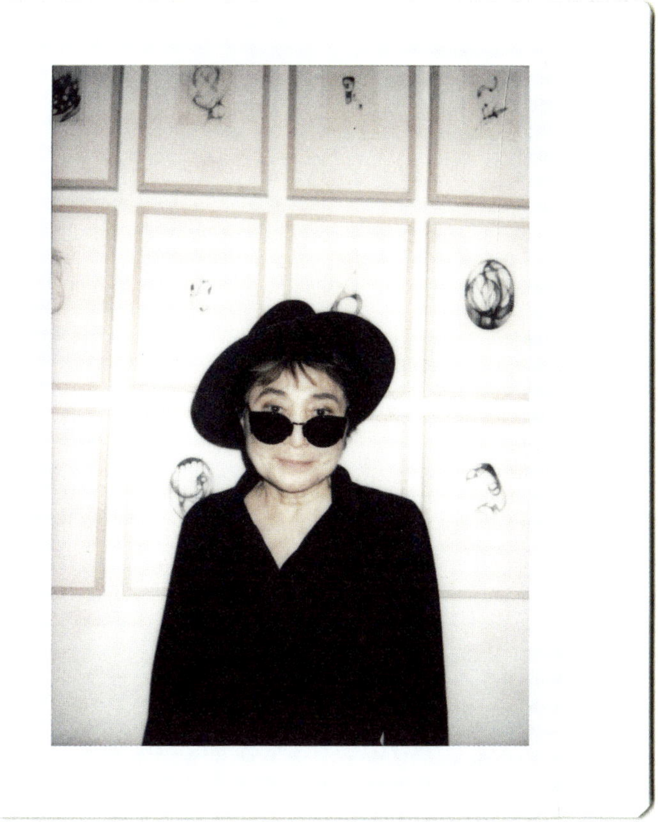

YOKO ONO

NEW YORK, 2016

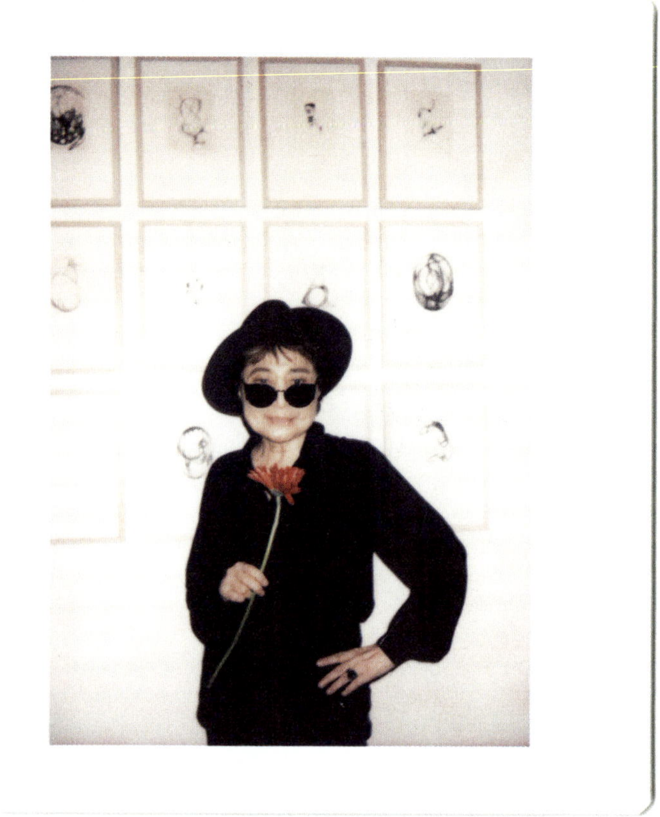

Yoko Ono is an artist whose thought-provoking work challenges people's understanding of art and the world around them. Born in Tokyo in 1933, she moved to New York in 1953 following her studies in philosophy in Japan. By the late 1950s, she had become part of the city's avant-garde, and in 1960, she opened her Chambers Street loft, where she hosted a series of radical performances and exhibited realizations of some of her early conceptual works. Since then, Yoko has given countless concerts, made several films, released more than a dozen albums, and exhibited her work in numerous museums and galleries worldwide.

It was 10:45 a.m. on a cold January day in New York, and I was waiting for Yoko to arrive at her studio, whose walls are filled with her iconic *Grapefruit* drawings. I was surprised to hear that the eighty-six-year-old elder stateswoman of cool was driving her car to get there. She entered the room decked out in sunglasses and one of her trademark hats, which she left on throughout our conversation. Through the top of her glasses, I could see her eyes: I was trying to see her more as a fellow artist than the historical icon and ground-breaking, influential artist that she is today. However, it's never been possible to divorce her life from her art. Perhaps the blend of the two is what has made both her work and her life so extraordinary.

HUGO HUERTA MARIN:
Yoko, I will start shooting questions now.

YOKO ONO:
Well, go ahead. Because you know—I don't smoke, I don't drink (*laughs*).

HHM: (*laughs*) Your mind is clear! So, to start with, can you tell me about the genesis of your historical performance *Cut Piece*?

AS AN ARTIST, WHEN YOU THINK ABOUT AN IDEA, YOU DON'T USUALLY THINK ABOUT THE RISKS THAT IT CAN REPRESENT

YO: Well, one day I thought to myself: "Why don't I do that?", and I simply did it. I first performed it at the Yamaichi Concert Hall in Kyoto. As an artist, when you think about an idea, you don't usually think about the risks that it can represent, or anything. It was a bit frightening, because a guy came toward the stage as though he was going to stab me with a pair of scissors. The audience began to scream and I remember asking myself: "What is he doing?", but I wasn't scared at all. I needed to concentrate, and go inside myself to meditate. So, it was very strange, but at that time, I didn't realize that it was a frightening scene. After the performance in Kyoto, I did *Cut Piece* in Tokyo, New York, and London, and much later in Paris. I would assume it was annoying for some people, because I kept doing it.

HHM: What was your relationship with New York at that time?

YO: Well, I created a place for artists and musicians to express themselves—a kind of space for concerts and performances—and we held the first "loft" concert in New York. I thought, "Why don't we do it in a loft?", because at that time, the only three places in New York that allowed artists to show their work were Carnegie Hall, Carnegie Recital Hall—which was a very small venue—Town Hall, and nowhere else. That was it! And you had to be pretty famous to get in. I had so many friends who were great artists, and we didn't have a space to present our work, so I thought, "Why don't we have a place for us to do the concerts, instead of waiting until Carnegie Hall says we can do it?"

HHM: The avant-garde.

YO: Exactly—that was totally unusual at the time. No one was giving concerts in a loft, and so many of my friends advised me, "Yoko, don't do it in a loft, nobody will come, you have to do it in midtown." Well, if I had had the chance to do it in midtown I would have, but I didn't have the financial resources. It was also around the same time that artists began using lofts as studios. I think there were two or three people who did that in those days. So, I started looking for places without success, but Minoru Niizuma—who was a sculptor back then—had heard that I was looking for a place and wanted to show me some spaces. One Sunday, we went downtown and he showed me the loft. It was in an old building on Chambers Street, and I remember there was a ski shop on the first floor, but I still thought it was very good. Once we were there, the owner told us that Yukiko Katsura—a very famous Japanese artist—was already interested in taking it, and if she didn't want it, then I could have it. That night, I went home and kept thinking, "Oh, please let me get it!", because it was only fifty dollars and fifty cents. That's very cheap, you know, but for me to raise that amount was a big deal. I said okay—I was ready to pay it.

The following day, I grabbed the money and ran back there. The owner told me that Yukiko Katsura hadn't taken it, so I got it. I managed to get an old piano, and Richard Maxfield called me saying that La Monte Young wanted to join me. That was how La Monte and I started doing things together, and those were very exciting times. Now, going back to that first concert, I was very surprised, because I didn't think anybody would come, as it had been snowing heavily. But against all the odds, they came: John Cage, Peggy Guggenheim, [Marcel] Duchamp, David Tudor, Max Ernst. They all came wearing big coats and all—it was great.

HHM: What is your relationship with New York nowadays?

YO: Well, it is the same old thing, except that I don't have to get a loft to do it (*laughs*).

HHM: (*laughs*) What was your relationship with Japan like at that time?

YO: Well, I performed *Cut Piece* for the first time in Kyoto. I didn't go to Japan for a long time, unless there was a reason I had to go there, such as a concert or something, so I went once every five years or something like that. But now, I go back every year. I've always had a certain relationship with it, but it wasn't as strong as my relationship with New York. New York became very important to me and my career, because that is where I started creating things. I created an actual environment, so I was very excited.

HHM: Would you say that your ideas still come from a similar place?

YO: The inspiration is different. I mean—Keith Haring created hundreds of drawings in the New York subway, you know. I used to do my work in my loft—and we all had to find a way to do it—because it has never been easy for artists. Now, I am just very lucky that people ask me to perform a concert or a show, and I do it.

HHM: Is it your intention to raise awareness through your work?

YO: From the very beginning—very early in my life—I kept telling all my friends about things that I found interesting. I felt I had to tell the world about the things that were going on. I was always connected to the world. I don't know why, and I didn't have the means to do so, but I kept saying things like, "This has to happen," or "People have to know about this," you know what I mean?

HHM: You always had the urge to communicate.

YO: Always had that.

HHM: Your work is largely concerned with oppression against women. Do you consider yourself a feminist?

YO: Well, it's a very difficult word to define now. Of course, I always felt that I was a feminist, but nowadays, there are terrible misconceptions associated with the word. People go crazy about it. But of course, I am a woman.

HHM: Light is a recurring theme in your work. Is the concept of utopia implicit in your oeuvre?

PHILOSOPHY IS IMPORTANT FOR EVERYBODY. IT IS HOW YOU CHOOSE TO SEE THE WORLD

YO: Are you talking about utopia or are you talking about *Nutopia*?

HHM: Utopia.

YO: Well, no. I think that light is our race.

HHM: And would you say philosophy is an important influence for you?

YO: I think that philosophy is important for everybody. It is how you choose to see the world.

HHM: There seems to be a strong relationship between the language and the material that you choose to use, such as bronze, marble, water, air, etc. How do you decide on one specific material?

YO: It all depends on the piece, really. And when I think about the piece, I immediately think about the material. They go together.

HHM: Also, working with language has always been extremely important for you. Why have you decided to incorporate instructions along with some of your work, as in *Grapefruit*?

YO: I first started as a poet. But also, even when I was a very young woman—I mean, it sounds crazy because I think I am a young woman now (*laughs*) … When I was an infant, I always wanted to do something. And whenever I wanted to do that something, I always thought about it in terms of material; not just for artworks, but also for music, films, and all the things that I do. I always think about what I need to use in order to create.

HHM: A method.

YO: Yes. One of the most important things I learned at school was to listen to the sounds in one's own environment. We got homework in which you were supposed to listen to the sounds of the day and translate them into musical notes. This made me constantly translate the sounds around me into musical notes as a habit.

HHM: Talking of the instructions incorporated into your work, would you agree with Marcel Duchamp when he said that "the audience does half the work"?

YO: Well, I must say that Duchamp didn't have that kind of communication with the public. What Duchamp did in those days was incredible. He used these daily ordinary materials and established them as art. But his work was done, and that was it—that is where he stood. I, on the other hand, wanted people to join in and interact with me. So that is different, I think.

HHM: Would you say that activism is the core of your work?

YO: There was not even a word like "activism" back in those days, but I think I was very much concerned with it. I wouldn't say I was the only one; there was a large group of people who were always thinking about that kind of thing.

HHM: Is spirituality a major aspect in your work?

YO: I think spirituality is a major thing for all of us.

HHM: What is your concept of beauty?

YO: I think everything is beautiful.

HHM: Everything? Even the ugly?

YO: Yes, everything.

HHM: On what basis do you begin a new project?

YO: I think doing something that has already been done is a waste of time. Artists are not here to repeat themselves, but to do something totally new, so they can give something different to the audience. Take Matisse or Duchamp, for instance—they were way ahead of their time.

HHM: In that sense, what are the advantages or disadvantages of doing something completely new?

YO: I think that everything that is new is an advantage in itself.

HHM: What are your thoughts on the rise of the artist as celebrity?

YOU KNOW WHAT? EVERY PERSON HAS THEIR OWN OPINION ABOUT ME AND MY WORK, AND THOSE ARE THEIR IDEAS, NOT MINE. ONCE I'VE COMMUNICATED MY ART, I'VE DONE MY PART

YO: Well, not many artists are celebrities. In fact, artists have never been celebrities—until now. In some ways, becoming a celebrity is good because it makes it easier for them to communicate, and that is what artists want to do. But at the same time, there is some heavy luggage given to you (*laughs*).

HHM: Where do you go to be alone?

YO: I am always alone.

HHM: At what point in your career did you feel that you were a successful artist?

YO: I don't think I am successful yet.

HHM: Do you worry about being overexposed?

YO: Not at all (*laughs*). You know what? Every person has their own opinion about me and my work, and those are their ideas, not mine. Once I've communicated my art, I've done my part.

Then they make their own judgment. I just keep repeating that to myself by saying, "Make it, make it, you can make it," and that has been a very long road.

HHM: Do you have any recurring dreams?

YO: That this world will become a peaceful place. I believe in world peace and love. All of us should love each other—that would change the whole world. But right now, it's not like that, and therefore we are all suffering.

HHM: Duchamp once ended a symposium by saying that he thought the great artist of tomorrow "cannot be seen, should not be seen, and should go underground." Would you agree?

YO: I don't think that we need to go underground intentionally. When you are true to yourself, it doesn't matter if it's underground or aboveground; you are just being yourself.

HHM: What is the most honest thing you can say about yourself?

YO: I am a woman.

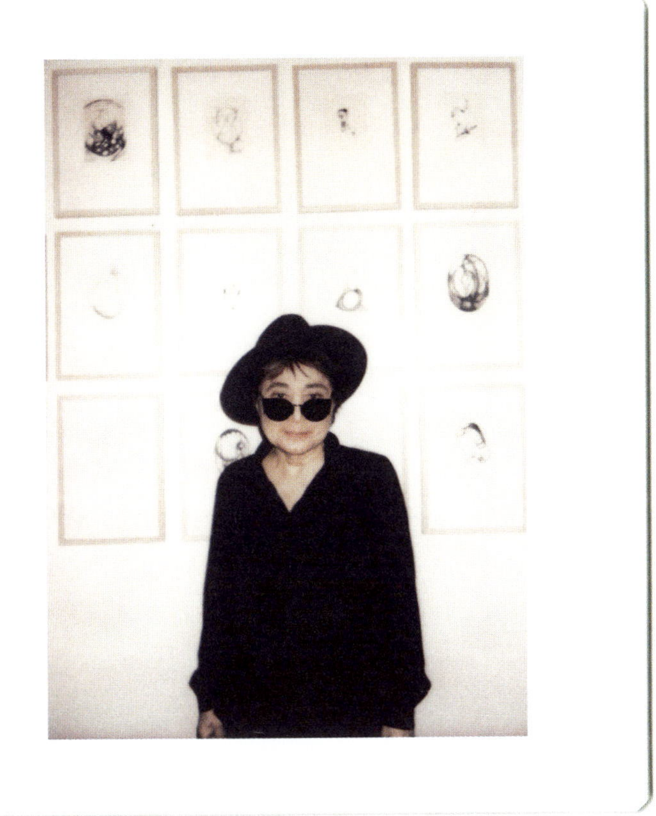

TR

A

TRACEY EMIN

NEW YORK, 2015

C

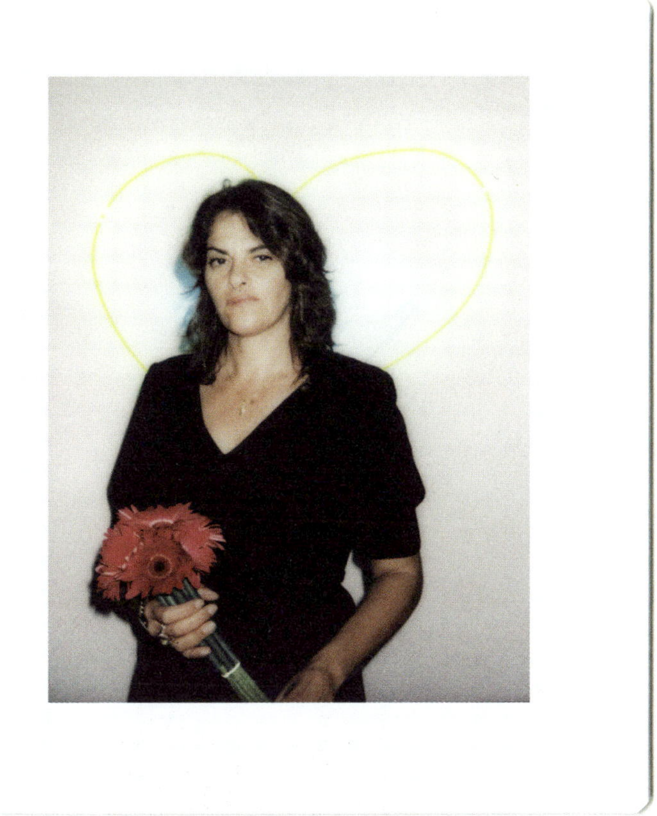

EY

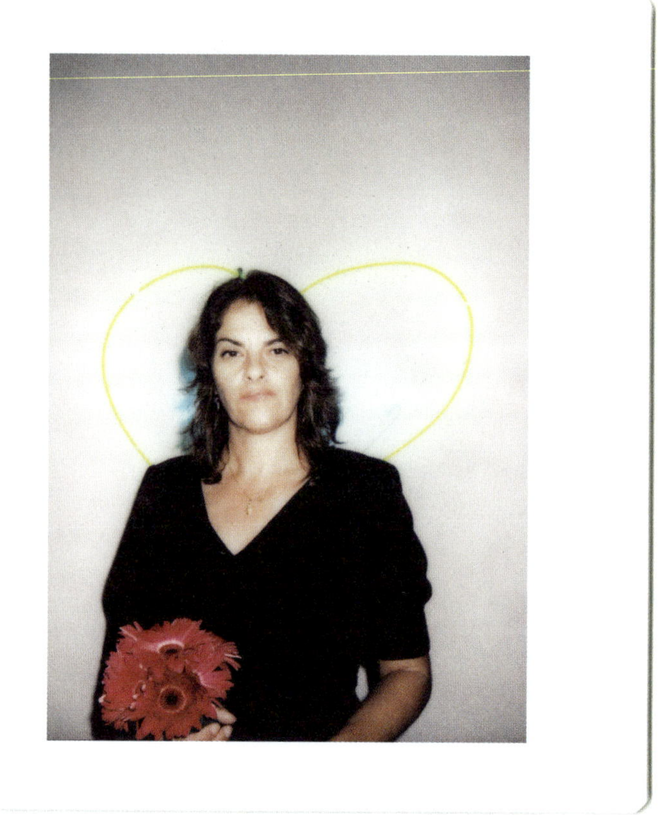

Tracey Emin is a British artist who was born in 1963. She creates work in a wide range of media, including painting, drawing, film, photography, sewn appliqué, sculpture, and neon text. Her art is primarily expressionistic, a cypher for memories and emotions that can be frank and poetic, intimate and universal. Using her own experience—and frequently her body—as source material for the work, she explores ideas of self-portraiture and narrative disclosure. Hers is a unique form of confessional art that has a non-voyeuristic intimacy, since her stories are neither tragic nor sentimental and often resonate deeply with their audience.

I met Tracey at the Lehmann Maupin gallery in New York. The room, which seemed to be the right spot for our encounter, was filled with her neon installations. In person, her energy is that of an Amazon, but is also combined with great warmth and charm. She possesses an incredible combination of courage and daring, as well as vulnerability and openness. Perhaps it may be this that makes her able to create such menacing, interesting work. At her core she is equally unafraid of failure and success, and her art is one of disclosure: It reveals her hopes, frustrations, and victories in candid, and at times scandalous, work.

HUGO HUERTA MARIN:
In your embroidered works or neon installations, is it you speaking to the viewer? Where does Tracey Emin end and this omnipresent and shapeless voice begin?

TRACEY EMIN:
I have different words that come into my mind. Sometimes it is a straightforward sentence or statement, but other times it is a dialogue or a conversation. Often it depends what the work is and why I am making it. Neons are

MY WORK IS ABOUT ME: IT IS HOW I THINK, HOW I BREATHE, HOW I MOVE, WHAT I WITNESS, WHAT I PAY ATTENTION TO

typically left open-ended for the viewers to enjoy and interpret the ending for themselves. The blankets, on the other hand, are much more informative, with short paragraphs on them—they are more like storytelling. Then there is my writing, which of course is full-blown writing: a different category altogether.

HHM: Philosopher Roland Barthes' essay "The Death of the Author" argues that writing and creator are unrelated. Do you think this theory applies to your work?

TE: I am incredibly present in my work, so I have no choice. My work is about me: It is how I think, how I breathe, how I move, what I witness, what I pay attention to. It would be very difficult for me to try and pull myself out of the work. It would be virtually impossible.

HHM: In that sense, does your half-Turkish heritage influence your work to some extent?

TE: I think not being Anglo-Saxon influences my work, whether it's the Turkish side or not—because my mum's grandfather was a Gypsy, so from my mum's side I come from this full-blown Gypsy family. Then I've got the Turkish family that comes from Sudan, Africa, so I don't think it's one thing or the other. I just know that I'm not a conservative Anglo-Saxon, and I'm definitely not a white Anglo-Saxon.

HHM: Your work is both vulnerable and confident. Which word do you think describes it best?

TE: Couldn't describe myself better if I tried. Vulnerable and confident.

HHM: Is your work about sex or love?

TE: My work is about love. It has always been about love. My work has never been about sex.

HHM: What is your position on pornography?

TE: I've only seen two porno films in my life: one involving animals, the other one by mistake at a nightclub as it was being projected on the ceiling. I've looked through one porno mag in my life and that's it. I'm not interested in it. I do like erotic, sexual things, but not in a corny way. I collect Edwardian erotic photographs, not to get off on them, but to use them as inspiration. I find them very beautiful. I've never enjoyed pornography.

HHM: You are frank about needs and desires. What is your opinion on the risk of your thoughts not being considered acceptable?

TE: That's something that worries me because, at times, I feel like I'm outside of everything and that my thoughts are unpalatable. I think a lot of artists feel that.

HHM: As a result, has your work had any repercussions in your personal life?

TE: I have very little personal life because of this. It is a sacrifice that I must make to carry on working.

HHM: Do you believe in art, or do you believe in artists?

TE: I believe in art. Art is like an entity—it's like God, it's like love. Art exists as a "thing" that floats in the ether and artists pick up on that, like some kind of medium. We transfer that feeling.

HHM: Would you say spirituality or religion is assumed in your work?

TE: My work wouldn't exist without them. I had an exhibition called *I Need Art Like I Need God.* I think that says it all.

HHM: Do you see art as a new form of religion, and museums and galleries as the new churches of our time?

TE: Yes, I definitely do.

HHM: Therefore, what is the difference between showing your work in a place like Times Square and showing it at a gallery or a museum?

TE: Times Square was fantastic; it was a once-in-a-lifetime experience. I will never forget seeing all of my neons projected up in Times Square. I've had many good gallery and museum exhibitions, but to have something like that—with all the yellow taxis passing through, and it's just there, and it's happening and living in the real world—it was exciting and different. It's not comparable to a museum or a gallery.

HHM: What do you think of art as "spectacle"?

TE: Bores me. Bores me to death.

HHM: What was your experience like as a member of the "Young British Artists" in the nineties?

TE: I can't believe we got any work done in the nineties, but somehow we did. Every night we stayed out until 5 a.m. but we also got up at 10 a.m. the following morning, so we had very long days. It was fun, a lot of fun, and I've gotten some good friendships out of it, but it was a long time ago: twenty years ago. Life is nothing like that now.

HHM: Is London still at the cutting edge of the art world?

TE: London has had flares of being at the cutting edge, but really, it's New York. New York will always be the head of Modernism, because it invented Modernism. It is an incredibly powerful city. What's great about London is that it has a kind of youth about it, a vitality. Maybe New York has a tiredness and a grandeur already. They are very different places. Some

I HAVE NEVER CREATED ANYTHING TO SHOCK ANYBODY. SOME HAVE BEEN SHOCKED, BUT I NEVER DID IT INTENTIONALLY. THAT'S NOT MY IDEA OF ART

people would say that Asia is now at the cutting edge, so it depends what your perspective is, and where you live.

HHM: What is your opinion on using shock as a form of strategy?

TE: I think it is a really foolish, immature strategy. I have never created anything to shock anybody. Some have been shocked, but I never did it intentionally. That's not my idea of art.

HHM: How would you describe your relationship with the media?

TE: I think my relationship with the media is the best it could possibly be. Sometimes I feel that my privacy is invaded—when I'm walking down the street looking scruffy and someone throws a camera in my face—but it comes with the territory. The same applies when a group of schoolgirls are screaming and wanting my autograph. That's a nice feeling. Both things actually come together.

HHM: Would you collaborate with fashion magazines, or any big-name brands?

TE: I've done it. I've collaborated with Marks & Spencer and almost every fashion magazine you could think of. I used to write for *GQ* magazine, and I am presently its Feng Shui editor. I wrote a column for *The Independent* newspaper for four years, I modelled for Vivienne Westwood, and I am friends with lots of different fashion designers. The fashion world isn't something I am terribly interested in now, but it is something I think is very interesting for other people. The only reason I'm less interested in it now is because I'm much older and I'm not a size six. It's not the nineties.

HHM: Do you think there is an abuse of feminist discourse nowadays?

TE: No, I don't. I don't think there's enough feminist discourse.

HHM: What is your worst fear?

TE: My worst fear is never going to happen, but it would be burying my children.

HHM: What are your thoughts on the rise of the artist as celebrity?

TE: There aren't that many artists that rise to celebrity. If Jeff Koons was walking down Liverpool Street now, no one would know it was Jeff Koons. Andy Warhol, Salvador Dalí, [Pablo] Picasso—there have been a few of them out there. But on the whole, some of the biggest celebrities in the art world now are actually gallerists.

HHM: There is one name that keeps coming up whenever I read about your work … Why is William Blake so emblematic to you?

TE: I think William Blake is emblematic, romantic, passionate, charged, energized, forward-thinking and timeless.

HHM: Where do you go to be alone?

TE: Several places. I go to my studio on the weekends and I work, or I go down to my swimming pool and swim during the week. But the most significant place I go for solitude is my house in France, which is in the middle of a nature reserve and quite close to the sea. I have a small studio there. I don't speak French, and I don't have any neighbors. It's pretty remote.

HHM: At what point in your career did you feel that you were a successful artist?

TE: In 1997, I went to my opening at the South London Gallery and I couldn't get in. There were big queues going down the street and I thought that maybe I had gotten there too early or something, but it was just because there were too many people. I couldn't get into my own show. That was pretty good. That was the deciding moment for me. I thought: "This could work; I could do this."

HHM: Do you worry about being overexposed?

TE: To be honest, yes I do. I always look at actors who have a new film coming out, and you see them everywhere. At first, I'm really interested in them, but by day six, I've had enough. I think it's how the media exposes things.

I personally don't have a publicist, I don't have PR, and I don't look for publicity. Everything generates itself; the work generates itself. Even if I've been out of the limelight—for example, if I've been in France for two months—the newspapers will always have something to say about me. So, there's that kind of exposure. The other kind of exposure, where your work gets too much attention and people start to diss it and want to pick holes in it because of your success—there's that problem as well. Eh, it's not that bad though. I can live with it.

HHM: What inspires you the most?

TE: Nature. The purity of nature—whether it's a waterfall, a lake, a mountain, a person, flowers, or animals. That has got to be the honest answer. And having experiences within that: that's the truth.

HHM: Do you have any recurring dreams?

TE: I do have recurring dreams, but the other night I had a terrible nightmare that a woman was standing by my bed and trying to steal my necklace. I started to fight her off and then she tried to strangle me. When I woke up from the dream, I physically felt the pain around my neck. It was really scary. It freaked me out. I don't want to have too many recurring dreams like that.

HHM: Marcel Duchamp once ended a symposium by saying that he thought the great artist of tomorrow "cannot be seen, should not be seen, and should go underground." Do you agree?

TE: Just like he was?! Maybe he was saying it because he had such a high profile, and he knew how harmful it could be. I think a lot of artists are taken far more seriously if they are just quiet and don't have a visual profile. Everyone seems to think that they are much more serious than, say, someone like me. But life is for living. You are only here once, and I'm certainly not going to be starving in my attic to have people take me seriously. I'm going to do what I want to do and enjoy my life to the fullest.

HHM: What are your thoughts on the big international art exhibitions like documenta or the Venice Biennale?

TE: I represented Britain in the Venice Biennale, and it was quite an experience—quite amazing on the one hand, but somehow soul-destroying on the other. I wasn't prepared; I don't think I'd ever be prepared for something like that. To be on that international stage is difficult. After you've done it, you have all these ideas about how you'd do it differently. It's like being pregnant and then you have an abortion. You only have three weeks to make your mind up, and the rest of your life to regret it—if that's the case.

HHM: What is the most honest thing you can say about yourself?

TE: Got a really good sense of humor.

TRACEY EMIN

CA

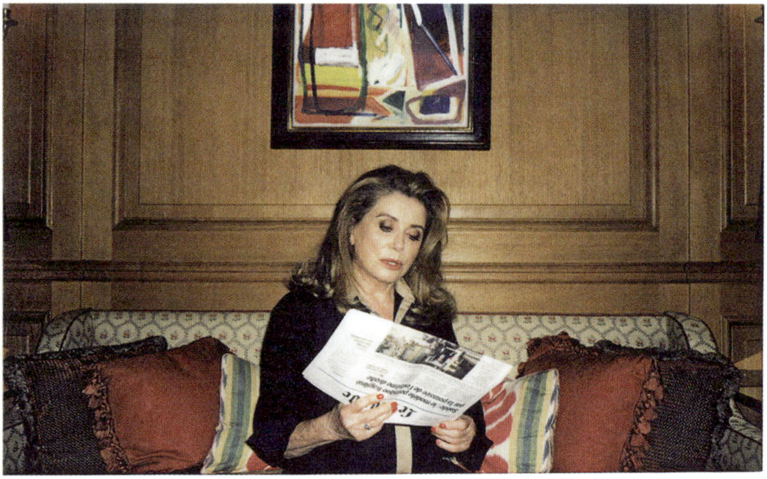

CATHERINE DENEUVE

PARIS, 2018

TH

ER

INE

Catherine Deneuve was born in Paris and is considered one of the greatest European actors. She gained recognition for her portrayal of complex characters for various directors, including Luis Buñuel, François Truffaut, and Roman Polanski. In 1985, she succeeded Mireille Mathieu as the official face of Marianne, France's national symbol of liberty. A fourteen-time César Award nominee, she won for her performances in Truffaut's *Le Dernier Métro,* for which she also won the David di Donatello for Best Foreign Actress, and Régis Wargnier's *Indochine*.

I met with Catherine Deneuve on a warm day in September at the Hotel de l'Abbaye Saint Germain in Paris. I was sitting on a couch near the lobby when I noticed people around me freeze. Entering the hotel was Catherine Deneuve in a fur coat, Jackie O sunglasses, and a Birkin bag … glowing. In person, she is every inch the star. Candid, fun, and remarkably clever, without tiptoeing she gave me 100 percent, chain-smoking all the while. Catherine Deneuve needs no introduction; she is a monument to French poise. An icon not only of French cinema, but of France itself.

HUGO HUERTA MARIN:
Let me start off by talking a little bit about films. Was there one film that had a big impact on you early on?

CATHERINE DENEUVE:
I was very young when I first saw [Sergei] Eisenstein's film *Ivan the Terrible* … It was like traveling to a foreign country.

HHM: When it comes to your filmography, is there a film project that stayed with you or that you would like to be remembered for?

CD: Probably *The Umbrellas of Cherbourg* and *Repulsion*.

HHM: *Repulsion* was a film that opened the door for bigger conversations in cinema. How did the critics receive the movie back then?

CD: As far as I remember, quite well. The film was made in England and I remember the critics were really positive. It was also praised for the music—the music was fantastic.

HHM: Do you think films like *Repulsion* or *Belle du Jour* were considered transgressive for their content or because of their violation of taboos?

CD: I think both. If we are talking about *Belle du Jour*, yes, it was breaking taboos at the time. Women's fantasies, phantasm …

HHM: If these movies were released today, do you think they would have the same impact?

CD: No. I mean, perhaps if they were filmed by a good director … But things have changed and people have so many references now. Everything is so exposed that people are more familiar with very strong images and themes. Everything is on television and on the internet now. So, I think they would be well received, but they wouldn't be as shocking as they were back then.

HHM: Nowadays, what makes a good script or an interesting project to you?

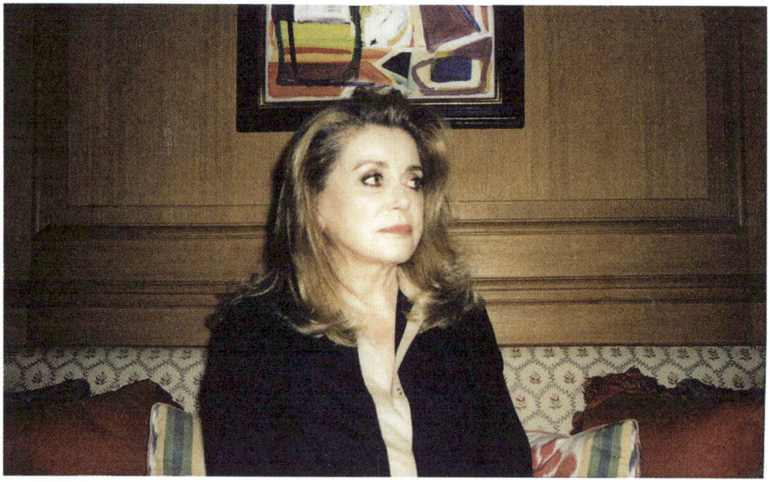

CD: A good script is a good script. It is difficult to explain but what makes a good script is a good story—it has to do with the characters, the theme, the development of a scene, the dialogue … In the end, I don't know what it takes to make a good script—it is good or it isn't. But it is quite evident when you read it; you just recognize it. I recently saw a very good film, almost like a one-shot film.

HHM: Which film was it?

CD: A Danish movie called *The Guilty*. It is about a man … You only see one man in the entire film. At one point, you see two other faces, but the entire film is about one man and a phone. It is incredible.

HHM: In all of film history, who do you wish would have directed you?

CD: [Joseph Leo] Mankiewicz.

HHM: Are there other film directors whom you'd like to work with?

CD: Of course, a lot! I couldn't even tell you names because there are just so many great directors: French, American, Japanese, Korean …

HHM: Is there one specific name that have your eye on?

CD: At the moment, yes, because I am going to do a film with him … His name is [Hirokazu] Kore-eda. Do you know who he is?

HHM: He got the Palme d'Or this year at Cannes, didn't he?

CHANCE AND THE UNKNOWN ARE ALWAYS THERE WHEN YOU ARE ACTING

CD: Yes. I love his films. He is doing a film in Paris and we start next month. I am very curious and very anxious to start.

HHM: What role do you think an actor plays in society?

CD: It's very difficult because in the past, you could see people really focusing on one actor or one actress, but I am not sure it is like that anymore. I have the impression people are now following a director or a film instead of following actors, but people still talk to me in the street or during festivals, and when they come to me, it is very strange because they want to thank me for what I have done. Being an actor means you are part of something, of course, but you are not an artist, like a painter or a musician. But, you know, people are grateful because you somehow *incarne* things the public would like to see or would like to be. What is the translation for *incarne*?

HHM: Embody?

CD: Yes. You play a character and people really think you become that character, because when you watch a film, you want to be taken somewhere else, through someone else.

HHM: The artist as a cultural reflector.

CD: In a way, yes.

HHM: What role do chance or accidents play during a performance?

CD: It's part of life, it happens … Not all the time, but it happens. It has to be taken as something that you can potentially do something with or you can just go through it. It is difficult to know but, of course, chance and the unknown are always there when you are acting.

HHM: The concept of beauty is crucial in the film industry …

CD: It is very different from what it was twenty or thirty years ago. Very different.

HHM: How has it changed?

CD: When I first started making films, a while ago, the actor's physical appearance was very important. Today, it has more to do with style, personality, and being different—being special, being unique. Just being beautiful is not enough.

HHM: I am very interested in the subject of beauty in cinema, and it is interesting to watch filmmakers portraying beauty in their films, particularly when watching French cinema vs American cinema.

CD: What would you say is the difference?

HHM: In my opinion, French cinema always has a kind of intimacy …

CD: Oui.

HHM: Whereas, American cinema …

CD: American cinema has to be striking.

HHM: Exactly. I also think, in general, European cinema takes more risks.

CD: Yes, I think so too.

HHM: For instance, I remember watching [Luis] Buñuel's film *An Andalusian Dog* for the first time, and how the scene where a razor slices through an eye struck me. In this sense, do you think the concept of attraction and repulsion can get along?

CD: (*laughs*) Yes, I think so. I think they can go together, but we are not talking about the concept of beauty anymore. But very often, what repulses you appeals to you as well.

HHM: What is your concept of beauty?

CD: My concept of beauty is a sort of harmony between what something looks like and what it is. It is a balance between the look and the content of things.

HHM: How do you think art influences film?

CD: I think cinema reflects society, and art is part of society as well. So, it has to do with the influences you have—even unconsciously—from what surrounds you, what is shown to the world, what the media decides to put in the newspapers or in the magazines, and your eye becomes used to it. It is difficult to keep your own, true perspective, but it is part of life.

HHM: Film and the many disciplines of art become the parameters of the state of society.

CD: Yes, and I think that has been part of our lives for a very long time.

HHM: Do you think the narrative in filmmaking has also changed over time?

CD: Of course. Again, the stories are always a mirror image of society, and cinema has been following the way people live, the way they relate to others, and the way they show their feelings. Nowadays, people get divorced more easily, women are free to express themselves, you are not allowed to smoke in films anymore, people have cellphones—that has changed plots completely. So, a lot has changed with time and cinema has been following it. Filmmakers don't tell the same stories. What was shocking thirty years ago is very different from what is shocking today.

HHM: But now and then, people don't like to see or be confronted by films

CATHERINE DENEUVE

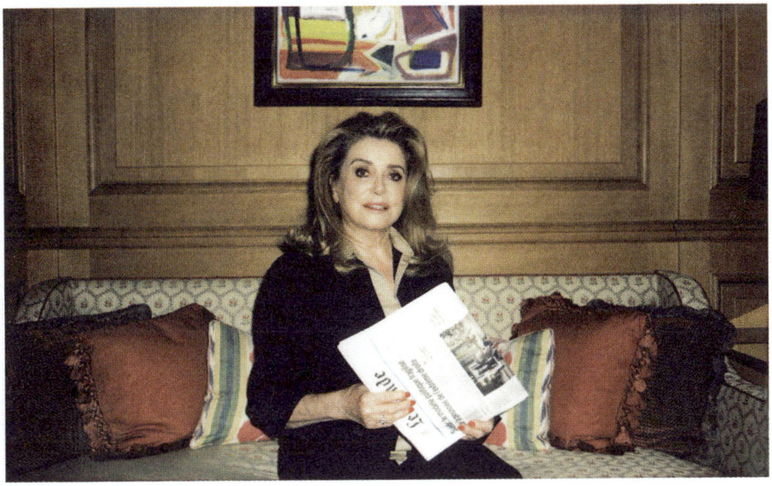

reflecting social conduct or social stories reflecting themselves. In that sense, I can think of controversial stories from filmmakers like Lars von Trier …

CD: He is very special, I must say.

HHM: How was the experience of working with him?

CD: It was very strange because he is very … He has this humor and sometimes, that gets him into trouble, you know? I saw him this year at Cannes and we had lunch together and he was very different from the time I met him when we worked together. So, I don't know how is it working with him today, but I am not sure he always says what he really thinks … I believe he says what he thinks is useful for him in the context of a film. I am not sure he is that frank or direct when you talk to him. I had dinner with him several times and he speaks about very personal things, but still, I can't help but think he is doing it on purpose …

HHM: It correlates with the discourse he has toward women in many of his films.

CD: But he is also provocative … Like what happened in Cannes some years ago. He apologized the same day but it was too late, and frankly, it was a shame because he was showing one of his best films—*Melancholia*. So, what he says about women, I don't know if it is true … When you see his films, you can see that he likes women. Some directors who seem to like women are sometimes very misogynistic. They don't even know it, but they are.

HHM: The canon of art is the canon of lauded misogyny …

CD: Yes. I am not sure I would like to know what [Pablo] Picasso really thought about women (*laughs*).

HHM: (*laughs*) Going back to the subject of film and its references, I remember a specific film that struck me at a very early age, *The Hunger*.

CD: Oh, yeah, but that is something else. I like the film very much …

HHM: It has an uncanny aesthetic. What do you think is the relationship between film and fashion?

CD: Well, I think it is important, but I am not sure fashion defines the story, because when you work on the clothes for a film, they have to be inspired by something. It depends, of course, on the subject of the film, but I don't think fashion influences the style of a film. Have you seen *Velvet Goldmine*?

HHM: Glam rock.

CD: Glam rock in England, with all the music, the fashion, the singers, and the bands. In that film, you can say there is an influence both ways; otherwise, I am not sure cinema is influenced by fashion. It is, again, something that is part of our daily lives, you know, the evolution of society. Your eye is following everything and then using or disregarding it. I think it is very difficult for artists to remain on their own path.

HHM: What is your relationship to fashion?

CD: So, so (*laughs*). It depends …

HHM: (*laughs*) You are considered a fashion icon, and with regards to fashion photography, you have been portrayed by the greatest photographers of the century. But I am curious to know how it was working with Man Ray?

CD: Man Ray? It was a one-of-a-kind experience. You know, we only did one photograph and he didn't talk much. I didn't know him before and I didn't know more about him afterward. It was an interesting experience but it was very short. I was surprised by the way he worked, and to be in his atelier with all those objects he made. I was curious about all those things.

HHM: What inspires you the most?

CD: I suppose the way I look at people. I always have my eyes open. I am more of an observer than a talker.

HHM: What is the most honest thing you can say about yourself?

CD: I don't say everything … But I always say what I think.

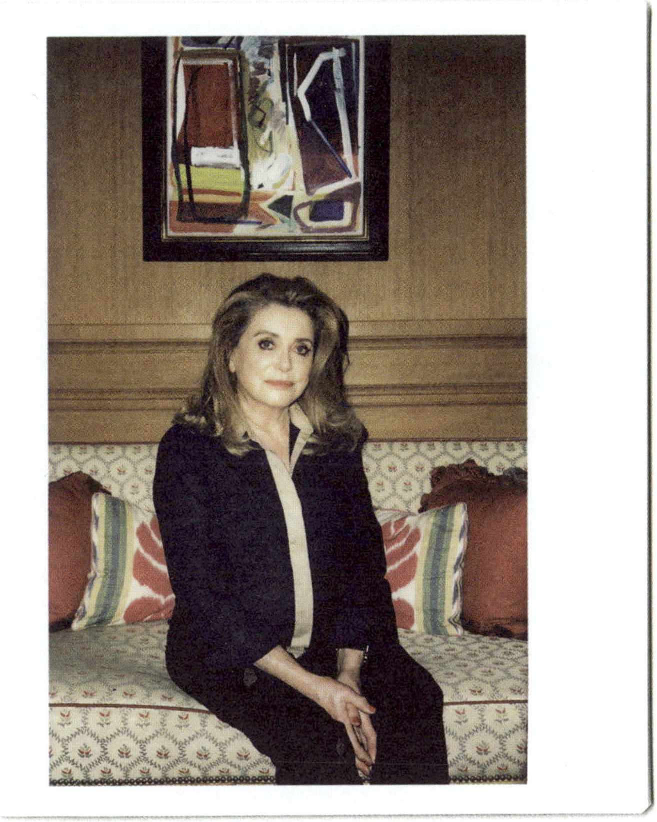

SH

I

R

SHIRIN NESHAT

NEW YORK, 2014

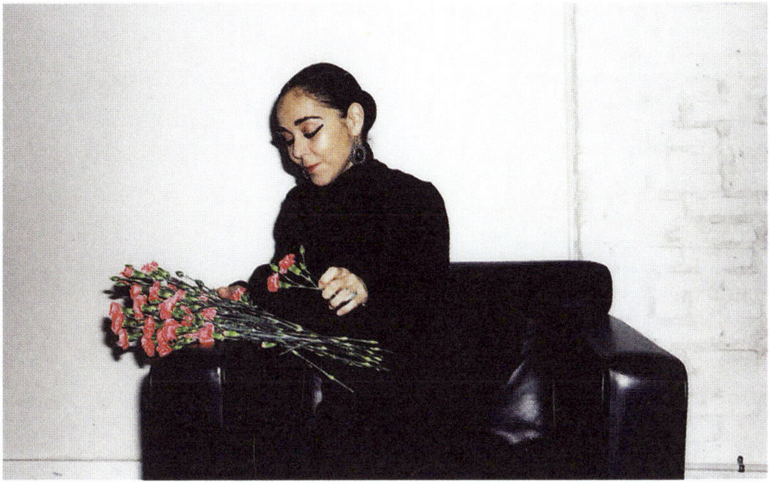

IN

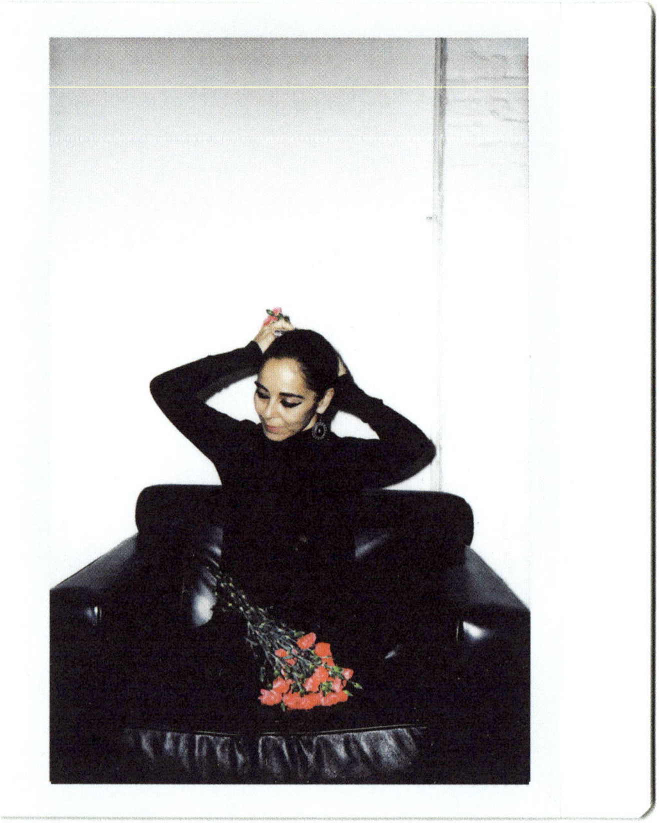

Shirin Neshat is an artist born in Qazvin, Iran, in 1957. She moved to the United States in 1974 and has since consistently probed issues of gender, power, displacement, protest, identity, and the space between the personal and the political with a singular and powerful aesthetic. Her work explores the separate experiences of men and women with the energy of myth, while later projects capture universal themes of ritual and loss. In 2009, Shirin Neshat directed her first feature-length film, *Women Without Men*, based on the novel of the same name by Shahrnush Parsipur. The film received the Silver Lion Award for Best Director at the 66th Venice International Film Festival.

I first interviewed Shirin five years ago in the naturally lit living room of her apartment in downtown Manhattan. I was mesmerized by the soft, melodic, almost fragile voice stating strong, defiant, and rebellious concepts. The complexities of her work have captivated me ever since, and we've cultivated a friendship that has grown over time. Five years later, Shirin remains the same. Women and political and social turmoil fascinate her, and she takes on huge and complex projects that challenge her both as an artist and a person. Since the early 1990s, Shirin has been lauded for her photographs, films, and videos that explore the lives of Iranian people, particularly women. The artist has gone her own way, creating work that feels particularly relevant today.

HUGO HUERTA MARIN:
It seems that there is a constant element of contradiction and paradox in your oeuvre. Why is contrast a key concept in your work?

SHIRIN NESHAT:
You are absolutely right. All of my work has dealt with some notion of opposites: male/female, personal/social, magic/realism,

black/white. For a long time, I tried to understand why it is this way, but I now realize it is probably because I feel so divided between my inner and outer worlds, who I am as a person to others, and how I feel inside. I am full of contradictions: strong and rational and yet very fragile and vulnerable. I guess I also see everything in life as some form of contradiction. We are surrounded by so much beauty and humanity, but at the same time, ugliness, violence and pain.

HHM: Is nostalgia a part of your work?

SN: Without a doubt. Nostalgia, separation from my family, the feeling of abandonment, my continuing unresolved relationship with Iran, and, most importantly, a life in exile have each played a great role in the formation of my vision. My depiction of Iran is clearly from the point of view of an Iranian artist who has not been to her country for a long time and is full of nostalgia.

HHM: In that sense, how has the Islamic Revolution influenced your art?

SN: The Islamic Revolution has influenced both my personal and artistic life. Along with millions of other Iranians, I was forced to stay away and be separated from my family in Iran after the 1979 revolution. I have had to cope with grief, nostalgia, anxiety, and rage, which became the impetus of my decision to be a committed artist. If the Islamic Revolution hadn't happened, perhaps I wouldn't be an artist.

HHM: Your work has moved from photography to video to cinema, all

I AM FULL OF CONTRADICTIONS: STRONG AND RATIONAL AND YET VERY FRAGILE AND VULNERABLE

with a strong and unique essence. Do you have a particular formula when it comes to your work?

SN: I have not been good at repeating myself. I have a tendency to keep moving from one form to another. This pattern must have something to do with my nomadic character and lifestyle. Once I feel too comfortable with any medium, I get bored. Then I rebel against my own signature work and turn in the opposite direction. I like being a beginner; like a student. It's terrifying to keep reinventing yourself, but also exciting to see yourself on the edge, not quite knowing what you're doing, and whether you will fail or not. I started with still photography that was mostly inscribed with calligraphy, but after a few years, by the time the work was being discovered, I felt somewhat exhausted by what I was doing, put a stop to it altogether, and turned toward video installations. But then, when people began to define me as the media artist who was making double-channel video projections, I gravitated toward cinema. I am not necessarily gifted at any particular medium, but am a restless person who needs to strive constantly, even at the risk of failing. It can be too much work, and not being familiar

IRANIAN PEOPLE DON'T SHARE THE SAME FREEDOM OF EXPRESSION AS AMERICANS DO, SO WE ARE TRAINED TO USE METAPHORS AND SYMBOLS IN ORDER TO SAY WHAT WE OTHERWISE CANNOT EXPRESS

with the language of the new medium can be extremely difficult at times. Yet, I somehow cope and never quit. I believe that the challenges and the process become more important than the actual outcome.

HHM: You employ symbols associated with your culture, like the Farsi poetry used in your portraits. How does this symbology relate to your work?

SN: I come from Iran, a country that is known for its rich history of poetry and mysticism. Perhaps this is due to our long history with dictatorship, which forced Iranians to rely on poetic, symbolic language to say everything that we weren't allowed to express outwardly. Allegorical language has been the most natural expression for us. I remember that when *Women Without Men* was released back in 2009, an American critic wrote how perplexed she was by the amount of symbolism used in the film. She obviously missed the cultural nuances, and how Iranian people don't share the same freedom of expression as Americans do, so we are trained to use metaphors and symbols in order to say what we otherwise cannot express.

HHM: Is beauty a major aspect of your work?

SN: Absolutely. I'm influenced by classic Islamic art, where the notion of beauty plays a great role, and has been defined as a mediator between humans and the divine. If you look closely at my work, symmetry, repetition, abstraction, void, geometric compositions, and, most importantly, the incorporation of text within image all borrow from the Islamic tradition in art and architecture. But I always depict beauty in the presence of horror, disturbance, pain, and violence, which is informed by the socio-political material of my narratives.

HHM: Looking at your video- and film-based work, it seems that the concept of space also plays an important role.

SN: Space has been a particularly important aspect of my work, as it helps define the narrative by setting up the mood, the character, and the historical and political backbone of a story. For example, in my video *Soliloquy*, which was shot partly in Turkey and partly in the USA, the architecture became central in identifying Eastern and Western cultures' conflicting values and ideologies. In the West, we filmed magnificent, monumental modern architecture in Albany and New York City, representing the grandeur and capitalistic nature of America; in the East, we chose an absolutely beautiful mosque with a big dome in Turkey. Another intentional use of space and architecture is evident in the movie *Women Without Men*, where we had four women from four different economic classes, and we were tasked with recreating Iran in the fifties in Casablanca, Morocco.

HHM: What role does cultural identity play in your work?

SN: I've learned to work nomadically, which is probably the only positive aspect of being a self-exiled artist. There is a tremendous amount of adventure in traveling to various countries and making work that purports to have been shot in Iran. We have traveled as far as Mexico, Morocco, and Turkey to look for places that have aspects of the Iranian landscape and architecture. There is a long history of artists living and working in exile, such as [Andrei] Tarkovsky, who left Russia and worked in Sweden and Italy. [Sergie] Eisenstein and [Luis] Buñuel went to Mexico and made many films. Many Iranian artists, musicians, and filmmakers have had to leave Iran recently because of the political situation, and are making work abroad. However, what is interesting is that even if I go to Mexico and make a work that tries to look as if it is taking place in Iran, it will still have the flavor of Mexican culture and the Mexican people. You learn to integrate different cultures into your own, and this becomes your trademark. I have grown to appreciate this nomadic way of working and I therefore have no interest in working in Iran.

HHM: What word would best describe your work?

SN: Rebellion. On a personal level, my artistic nature leads me to rebel, which is also evident in my female characters. My work is mostly about women living under oppression and difficult cultural and political situations, and my characters are always represented as defiant, resilient, and rebellious.

A good example of this is evident in *Turbulent*, where the female singer turns her repression into a creative force when she sings in a guttural and powerful way, and breaks every rule of classical music, while the male singer remains within the framework of traditional music. In *Fervor*, the female protagonist, who is conflicted between her temptation toward the opposite sex and religious taboo, walks away in protest from the crowd. Lastly, in *Women Without Men*, every female character, regardless of the nature of her problems or aspirations, takes her life into her own hands, turns away from society, and takes refuge in an orchard that is unworldly and free of social, religious, and cultural inhibitions.

HHM: You are considered a symbol of resistance to Iranian repression …

SN: I think that's probably an overstatement. I don't view my work as a form of resistance. I believe it is very symbolic, and functions in the realm of fiction. If that wasn't the case, I would have been an activist rather than an artist. Although I believe in the power of art, I think that in the bigger picture, I don't have as much of a presence and a voice as people might think—though I am very flattered when people think that my work inspires other Iranian women.

SHIRIN NESHAT

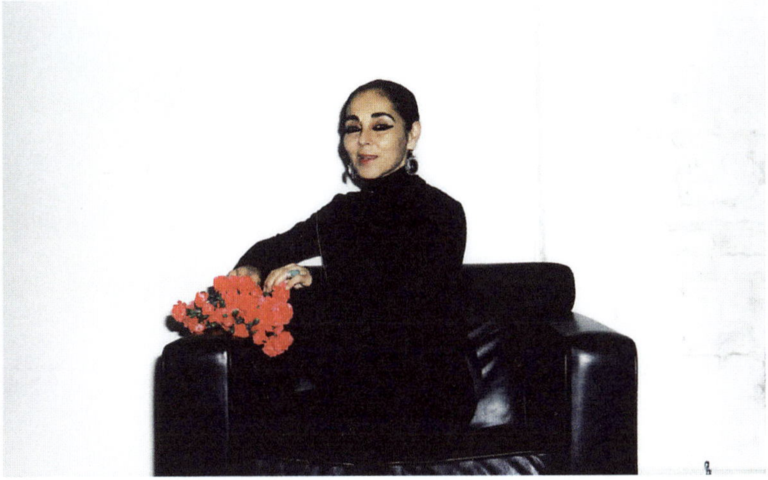

ON A PERSONAL LEVEL, MY ARTISTIC NATURE LEADS ME TO REBEL, WHICH IS ALSO EVIDENT IN MY FEMALE CHARACTERS

HHM: Following on from that, you have talked about the reaction of Iranian women when placed against the wall. Can you share your thoughts on this?

SN: First of all, in my opinion, on a biological level, women are conditioned to be strong since they bear and nurture children. Women seem to handle crises better than men. I've learned this by observing my own immediate family. My mother and sisters have lived through incredibly stressful situations—politically, personally, and economically—but they are fighters, and although the males in the family seemed to rule on the surface, the women were the ones who kept the family together. Similarly, as I said earlier, I'm so inspired by Iranian women in general because they have confronted and revolted against the authorities in subtle yet subversive and defiant ways. In fact, Iranian women remain the biggest threat to the government to this day, as they refuse to comply with the religious and social codes.

HHM: Do you believe your work will resonate for young Eastern artists in the future?

SN: I just came back from a trip to the Middle East. I traveled to Beirut and Qatar, so I met many people. I had my first Middle Eastern exhibition at MATHAF, a contemporary art museum in Doha, and gave a workshop and a lecture at the American University of Beirut. It was surprising to see how many young people—particularly women from Muslim communities—follow my work. I was deeply moved by their reaction, which was mostly positive, though there was, of course, a lot of criticism of my work by those who didn't agree with my aesthetic or point of view. But it was good to see how through social media, young people, in particular, have been informed and affected by my work.

HHM: Looking at all the different meanings that your work holds, would you say there is a lack of spiritual approaches in contemporary art?

SN: If anything, I believe there is a lack of content or meaningful art around. Then again, artists make art for different reasons. Some make art for the sake of art, as a career, and are concerned less with content and meaning, but are more interested in the aesthetics. Even when teaching young students, you can tell they are really struggling to find themes that are substantial and relevant. It's as though they are sheltered within their lifestyles and the school environment and are therefore unable to express anything profound.

HHM: The comfort zone.

SN: Yes, that's correct. The comfort zone doesn't go well with art practice. At least, it doesn't sit very well with me. I have taught privileged young students at Ivy League schools who have not seen the world, have not struggled politically, are not well-read, and are not knowledgable. Therefore, their themes often become one-dimensional and irrelevant. But in general, I think an artist's lifestyle nurtures the work they create. You have to put yourself at the mercy of life and experience things in order to find your subject.

HHM: Marina [Abramović] often used to joke that "the more fucked up the childhood the better the artist."

SN: (*laughs*) When an artist has nothing to say, that is reflected in their work. It is not only about the artists. I also think that a lot of people in the art world, including critics, appreciate art that is simply an elaboration of various movements in art history, and don't necessarily require content or meaning.

HHM: What are your thoughts on the rise of the artist as celebrity?

SN: And being very wealthy? I think this is a real issue and a dangerous one. The truth is, every artist faces some degree of ego and narcissism. We all want everyone to praise our work. Unfortunately, that is human nature. But I remember a friend once told me, "Never take praise too seriously, and never take rejection too seriously." Personally, I try to keep a certain amount of distance from the art world, in order to stay sane and healthy. The competition can be overwhelming. But I believe every artist has their own way of dealing with such challenges when they reach a certain point in their career.

YOU HAVE TO PUT YOURSELF AT THE MERCY OF LIFE AND EXPERIENCE THINGS IN ORDER TO FIND YOUR SUBJECT

HHM: Where do you go to be alone?

SN: To the movie theater. Or I go for a walk in the park. I'm currently working on a script, and I really enjoy the process because it can be a completely solitary experience.

HHM: Do you worry about being overexposed?

SN: I do worry, and so I do few and select exhibitions. I don't work with many galleries. In fact, I am only represented by one gallery in New York City where I exhibit every five years. Otherwise, I only have shows in museums once in a while.

HHM: What inspires you the most?

SN: When I see a great work of art, or a film. It restores my faith in the power of art. A good friend of mine once gave me a list of film masterpieces to see and said: "Make sure you write down the date and hour you watch these films, because your life will never be the same again."

HHM: Do you have any recurring dreams?

SN: Yes. I write my dreams down and recently, I've turned some of them into video installations. I've recently come to realize that in almost all of my dreams, my mother appears. It may be due to the fact that my mother plays a great role in my life. She is getting very old, and although we mainly speak on the phone, I am addicted to her unconditional care, love, and affection. I sometimes think that she is my last real connection to Iran and if she leaves the world, my relationship to Iran will end permanently. So, the anxiety and fear of losing my mother seems to be a subject that keeps haunting my dreams.

HHM: Marcel Duchamp once ended a symposium by saying that he thought the great artist of tomorrow "cannot be seen, should not be seen, and should go underground." Would you agree?

SN: Maybe that was the case in Duchamp's time, but today, I believe that the artist's persona—lifestyle, political views, and how they present themselves—are just as important as their work. These days, it's nearly impossible to look at an artist's work without studying the artist's character.

HHM: What are your thoughts on the big international art exhibitions like documenta or the Venice Biennale?

SN: I believe that being part of these big international exhibitions can validate an artist's work and put them on the map. On the other hand,

I've participated in many big international biennials, and I still enjoy it, but when a curator presents an artist's work in this larger context, it reflects more on them as curators than the nature of an artist's work.

HHM: What is the most honest thing you can say about yourself?

SN: I am extremely vulnerable—and I don't mean that in a negative way. I like this vulnerability because it keeps me on my toes.

A

ANN DEMEULEMEESTER
LONDON, 2018

NN

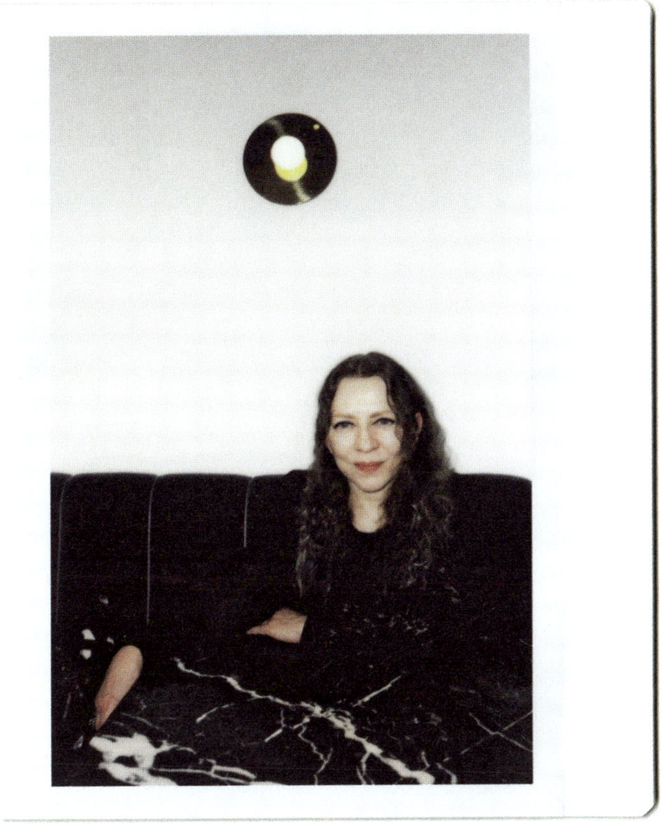

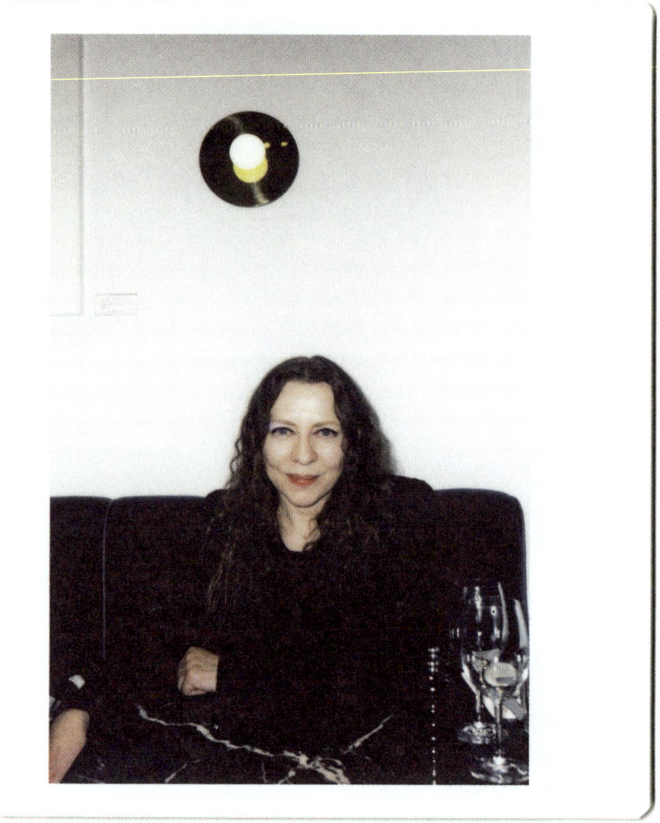

Ann Demeulemeester is a Belgian fashion designer. For her, fashion is a form of communication. Her complex visual language of contrasts expresses a whole gamut of emotions. The tension in her clothes is highly poetic—simple, the same way a knife is simple; serious but not severe, meticulous and experimental.

Ann arrived at our meeting at The Laslett hotel in London at exactly 10 a.m. She looked nothing like the other women in the room. Dressed in head-to-toe black and red lipstick, she carried a huge black 1,010-page book that chronicles thirty years of her work in fashion. I was surprised to find out it was a gift for me. She said she brought it because she knew I loved books, although this was the first time we had met.

Ann wants no part of celebrity culture and isn't interested in trends. She couldn't care less about talking about the famous people who endorse her fashion, but was thrilled to recount the story of when she was invited to dress a sixteenth-century Madonna. Over the years, the essence of her romantic vision has remained the same. That is the way Ann is: She plays by her own rules.

HUGO HUERTA MARIN:
I was interested in reading about the beginning of your career and the group of designers associated with Franco-Belgian Deconstructivism, the Antwerp Six.

ANN DEMEULEMEESTER:
Well, you know, there was no such thing as the Antwerp Six—the media started calling it that, but we never had the intention of making it into a group. We studied together in school, we were all very ambitious, and nothing like "Belgian fashion" existed yet. So, the advantage was that we could start from zero because there was no tradition we had to carry on our backs. After school, we all had the intention of starting

ANTI-CONFORMISM MADE THE LINK BETWEEN THE DIFFERENT DESIGNERS THAT FIRST PUT BELGIUM ON THE MAP

something new, and everyone—with their own ideals—did it in their own way. We each made a little collection, and to save costs, we rented a truck together and went to London. Once we got there, we rented a stand at the British Designer Show. We were all next to each other, sharing the same space, and as of the first day, it was crazy. The press discovered us and nobody could pronounce our names, so they would just say, "Do you know about these six new designers?" Nobody was expecting six new designers to be on the scene—especially ones from a country nobody in "fashionland" has heard of. So, that's the story of the Antwerp Six. Having said that, I think it had an impact because it was a combination of individuals defending what they were standing for.

HHM: Is there something like a "Belgian school" or a "Belgian eye" for fashion?

AD: I don't know if there is a "Belgian school" for fashion—it is not evident to me—because I think I am very different from the others. But anti-conformism made the link between the different designers that first put Belgium on the map.

HHM: You were the creator of a new aesthetic in fashion when you first started. Would you say your ideas still come from a similar place?

AD: Yes. They come from my feelings. I have always followed my intuition throughout the years. I have never had a strategy; I just tried to be honest. I have always tried to understand and analyze the relationship people have with their clothes, and how people present themselves to the world—that is what got me started.

HHM: You were more interested in individuality.

AD: Exactly. In fact, I first started drawing portraits and from that came the interest in what people were wearing. To some extent, I thought it was my task to propose a new vestimentary code, and I wanted to charge clothes with emotion or let them talk for the people wearing them. I needed to create a kind of communication with other people from different parts of the world, so I started sending out my work and I was able to meet people I would have never met otherwise. That was probably the most beautiful thing about it—I was able to find soulmates through my work. I was able to charge their clothes with love, with beauty, with innocence, with strength, with self-confidence, with whatever I was feeling or I could give, and that was really special. On the other hand, there was always anonymity when I sent out things and you don't always know what your work means for other people, but I was rewarded by discovering that my dream was also the dream of another woman, of another man—it made me realize that we are all part of the same chain of creation.

HHM: Do you think the mindset of an artist changes after they have success or recognition?

AD: It follows you. I am not the same person I was thirty years ago, but I have always followed my feelings.

HHM: Did this principle break for you at some point? Why did you stop designing?

AD: At some point, I asked myself: "What now?" As a young girl, I had certain dreams that I wanted to achieve. I worked very hard, gave everything, and suddenly, I had achieved what I always wanted and asked myself: "Do I need more? Do I need more fame? Do I need more money? Do I need more shops?" And the answer was no, so I just followed my intuition and I decided to stop. I thought that perhaps it was possible to do more things in one's life—it was a very risky thing to do—but I jumped. I was also tired. I realized that in fashion, you cannot choose how much you produce or show to the world. You can't show your work when you are ready; you always have to be ready on certain dates. In the nineties, you could still do four collections a year—for men, for women, summer, and winter—but now, it's just crazy. The fashion industry demands new collections all the time and I just don't work like that—it's really strange to me. You are born as a creative person and you do your best, but in fashion, you also need a business to survive. You have partnerships with business people, and I guess it's normal that creative minds sometimes clash with business minds, but I am the kind of person who goes my own way.

HHM: It's interesting to see how many fellow artists are showing resistance and rebelling against the system …

AD: It is a war against the system. It is not that I am tired of making beautiful clothes, it is just that I am tired of the system. Absolutely.

HHM: Were there any ideas that didn't come to fruition because they seemed too extreme?

AD: No, not really. I don't have frustrations in that sense. The only frustration was that sometimes, I wanted to show my work in a different way, but that aspect of fashion is very limited. You are supposed to do a fashion show on a certain date, at a certain time, and with certain kinds of people … and that is something that I would like to change. Once I wanted to have a show with very little light, almost in the dark, but the answer was always no, because there would not be enough light for the press to take photographs for magazines. Oh, big drama!

HHM: *(laughs)* How did your mindset change from one collection to the other?

AD: That was always really natural, because no collection could have been there if the one before it didn't exist. I always started with what I could not finish in time for the previous collection and that would put me on a new path to start a new collection.

HHM: I am curious to know about your relationship with color. What do you find interesting about working with black?

AD: For me, it is the most poetic color. I don't know if it is a color—it is a non-color—but in the end, working with black is a way to get to the essence of things. You have light and you have dark, you have white and you have black—it is as simple as that. You can see everything you want to see through a black-and-white picture. Everything you need to explain—a silhouette, a contrast, a mood—it's all there. It also came in an instinctive way because I love to work with shapes and cuts and for me, making a garment is like sculpting—you need to make a three-dimensional form and that form has to envelop a body, and you have to be able to reshape it and put an accent where you want to add or hide certain things. In a way, you make a second body, and when you are searching for shapes, you don't want to be distracted by a flower or a stripe, so you take the purest thing—white cotton or black wool—and you start making the shape and cut until all the volume is right and there is tension in the shape and movement where needed. I think that nowadays, 99 percent of clothes are made with the same pattern and just vary in color and decoration. But I am much more interested in architecture than in decoration.

HHM: Do you think red could be black?

AD: Absolutely.

HHM: There is a certain power in fashion that confronts gender and sexuality. What role does sex play in your work?

AD: I think when I started—and it is difficult to think about it now, thirty years later—it was an important concept for me because I couldn't find what I thought was sexy in fashion. What they called sexy, I thought was vulgar, so I had to invent a new kind of sex appeal in clothes. I started to make a new kind of erotic translation of what I found attractive. I did not think so much in terms of man and woman; rather, I thought in terms of beautiful human beings, because I think everybody has masculine and feminine elements, and it is where they meet that it becomes interesting and intriguing. All of that was very inspiring to me. It was great to find the freedom to do it in a different way and not how it was perceived in the world back then.

HHM: There is also an aspect of tension and duality in your work.

AD: Yes, working with contrast makes things intriguing. I cannot live with only black, I need white in the same way, and I think it relates to everything. To be complete, you need to work with opposites and contrast, and finding a balance in between these two poles can make something beautiful.

HHM: What is your concept of beauty?

AD: I don't have one. It's like thinking that there is a recipe for beauty—I don't think there is one. I think being real is the most beautiful thing.

ANN DEMEULEMEESTER

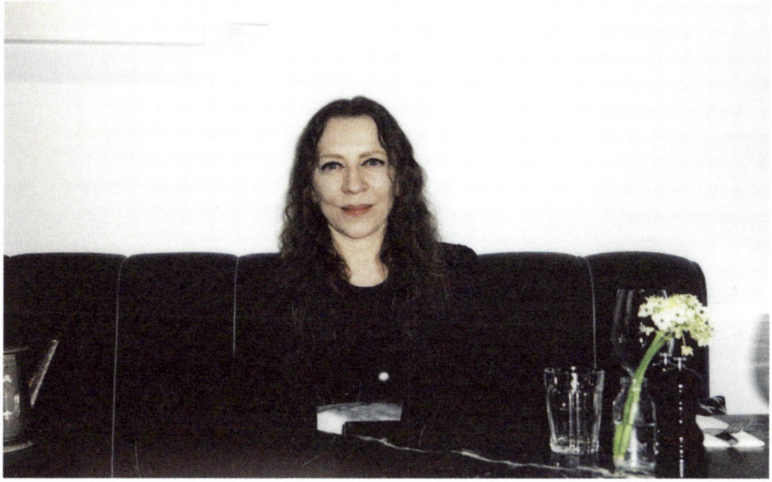

WHAT THEY CALLED SEXY, I THOUGHT WAS VULGAR, SO I HAD TO INVENT A NEW KIND OF SEX APPEAL IN CLOTHES

HHM: You attended art school before moving into fashion. What do you think is the link between visual art and fashion?

AD: I can only speak for myself. I am not interested in analyzing art and fashion in a journalistic way but I am always inspired by great artists. When I see something that strikes me or perhaps makes me sick or that I feel in my gut, it gives me the energy to create good work—I call it a transmission of energy. It happens to me with art but also with music or when I see a beautiful film.

HHM: Are there any movies that have had an impact on your work?

AD: Perhaps François Truffaut's *L'Enfant Sauvage*. It is a movie about a wild child who is found in the bushes and a doctor who tries to bring him into the civilized world. I must say, the story was very inspiring to me.

HHM: There is also a strong relationship with music in your work.

AD: Well, when I first started, I sent out my work and soulmates found me—Patti [Smith] and Polly [Harvey] were two people that found me in this way. I didn't organize it, they came to me, and that was incredible because I loved what they were doing, and having them wearing my clothes was like closing the circle—it was amazing.

HHM: What is the story behind these collaborations?

AD: How I got to know Patti is a beautiful story. Back in 1991, it was very important for me to choose the music I would play in my first show in Paris. I decided to play Patti's because her music was there for me for years and years. After that, I would often end up using the music I was listening to while preparing for the shows. After that first fashion show, I sent her two white shirts to thank her for making her music, and I wrote her a letter—it just felt right to do it … Then, I got a letter back from her and it started like that. I wrote back and I think that for ten years, we wrote letters to each other. Later on, during a difficult moment in her life—her husband had just died—Bob Dylan got her back on stage and many of her friends went to see her to give their support. I made clothes for her and I went to her concert. I just wanted to see her singing but somebody grabbed me and brought me backstage, and it was beautiful. It was like meeting somebody I had known all my life … And with Polly, it was kind of a similar situation but later … I loved was she was doing and I used her music in my fashion shows. Then, at a certain point, she asked me if I could make clothes for her—and I did, and we had this beautiful friendship. In fact, I am visiting her in London now.

HHM: Sometimes, fashion becomes as much of a statement as songs for musicians. Do you think a piece of clothing can be political?

AD: Well, clothes can't be political; ideals and thoughts are. The way you dress is only a message that you send out. It's how you present yourself to the world. People don't meet each other naked, they meet each other with clothes, and the clothes can tell a story; they can show your conviction, dreams, happiness, anger, madness …

HHM: Or devotion … I wanted to ask you about the story behind the sixteenth-century Madonna you dressed at St Andrew's church. How did that happen?

AD: That is a beautiful story—I think she is my most precious client (*laughs*). One day, I was working and I got a phone call from a priest. He said he'd heard that I was one of the finest fashion designers in Belgium, and that his sixteenth-century Madonna needed a new dress. He wanted to present her to younger people so they could see her as a friend. I must tell you that in that moment, I got chills and I decided to do it. He gave me one month. I made an appointment with him and I went there. He placed an enormous ladder in front of her so I could see her closely, and there she was. She had a big velvet dress and crowns on. We put everything away and there was this little delicate, wooden statue—it was so special. I tried to create something that made her look more fragile, more human, and close to nature. Afterwards, I went back to work there.

I was all alone in the church with this Madonna, dressing her. I don't know how many meters high I was, putting a fragile little silk cloth on that statue. I must say, it was almost like a spiritual moment. I made a bustier with feathers and I put it around her. Since then, she has been standing there and every ten years, I go there and wash her clothes.

HHM: Fashion that embraces sacred images and customs continues the relationship between art and religion.

AD: Yes.

HHM: What are your thoughts on the juxtaposition of artist and celebrity?

AD: Being a celebrity is like a profession nowadays, isn't it? It doesn't mean too much to me. I am a worker, I am a maker. I don't see myself as a celebrity.

HHM: Where do you go to be alone?

AD: Nature. I love to work in the garden.

HHM: What inspires you the most?

AD: What is inspiration? That is the most difficult thing to define. I think it's something that is given to you. I don't know where it comes from but I think that from the moment you are born, you have all these experiences in your life and everything you see or hear, or whatever distracts you, is somehow in your hard disk and in your memory, and after fifty years, there is a lot on that hard disk. At a certain point, when you need inspiration, some things can surface. Why? I don't know but they come in an uncontrolled way.

HHM: What was the first record you ever bought?

AD: I can't remember but I can tell you that the first record that really meant something to me was *Horses* by Patti Smith.

HHM: What are your thoughts on the big blockbuster fashion shows like the ones at the Met or the Victoria and Albert Museum?

AD: I think every show is very different. They have asked me to do a big show about my work and so far, I haven't found the courage to do it …

HHM: Why?

AD: I don't know. It's like looking back while you are still in the middle of something. So far, I have always said no but who knows, maybe one day … On the other hand, I have saved everything I have ever made. I have an enormous archive and this is also why I could quit—when young designers go there, it's like entering Ali Baba's cave. They can take things out and put them back on the runway and it just works. It's good that my label—with all the work I've done—will be able to continue somehow.

HHM: What is the most honest thing you can say about yourself?

AD: I always do my best.

ANN DEMEULEMEESTER

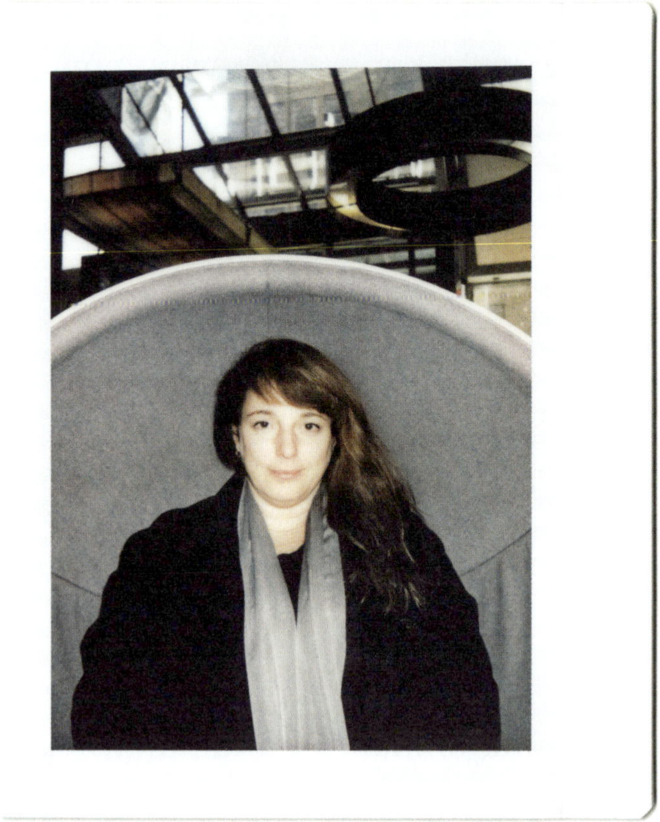

IA

TA

N

TANIA BRUGUERA

BROOKLYN, 2015

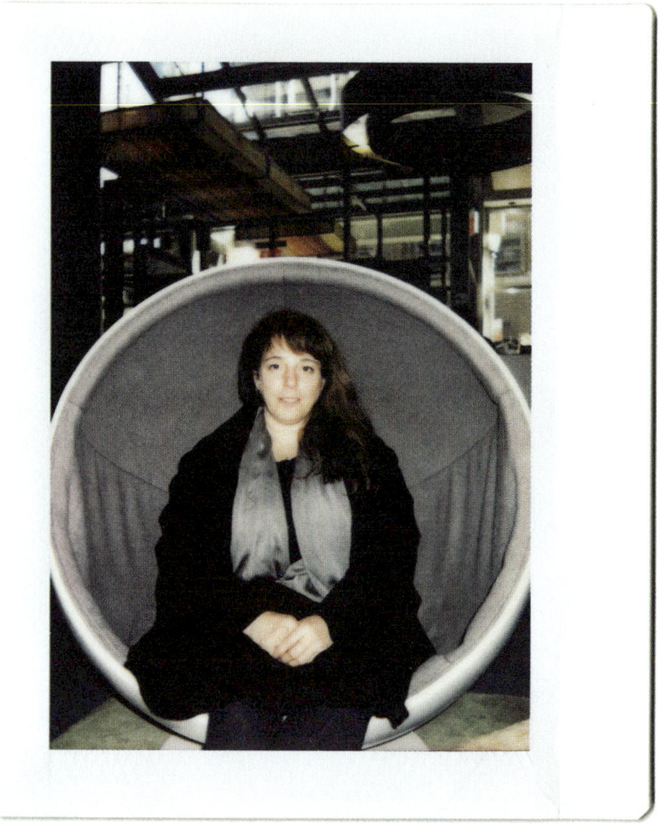

Tania Bruguera is a Cuban interdisciplinary artist working primarily in performance, installation, and video. She has participated in documenta 11 in Kassel, Germany, as well as in several biennales in Venice, Johannesburg, Sao Paulo, Shanghai, Havana, and Site Santa Fe. She is also the founder of Arte de Conducta, the first performance studies program in Latin America, which is hosted by the Instituto Superior de Arte in Havana, and of the Institute of Artivism Hannah Arendt. Tania toys restlessly with the idea that individual stories should be understood within the context of social and historical experience. This approach, however, is not the result of a deliberate scheme to devise an essential pattern or formula. On the contrary, she weaves a dense and intricate fabric out of apparently disconnected issues. These open up into a project both intellectual and quotidian that engages the viewer in a constant exchange of signifying possibilities.

I met Tania at a coffee shop in Brooklyn on a winter morning. We had this conversation in Spanish, while we talked about art and politics in Latin America. That talk made me think again about one of the greatest realizations I had had in recent years: that art is a tool for social change. But Tania is an old hand at such effects: She makes people question the establishment, and perhaps that is why she is at the forefront of political art. She is a daring thinker and an astute political fighter who understands that real resistance only happens inside the flame.

HUGO HUERTA MARIN:
Would you consider censorship to be the core aspect of your work?

TANIA BRUGUERA:
The core of my work is based on the idea of how power works, especially in regards to censorship. So, in that sense, yes.

HHM: Would you say your work is about a wound but also about the healing process?

TB: My work is about a wound. It's about something that hurts, and it hurts because I don't understand it, or it seems unfair to me. On the other hand, maybe more than a process of healing, it is a process of giving hope to others by telling them, "Okay, your wound exists, but you also have the rest of your body; try not to concentrate on the wound." I would love to complete the healing process for others, but it is only the injured person who can do that.

HHM: What is the biggest challenge you have encountered while making a new piece?

TB: There have been so many … What was once a challenge later became a modus operandi incorporated into my artistic practice. The biggest challenge is the idea of power in itself. There was a time in my career where I transitioned from talking about problems to trying to solve them. I moved from a moment of representation to sharing concrete proposals that could possibly make a difference. I think that when this shift happened, the challenges associated with my work also changed. When artists complain or "weep" through their art while presenting no real solution—thus making it a barren process—art becomes comfortable for some governments and conservative societies. The great challenge comes, not when the artist identifies the problem, but when they decide to make a change by inventing parallel worlds. These, although imaginary, can be dangerous for the status quo. When

THE GREAT CHALLENGE COMES, NOT WHEN THE ARTIST IDENTIFIES THE PROBLEM, BUT WHEN THEY DECIDE TO MAKE A CHANGE BY INVENTING PARALLEL WORLDS

I refer to power, I am referring not only to the powers within government, but to the structures of power within the art world. Challenges keep changing. For example, when I was younger, the challenge at the time was to create an artistic language that could reach the masses —language that a neighbor, a secretary, or a curator at MoMA could understand. The next challenge, imposed by the work itself, was how I could become an international artist without losing the urgency of the work. Currently, I'm facing the challenge of talking to politicians as an artist. People in power—whether it's a president or ten thousand people on the streets—need to understand art as an instrument for social change. An artist needs to incorporate art into everyday political issues.

HHM: Is documentation an important element in your work?

TB: Yes, but I have neglected that part a lot. It's a nightmare.

HHM: It seems that you have had a war against documentation.

TB: It is nearly impossible for me to think about documentation when I'm doing a performance. In the moment, I'm not thinking about the future, or of the possibility of an exhibition about it the following day. I'm thinking about the present, and that's the beauty of performance art. In my opinion, the best form of documentation is the emotional memory of the viewer. Documentation cannot replace the experience, because that would defeat the purpose of performance art. The way I've tried to cope with this is seen in *Tribute to Ana Mendieta*, where I re-contextualized the work while attempting to preserve the original tension between the work and the viewer, and tried to see if those issues were still relevant or still creating friction. I did not attempt to replicate the original image, but rather to update the conflict that came from the original work. Sometimes this required creating a new image, different from the documented one. The interest lies in the transformative process of the work, not in the specific action or its image.

HHM: Can we talk about the genesis of the Ana Mendieta series?

TB: I was eighteen years old. I noticed that all the "important" artists we studied in school were men, and that there were no iconic female figures for me to look up to. Some friends showed me a postcard of Ana Mendieta, and a mutual friend told our group that the next time she came to Cuba, he would introduce us. But unfortunately, Ana Mendieta passed away before that could happen. Upon hearing the news of her death, I felt a strong emotional void, which was further exacerbated by the emigration of some people I held dear. During this time, another aspect of her work manifested: the trans-territorial character of national identity. I therefore decided to express myself through Ana Mendieta. Simultaneously, I understood that Cuba was not the image of a man who had had fifty years in power, or the pictures of the colorful masses. Cuba was a philosophy of life. That day I decided that my work would be Cuban—not through the use of its colors, landscapes, or national symbols, but because I felt it could be a different way of portraying the world.

HHM: Is she still an important influence for you?

TB: Yes. The way she has influenced me has changed over the years, but she still is an important influence on my work. In the beginning, I was very interested in her works on Jaruco and the idea of going out of the white cube and creating ephemeral art. Later, I became interested in how she dealt with politics. She was very political with regards to Cuba, feminism, and her own position within the art world. Ana Mendieta adopted Land art in her own way, and that was an important lesson. I am still influenced by works such as *Untitled (Rape Scene)*, or *People Looking at Blood*, where her work merges with the lives of others.

HHM: In those works, she studies people's reactions.

TB: Exactly. People can pass by her artwork and have no clue that it is fine art. It's influential on me because that's what I'm trying to do with my work—creating art that is incorporated into life. She did it in a masterful way.

AN ARTIST IS GIVEN MUCH MORE CREDIBILITY AND VISIBILITY THAN AN ACTIVIST, AND THIS GIVES THE ARTIST A RESPONSIBILITY

HHM: What differences are there between creating a work for a public space, such as *Untitled (Havana 2000)*, and creating a work to be installed within a museum context, like that of *Tatlin's Whisper #5* at Tate Modern's Turbine Hall?

TB: We can use the same work over again because MoMA bought it, and this is exactly what is happening right now. *Untitled (Havana 2000)* was made within the institutional context for a museum, as part of the Havana Biennale. This event occurs every three years as an exhibition space, and the energy of the place is very powerful.

HHM: The same happened with *Tatlin's Whisper #6*.

TB: Exactly, that would be a better example. I think there's something interesting about Cuban art and perhaps the art in other socialist countries. In these settings, art replaces spaces of freedom that cannot be found anywhere else. An artist is given much more credibility and visibility than an activist, and this gives the artist a responsibility—to think about all the things that occur inside and outside of the performance, and within or outside the institution as part of the function of the work. Another big difference is that when you create a work within the artistic context, you are somehow "protected" by the institution and it allows you to create a playful moment in that space, compared to what happens when you work outside the institutional context. In the latter case, there is no such "protection" of any kind and you must use a completely different language, because you are no longer talking to curators but to police officers. Outside institutions, symbolism is less speculated about, and therefore you have to work with the history and the tensions of the place and the context.

HHM: *The Burden of Guilt*, *Postwar Memory*, and *Tatlin's Whisper* are all such strong titles that seem to complement the work. How do you decide to name your pieces?

TB: Well, I was inspired by Marcel Duchamp. When I was a student, I identified the importance of titles. The art school I attended in Cuba was very conceptualist and contextualist at the same time. We were taught that the title of the work had to provide information which the direct experience didn't, in order to lead the public in some way—within all possible interpretations. For instance, the title *Tatlin* is understood to name a work about communism and utopia. The work eventually becomes an image, and images can change the meaning of the work. Therefore, you can find that interpretation in the title. This is why I translate the titles of my work: to preserve what I am communicating.

HHM: What is the difference between an activist and a political artist?

TB: Good question. In my opinion, the difference is that the activist uses strategies and tools that are effective and "proven." The artist is interested in creating new tools without being completely sure how they will work. We must be very aware that the work of the political artist must work politically, as it is very common to see artists who claim to be political artists simply because they use political images—that's not political art. The political artist is looking for a reaction and to engage people. I'm currently using a concept called "artivism"—wanting to change society like an activist, but through art.

HHM: Has making money changed the way you make art?

TB: What money? (*laughs*). I cannot say money, but let's say access and privileges that have the potential to have an institutional impact, and that is important. The privilege of being an artist gives me a certain responsibility of which I must be aware.

HHM: By giving voice to the voiceless, is the concept of resistance assumed in your work?

TB: Look, I think it's dangerous to say that I "speak for the voiceless." Everyone has a voice and has the ability to use it. The problem lies in those who do not want to listen. There is a tendency to individualize things, to focus on the person and not the problem. The art world must get educated and transform in order for political art to be properly achieved. Political artists should not become celebrities, because this will fuck up the work. When that happens, the authenticity, impact, and respect are stripped away, and it takes a lot of effort to earn that respect as a political artist. Political art is not meant to be consumed; it is meant to engage and transform.

I do believe there is a resistance to my work. It is an excellent word that should be used more often in these kinds of conversations because art itself is a battle. Having visibility does not mean that you are going to have an impact. There is a resistance in that you need to understand when the artist should be present, and when the artist should leave. In this way, a public space is created in order for other people to use. I believe, that as comfortable it is for the status quo to think otherwise, it is very dangerous for the artist to speak "for" others. The artist should speak "with" others.

HHM: Many artists who have grown up in totalitarian regimes and have based their work on their restrictions, for instance, through rebelling against them, then go to free countries like the U.S. and find that the art does not work anymore. It seems that freedom paralyzes it. Have you ever found yourself in this position?

TB: Yes. There is a certain myth about and fascination with censorship and its creative capacity. I think it is dangerous because it can rationalize the unjustifiable. Censorship forces you to focus and think of the essentials, but this does not mean you become a better artist. On the other hand, I don't think so-called free societies are necessarily free. In reality, freedom only exists within oneself, and not in society. I think we are living in a time of global totalitarianism. In some places, this totalitarianism manifests itself through legislative abuse and elsewhere through imposed and unquestioned economic systems. Censorship of freedom of expression has many variations. There are also many risks when the work is in reference to the removal of a specific context. The transition is difficult, and the work often loses levels of complexity because it is made for a new audience and a new context. A new structure of censorship can coexist along with the new creative space. During this process of adaptation, an artist's creativity may lapse.

HHM: You have talked about the "aesthetics of ethics." What is your concept of beauty?

TB: My concept of beauty manifests itself in an ethical gesture that proposes another way to operate in the world, and I call it "aest-ethics."

HHM: How do you think things have changed in the art world for Latin American artists over the last few decades?

TB: There is definitely more visibility, even though we still have to face many stereotypes. It is important to remember Latin American criticism. It explains the artistic process from a Latin American perspective. Often, critics from other places do not understand the social, historical, anecdotal, and emotional origins that a Latin American work refers to. For example, if you work with images of violence or poverty, some critics might interpret them in the wrong context, resulting in concepts like misery porn. It is important to fully understand the complexity of certain realities in order to present them to other groups of people who are not aware of them.

HHM: How would you describe your relationship with art galleries?

TB: Horrible. In 2011, I decided to leave all the galleries that were representing me and I stopped showing my work in museums altogether. I wanted to make a statement regarding my position concerning the inadequacy of institutions to exhibit works such as *Immigrant Movement International*. Galleries, in my experience, like my work as an artist, but once I decide to work with them, they want me to start doing things that are unnatural to me —I have often been asked to draw, paint, or make videos …

HHM: To make a product.

TB: Yes, a product. Working with galleries proves to be difficult because we do not agree on the definition and functions of art. Also, in my opinion, galleries are not very creative. If they can't come up with a traditional way of selling your work, they are either not interested in representing you, or they want to change the way you make art. They turn it into a boring business, just like the art market. On the one hand, I do not think that the artist is a producer, and on the other, who owns the work? Where does it circulate? What are its effects in these conditions?

HHM: What are your thoughts on the rise of the artist as celebrity?

TB: I consider it dangerous because I believe it is another form of dictatorship. The only benefit of being a celebrity is that your message reaches a much larger group of people.

HHM: Where do you go to be alone?

TB: In my head. And I'm there all the time (*laughs*).

HHM: At what point in your career did you feel that you were successful as an artist?

TB: When I succeeded in creating a community that would discuss the issues which I deemed urgent and that were not spoken about by other artists. For example, I created the *Behavior Art School* and the projects #YoTambiénExijo "I Also Demand" and *Arte Útil* "Useful Art."

HHM: Do you worry about being overexposed?

TB: Yes, because overexposure can damage the work in a significant way. It is also important to understand the use of exposure. Capitalist societies often work in a formalistic way and can make things superficial, and one can fall into that trap. The main purpose is not what you do, but why you do it.

HHM: What inspires you the most?

TB: I wouldn't use the word "inspires" but rather, what "motivates" me—and that is seeing injustice and knowing that things should and could be different, and that there is a possibility of change.

HHM: What is the most honest thing you can say about yourself?

TB: I'm scared—I'm scared of giving up and losing strength. I'm afraid of being afraid.

R

E

I

REI KAWAKUBO

TOKYO, 2019

Rei Kawakubo is a Japanese designer widely recognized as among the most important and influential designers in recent history. She has been making clothes since she founded her label, Commes des Garçons, in 1969. Since her Paris debut in 1981, she has blurred the line between art and fashion with regular and radical expressions. In recognition of her notable design contributions, an exhibition entitled *Rei Kawakubo/Commes des Garçons, Art of the In-Between* opened in 2017 at the Metropolitan Museum of Art in New York. The Japanese designer, whose inventiveness has endured for more than forty years, does not make public appearances and has only given rare interviews throughout her career. Her silence has given her voice more power and resonance than any fashion designer in the industry.

While I was living in Japan in 2019, I started to realize that people—particularly in Western culture—are uneasy or fearful of the concept of the void, while Japanese culture celebrates it. Therefore, I came up with the idea of conducting a one-question interview. In February 2019, Rei Kawakubo agreed to do it.

HUGO HUERTA MARIN:
It is interesting to contextualize fashion as a political tool. I can think of specific periods in time when clothes became as much of a statement as political ideas: people wearing studded dog collars that were made for real dogs, rubberwear, black leather … In your opinion, what makes fashion political?

REI KAWAKUBO:
I only ever wanted to make a business through creation, by making things that didn't exist before and fighting the establishment and the authorities that do not provide the proper foundation for this to happen. In that sense, fashion is political.

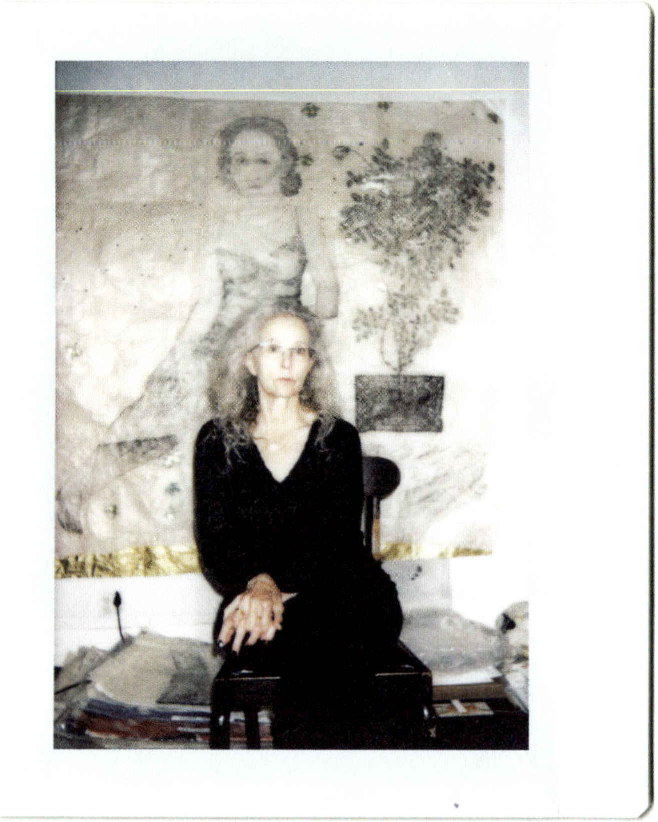

KIKI SMITH

NEW YORK, 2015

KI

KI

Kiki Smith is an artist recognized for her multidisciplinary practice, through which she explores the human condition. The body, mortality, regeneration, and gender politics, as well as the interconnection of spirituality and the natural world, are observed through a postmodern lens. Her expansive practice resonates personally and universally, manifesting in sculpture, glassmaking, printmaking, watercolor, photography, drawing, and textiles. Since 1982, Kiki has gained international acclaim and numerous accolades, awards, and honors. She has been subject of one-person exhibitions worldwide, including over 25 solo museum exhibitions.

When I arrived at Kiki's townhouse in the East Village, the first thing I noticed was a towering bright-red door. The line between her work and home life has always been thin. And once inside the house I was astonished by the works displayed randomly within the space: tapestries, sculptures, drawings, papers, letters, ephemera … An artist's studio that reflects a home, and vice versa. Many of the works I had studied in college; others I have seen hanging on the vast walls of New York's Pace Gallery. A true spectacle. Kiki Smith has created a visual iconography that is comprehensive and inimitable.

HUGO HUERTA MARIN:
You have worked with materials such as paper, glass, diamonds, wax, steel … How do you decide on a specific material for your work?

KIKI SMITH:
I don't know. The work tells me to. Either I'm working with a certain material and I'm curious to see what I can do with it, or it's simply obvious which material is the appropriate one to use. Everything is a mixture of the relationship between yourself and the material. Using different materials results in different

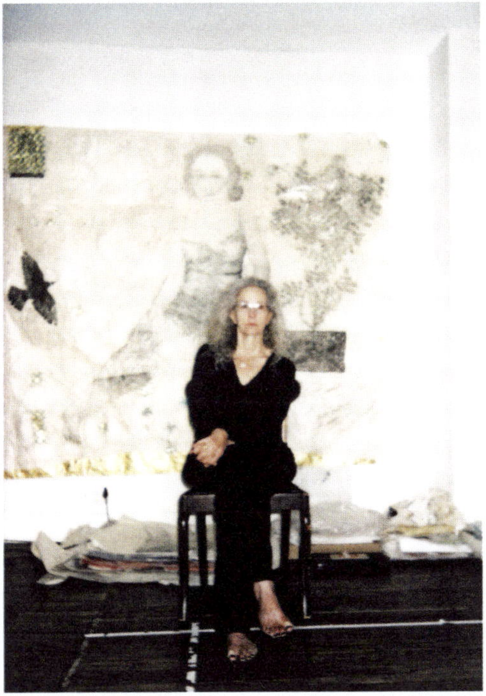

experiences, so I try to find exactly what experience and what material would be the most consequential or concise. I also sometimes realize that I need to work with more than just one material for the same piece or idea. This results in the creation of various versions of the same piece. It becomes, in essence, a dialogue between materials.

HHM: How would you describe the subjects of your sculptures?

KS: It changes and varies, depending on what I'm working on. More often than not, I would say that the thing itself is just an object, not a subject. It's less metaphorical or allegorical; it's just a thing, an autonomous thing that is not standing in for something else. It can have other kinds of meanings and different associations attached to it, but ultimately, it's just a thing, and its subject or object has to be itself.

HHM: It seems that the concept of beauty is a constant topic of discussion in your work. What is your concept of beauty?

KS: I don't have a concept of beauty. I like to make things as beautiful as possible. But one's definition of beauty can be like shifting sand, especially over the course of one's life. I find beauty in attention to details, even though they might seem sloppy. I'm always striving to make something beautiful, in a way that requires attention to the details. Beauty is important, and something I consider while creating new work. But at the same time, it's a very elusive, fluid, changing,

BEAUTY IS IMPORTANT, AND SOMETHING I CONSIDER WHILE CREATING NEW WORK. BUT AT THE SAME TIME, IT'S A VERY ELUSIVE, FLUID, CHANGING, SHAPE-SHIFTING THING

shape-shifting thing. I always attempt to make the thing find itself—what is most clear in itself. Sometimes it's beautiful, and sometimes it's not.

HHM: You have occasionally played with religious iconography and historical religious forms. Would you say that spirituality or religion is assumed in your work?

KS: That's something I've always been attracted to. Does it have spiritual content? I don't know. I can't say what is present in a work, but having been brought up Catholic, I was raised with the idea that objects hold meaning. The same holds true for Hinduism. Through the objects' construction, their physicality, and through all the different ways that things are attached to them, they hold their own reservoir of activity.

HHM: Do you believe there is a lack of a spiritual approach in contemporary art?

KS: Spirituality is similar to beauty in the sense that it's fluid and subjective; it's an elusive idea. I don't know what it means sometimes. I think people will always have questions—whether big or small—that continue to dominate a great deal of their lives, but I don't believe it's necessary for them to put these concerns into their artwork. I don't believe that art has a particular space or place, or that it's supposed to be doing something. I think it's just a way for people to synthesize their experience and their interests. In a way, they externally formalize some consciousness inside themselves, which can allude to anything, and that, to me, is what makes it successful. It is very broad, and people need different kinds of expression.

HHM: Do you believe your work has been considered transgressive for its content—when you show and make reference to semen, blood, and bodily fluids—or through its violation of implicit taboos?

KS: Lucy Lippard said, "Art recalls that which is absent," and I relate to that idea. One thing that art does—or at the very least, art is doing—is bring that which is hidden to the surface: things that are not spoken of in the public sphere. In my opinion, it's about our need for personal space. At certain points in my life, I needed some personal space and that allowed me to be more vocal about things that weren't openly discussed. I found them to be hindrances in my own personal life. The same can be said of things that are overtly problematic about the human body, or in our culture. But it can also be about details, aesthetics, or formal or informal things—it can be about anything. One can say it's transgressive, but on the other hand, it can also just be about feeling less oppressed by what is considered oppressive in our culture. Because culture is always much more constrictive than people are on the individual level.

HHM: Why did you choose the body as a subject in the first place?

KS: I was investigating the body until sometime in the nineties. During that time, my boyfriend was working at The Strand bookstore and gave me a copy of *Gray's Anatomy*, and I just ran with it. I loved it; I loved it as a language. The thing about creating art is that it's a great opportunity to learn about life, and to learn about different subjects. In this case, I just saw the cells and stomach and all that stuff. Although I didn't want to be a doctor or study medicine, I was still completely fascinated. In my opinion, being an artist gives you the opportunity—in a way—to walk around different kinds of spaces. But the landscape can change.

HHM: In that sense, is it wrong to describe your work as "visceral," as is often said?

KS: I wouldn't consider my work to be that visceral. I believe that my work is often just a set of ideas, but I would like for it to be more visceral. I suppose you could say that in the seventies, it was often through the material quality of the work that one could understand the message. For instance, the work of Richard Serra—or of any artist from that generation—was very material-oriented rather than illusionistic. It had clarity in that the material and the form were married in a very succinct way. I spent the first twenty or more years of my practice creating things using just the tangible aspects or qualities of the materials to create the meaning, which led me down a slippery slope at times. But I do enjoy works that are visceral and works that are physical, as there are many artists whose works are more physical than mine.

HHM: It's interesting to see how people interpret the same thing in different ways … Critics, curators, art historians, and viewers alter the rules of visual thinking and visual interpretation. And it seems that some people have trouble with the postures of some of your sculptures, such as *Tale* or *Pee Body*. What is the source of that imagery?

KS: In a way, they were inspired by anecdotes. I had a friend who I thought was very resentful about everything, sort of carrying around negative garbage in her mind, and it was very tedious and unpleasant to be around her. Somehow, from that idea, I thought: "It's like carrying around a tail of shit in the brain, and physically there is shit coming out too." It's a ponderous tale—like a story—so it is called *Tale*, T-A-L-E. It's something that is coming out of you, of which you can't let go. Some people hoard material things, and others hoard thoughts mentally. That was more of a statement. One also needs to consider the humiliation in carrying all of this garbage within. As for *Pee Body*, it was another sculpture I created with fluids exiting the body. It was about location … To elaborate, if your hair or anything else in your body falls away, they are no longer a part of you; you disassociate from them, or at least most people disassociate from them. It's about self, location, and the fluidity of that.

However, both sculptures were influenced by an object and a drawing. An object in a shape of a mass or a body and an appendage hanging like an arm. They were also influenced by one of my father's [Tony Smith's] sculptures, titled *Stinger*, where an arm juts out of a mass. I also created a similar sculpture that had what resembled menstrual blood—created with red beads—coming out of the body. For these sculptures, I had the idea of creating an object that had one static part while the other could be moved in any direction. Essentially, the object was like a drawing with lines undulating around, whereas the other part of it was completely static. So, I'm simply entertaining myself and thinking about the things that interest me. It's all of those things put together. In the end, it's not necessarily about its meaning—because I have no idea what it means—but more about my impetus for creating these sculptures. I don't deliberately create to attach meaning to my work. It's more about the curiosity about its results. What happens when you create something? Does it do anything back? Does it give you anything back?

HHM: Would you say a feminist discourse is assumed in your work?

KS: In general, I always say I'm a feminist as a citizen, but I don't want my work to have a didactic or ideological agenda associated with it. At the same time, my work is a reflection of my interests, concerns, and fascinations in my daily life. So certainly, when I've created sculptures of bodies and interior bodies or figurations, I created them from the point of a person or

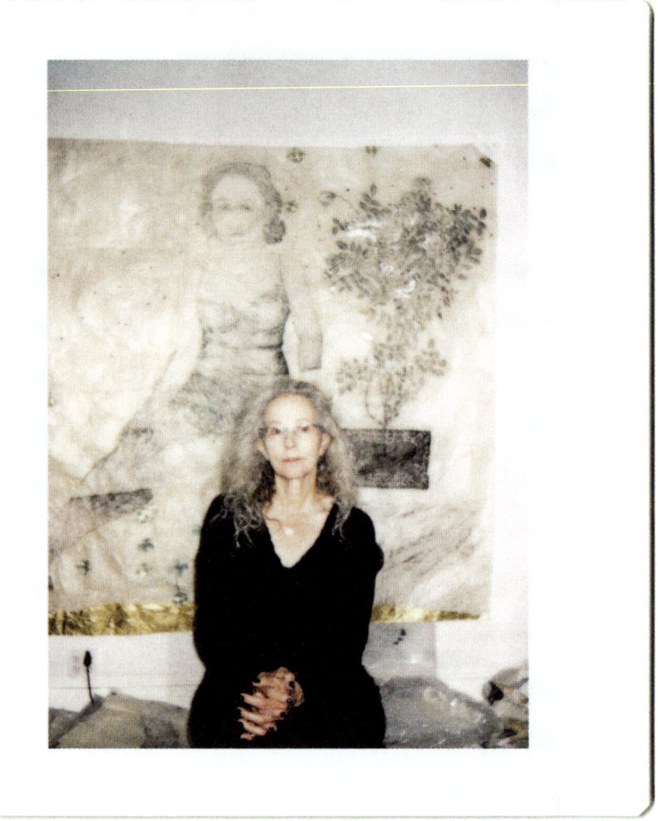

a female: an identified person living and meandering through the world. For the most part, I use the female form.

HHM: What do you think is the difference between how men and women create art?

KS: In general, I believe that female Surrealists and artists such as Frida Kahlo were inspired by their own individual experiences, and used their own bodies and their own images as a medium. I'm not saying that [Marcel] Duchamp didn't use his image, but he did so in the guise of a woman. In my opinion, the female artist's use of her own body in art is one of the major elements in the beginning of modern art, because it connects the microcosm to the macrocosm. It takes it from the personal to the political. I believe that Frida Kahlo represented the beginning of modern art. If one looks at artists in the seventies who used their bodies, one needs to consider that they might not have done so had it not been for these women using the self prior to them. Women from the 1800s over-represented themselves through photography, yet it still had an impersonal element. It was simply a way of using the self as a subject, but is also malleable.

HHM: Your work has also been compared to Nancy Spero's several times, in how you both portray the female body as a site of resistance and transgression.

KS: I admire her work immensely. She is like a hero to me. Her work has a very overt meaning, whereas mine moves around more, so it's sometimes harder to catch the impetus behind it. In a way, her work has a clear function of resistance—and she spoke eloquently about it. I am fascinated with how she worked, as printmaking was her expertise. I mean, she began as a young painter, but due to her life circumstances, she eventually moved toward printmaking. Personally, printmaking is fundamental to my work. So, I was interested in how she formally put her work together and fascinated by how inventive it was. She used images repeatedly, but each one was always unique.

HHM: You both use images as language.

KS: Yes. She was smart in the way that she used historical images, and by how she playfully created some of her own. She didn't use them in a way that made it seem as if she was confiscating or co-opting them. During the politically correct period in art history, people were not supposed to look at anything else, or create anything in relation to any other culture in the world. She fluidly did, but never in a way that was disrespectful. She was also wonderful in her use of language and image. That's something that I don't do as much, but I am fascinated by it. I love art and language together, and how words and images work together. That interests me greatly, even though it isn't evident in my work (*laughs*). She succeeds very well at that.

HHM: It seems that Mexican culture has influenced your work as well. You make reference to Jose Guadalupe Posada, Sor Juana Inés de la Cruz, and the rituals regarding the Mexican Day of the Dead.

IN MY OPINION, THE FEMALE ARTIST'S USE OF HER OWN BODY IN ART IS ONE OF THE MAJOR ELEMENTS IN THE BEGINNING OF MODERN ART. IT TAKES IT FROM THE PERSONAL TO THE POLITICAL. I BELIEVE THAT FRIDA KAHLO REPRESENTED THE BEGINNING OF MODERN ART

KS: Yes. In the eighties, I went to Mexico for the Day of the Dead and later travelled around Yucatán. My father had recently died, so the idea of the resurrection, or keeping the dead very present, was comforting to me. The celebration had a funny sweetness to it, and making things such as comical figurines of skeletons uplifted me. For about a year prior to that trip, my work had been solely about death, as I was confronted by the death of my father. But Mexico changed my work into being about life. I returned from my trip and made prints about life. One was called *How I Know I'm Here*. Also, when I look back on my time in Uxmal, I remember there was a sculpture of a Mexican god in the shape of a nose on the edge of a building—a body part used as a decorative motif. The idea of body parts as motifs inspired me, so I returned and made a room of tongues with terracotta

THE IDEA OF A SCULPTURE CREATED IN LAYERS HAS ALWAYS INTERESTED ME. YOU SEE IT AS A FACE, BUT ITS LAYERS HAVE DIFFERENT KINDS OF IMAGES

in The Clocktower, with films in Spanish about different parts of the body. I also went to Oaxaca and worked with James Brown and Alexandra Brown at Carpe Diem Press. We worked with printmakers and made prints of dead animals.

HHM: I wonder if you visited any of the archeological complexes in Mexico City or Oaxaca? The sculptures there are really powerful.

KS: Yes. One thing that I found to be very powerful was the sculpture of Coatlicue. Its shape is powerful, like a massive rock. In general, a lot of the sculptures from Teotihuacan are of faces that represent certain things. I believe they are pressed clay molds, but are very inspirational regardless. The idea of a sculpture created in layers has always interested me. You see it as a face, but its layers have different kinds of images. I created sculptures with layers for a couple of years, but I never made as many of them as I would have liked.

HHM: I was recently reading about Francis Alÿs's performance *The Modern*

Procession. Can you tell me about your experience of representing a living icon?

KS: When they asked me to do it, my first thought was that they had already asked ten people before me who had the sense to say no! But I love Francis Alÿs's work. I had met him a couple of times and found him to be a wonderful person. Because of those two reasons, I agreed to be a part of it. Then, I put on my best dress, and I'm not light enough for people to be carrying me around—and they had to carry me for miles. It was very funny, because I felt more like myself than I ever had in my life. I was very comfortable being carried ten or twelve feet up in the air. When we got to Queens, I got off. I changed back into my clothes and took the subway home (*laughs*)—I got back down to real life. I do believe there was an aspect that perfectly fit with my personality that made me feel so comfortable during the procession, because you know, I am not someone like Marina [Abramović] using the self or the body. I live a pretty plain, modest life—but it was very funny, as I thought I was definitely in my element.

HHM: What are your thoughts on the rise of the artist as celebrity?

KS: I think historically, artists have often been celebrities. Similarly, fame must be associated with the artist's work. It's good and useful for the artist and their work, but only if fame is a result of the work.

HHM: Where do you go to be alone?

KS: I'm always alone. I've lived alone for the most part of my life, and now I don't anymore. But I don't see that as separate.

HHM: At what point in your career did you feel that you were a successful artist?

KS: I suppose that feeling comes primarily from your individual experience of your work; you can put your energy into creating something and have it reflect back. As a result, it gives you some satisfaction, but it's only temporary. I know that in the nineties, people became aware of my work in that way. However, I think success in your work is short-lived. In a certain sense, I believe it is dissatisfaction that keeps you moving.

HHM: Do you worry about being overexposed?

KS: No, I don't think about such things. I live in New York, but for the last couple of years, I've been living upstate. I spend most of my time thinking about what I'm creating, and if it happens to fall apart, I have to figure out how to put it back together. I believe that in a way, the career stuff is not my business. My concern is to pay attention to my work and pay attention to my life, and remember the fact that we are here for a limited amount of time. At the same time, it's always nice to feel that you are doing something that has meaning to other people, that you've been useful in some way to something outside of yourself — that is a privilege.

HHM: What are your thoughts on the big international art exhibitions like documenta or the Venice Biennale?

KS: I haven't been to many, but I think it's wonderful when you can see artists from all over the world in one place. I think it helps artists compete with themselves, because the space demands the work be more ambitious or theatrical, or larger than the necessities of the work. Moreover, it also gives artists opportunities that they wouldn't normally have.

HHM: What is the most honest thing you can say about yourself?

KS: I'm complicated.

OR

L

AN

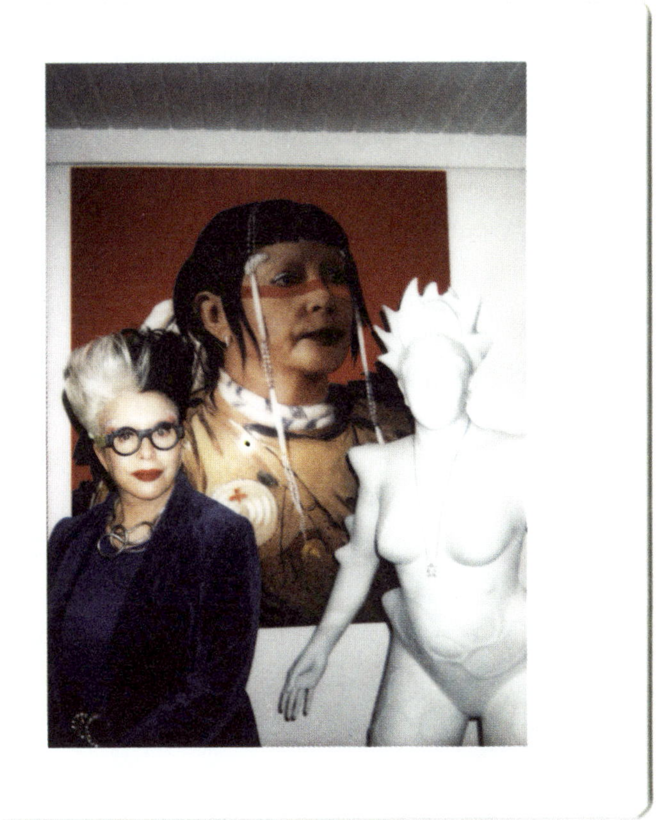

ORLAN

PARIS, 2015

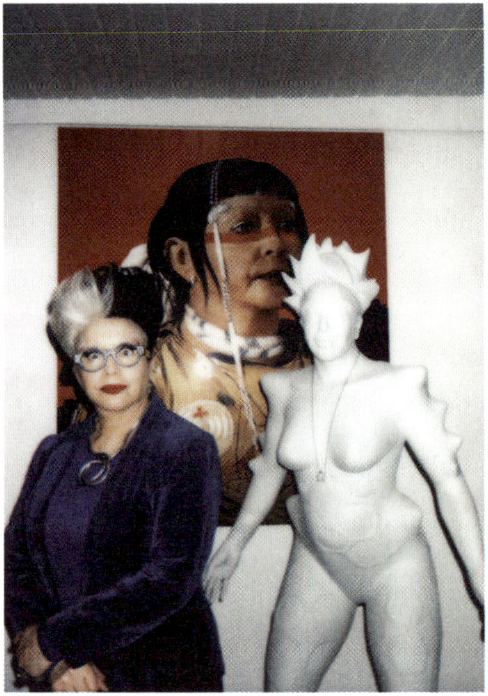

ORLAN was born in 1947 in Saint-Etienne, France. She adopted the name ORLAN, which is always written entirely in capital letters. She works in numerous mediums, which include photography, video, sculpture, drawing, installation, performance, and biotechnologies. However, she was the first artist to use plastic surgery as an artistic medium. After determining the use of her own body as a unit of measurement, her ideas became more radical with her surgical-operation-performances in the nineties. The aim of these performances was to dramatically alter her appearance against beauty standards defined by society. Each performance was built on a philosophical, psychoanalytic, or poetic text.

I met ORLAN in her Paris studio. Over a glass of red wine she talked about beauty and science. ORLAN displays her desire to redefine her corporeality and identity. Her work questions the religious, political, and cultural pressures on the human body that leave an imprint on its flesh, using scientific, technological, and medical discoveries while simultaneously challenging them.

HUGO HUERTA MARIN:
You are an artist deeply devoted to investigating the aesthetics of the body. So, let me start off by asking you, what is your concept of beauty?

ORLAN:
Beauty is a matter of dominant ideology. The standards of beauty that we designate for ourselves are valid only momentarily and only in a given place.

HHM: Would you consider the basis of these standards the core of your work?

O: My work questions the status of the body in society through all the political, religious, and cultural pressures which fall upon the flesh, especially—but not only—those of women. Therefore, my work questions the idea of beauty.

HHM: What role does sex play in it?

O: The work questions the cultural codes that dominate sexuality rather than sex itself. Although, I did *The Kiss of the Artist*—in which I was selling French kisses—and *The Origin of the War*, a counterpart to Courbet's *Origin of the World*.

HHM: Can we talk about the genesis of the surgery works?

O: I was reading a text by Lacanian psychoanalyst Eugénie Lemoine-Luccioni. Her book *La Robe* gave me the idea to create the series of surgical-operation-performances.

HHM: Changing your physical identity seemed unacceptable to many. Was it your intention to break social constructs or stereotypes?

O: It's about disrupting habits and preconceived notions and questioning my time. Most people do not realize that they've been living with ideas from fifty to a hundred years ago or more. Meanwhile, our lifestyles have changed so much, and so have our possibilities. For example, face transplants challenge the perspective on my self-sculpture work through surgery.

HHM: It seems that your work rejects the idea of tradition …

MY WORK QUESTIONS THE STATUS OF THE BODY IN SOCIETY THROUGH ALL THE POLITICAL, RELIGIOUS, AND CULTURAL PRESSURES WHICH FALL UPON THE FLESH, ESPECIALLY—BUT NOT ONLY—THOSE OF WOMEN

O: Tradition is always a good excuse to ensure nothing moves, to question all innovations, all the discoveries of our times, and to be closed to the present and all possible inventions and creations. Tradition has done a lot of harm.

HHM: Do you believe pain is important for an artist?

O: It can be, but it's not so in my case. Rather, my work is geared against pain, and toward the pleasure-body, as mentioned in my *Carnal Art Manifesto*.

HHM: In your work, you have employed symbols associated with different cultures, incorporating pre-Columbians, Africans, and Indians into your image. Is cultural identity a key concept for you?

O: The first part of my work covered Western culture, questioning Christian culture and my own identity. The second part—the surgical-operation-performances—served as a hinge for the third part of my work, as through these, I built myself a new image to introducc further new images in my work. In this third post-operative part, I grew interested by non-Western culture, which I also questioned through the use of pre-Columbian statuary, by making hybridizations between this statuary and my new face. This resulted in the creation of mutant bodies out of the earth and stone, in combining two civilizations and two artistic practices.

HHM: In that sense, theorist Guy Debord suggests that the present age prefers "the sign to the thing signified, the appearance to the essence." Would you agree?

O: Both can coexist.

HHM: How does your mindset change when you go from the operating table to making a sculpture?

O: I've never been interested in materials or fascinated by ancient and modern technologies. When I have an idea or a concept, I try to find the best materiality to represent its essence. Each piece brings everything back into question; brings me back into question.

HHM: Image and language are clearly important to you ...

O: Many of my works come from reading books. And every surgical-operation-performance was based on a psychoanalytic, philosophical, or literary text.

HHM: Which books from your library do you consider most valuable?

O: There are many. *The Fold* and *Difference and Repetition* by [Gilles] Deleuze.

HHM: Do you believe art has the responsibility to raise philosophical questions?

O: I think the artist has a responsibility. We are not oblivious birds in trees that simply tweet with no awareness of what is happening at the foot of the tree. We need to have—like any other citizen—a position on current events in the world and in society; we are not on the "outside."

HHM: Would you say sacredness and religion is assumed in your work?

O: I questioned my Judeo-Christian culture but I'm for a world without religion, which would have less hatred and war. John Lennon's "Imagine."

HHM: There is a clear correlation between fashion and your artistic practice. What is your relationship with fashion?

O: I have a conflicted relationship with fashion because much of my oeuvre features costumes and clothing. My baroque pieces are both sculptures and dresses, made with sheets from my trousseau or pleather. I have also made folded dress sculptures with craft and bubble wrap, marble, resin, or 3D printing. In each of my surgical-operation-performances, the medical team and my own team were dressed by Paco Rabanne, Lan Vu, Issey Miyake, or myself. On the other hand, I have also kept my entire wardrobe since I was a teenager, and from it, I created pieces that I hybridized with designers such as Maroussia Rebecq, David Delfin, and Agatha Ruiz de la Prada. These pieces were presented in fashion shows within a performance. In my exhibition *Un Boeuf sur la langue* at the Museum of Fine Arts of Nantes, I created a silk velour with which I designed dresses worn by black-painted mannequins. My main conflict with fashion is the violent pressure on bodies to follow a single disembodied body ideal. However, in life, one doesn't have a single body, but rather several bodies.

HHM: Do you consider yourself a feminist?

O: I've considered myself a feminist for a very long time. I have made many statements with a sign that says, "I am a man and a woman." At the time, I practiced humanist feminism. Nowadays, with everything closing in, I proclaim louder and clearer that I am a feminist. The millions of women in the world who don't have freedom of speech, who are enslaved sexually and domestically, who don't have access to healthcare, who may have been beaten, violated, killed — all these women need those who do have a bit more freedom to defend their cause.

MY BODY HAS BECOME A SPACE OF PUBLIC DEBATE. FOR ME, IT'S DIFFICULT TO HANDLE IT IN REAL LIFE, AS I'M OFTEN RECOGNIZED, PHOTOGRAPHED, AND QUESTIONED

HHM: How do you think things have changed for women in the art world over the last few decades?

O: There has been little progress. Being a female artist is still extremely difficult, especially in terms of recognition and in the way we are perceived.

HHM: Which younger artists do you feel connected to?

O: Emeric Lhuisset, Audrey Cottin, and Tania Bruguera.

HHM: What are your thoughts on the rise of the artist as celebrity?

O: My body has become a space of public debate. For me, it's difficult to handle it in real life, as I'm often recognized, photographed, and questioned.

HHM: Where do you go to be alone?

O: I am never alone, which doesn't keep me out of being in my own bubble.

HHM: Do you worry about being overexposed?

O: One can never be overexposed. We have death to disappear, rest, and be at peace.

HHM: What inspires you the most?

O: Reading, science, medical science, genetics, biotechnologies …

HHM: What are your thoughts on the big international art exhibitions like documenta or the Venice Biennale?

O: I enjoy both these big events—especially Venice, in which one can see many pieces from different parts of the world. But they remain events that only showcase those who in a sense have already made it, or those who are already in the art world.

HHM: What is the most honest thing you can say about yourself?

O: Do your best and let them say what they want.

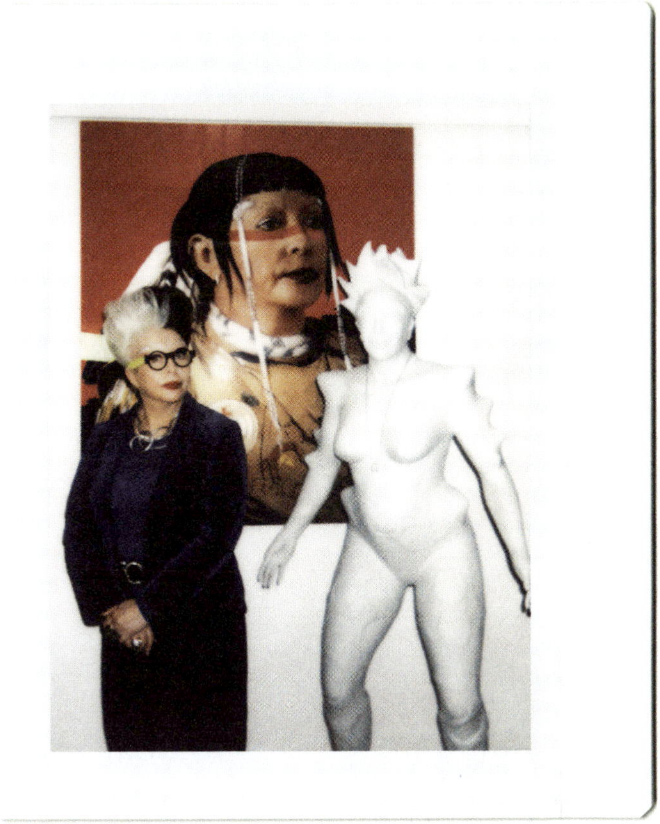

J

IAN

NE

UL

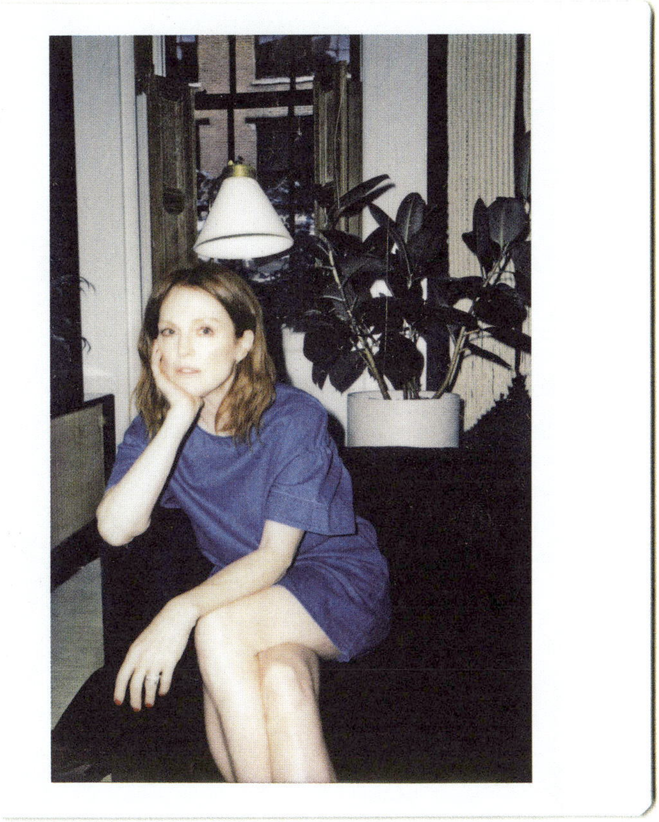

JULIANNE MOORE

NEW YORK, 2018

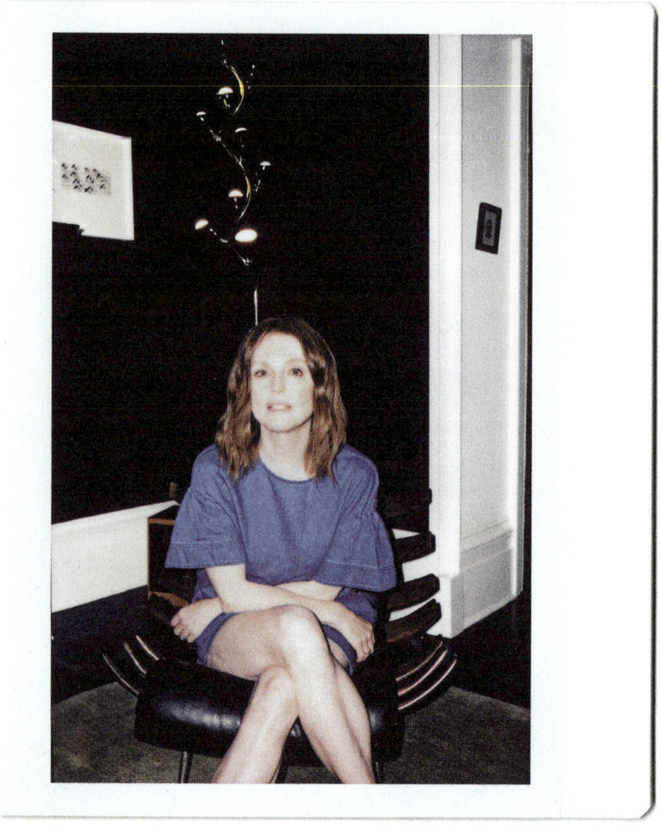

Julianne Moore is an Academy Award, BAFTA, and Emmy-winning actor, and the first American woman to be awarded top acting prizes at the Berlin, Venice, and Cannes film festivals. She is also a *New York Times* best-selling author for her children's book series *Freckleface Strawberry*. In 2015, she became founding chair of the Everytown for Gun Safety Creative Council, a creative community established to help amplify the movement to end gun violence in America.

I knocked on Julianne's door in the West Village and was surprised to be welcomed by her alongside her two joyful dogs. It was hard not to stare at the screen legend in a dashing indigo-blue dress. Julianne has made a habit of going against the grain, and her home mirrors that: It is a quintessential, beautiful brownstone whose art collection gives it a subtle, subversive twist. Likewise, in conversation, she enjoys taking risks; she exudes warmth but also has a certain edge. Julianne Moore is a brilliant actor and compelling conversation-alist who burns up and invites you to witness it at first hand.

HUGO HUERTA MARIN:
Let´s begin at the beginning. Are there any films that influenced you to become an actor?

JULIANNE MOORE:
I don't know if there were any, specifically. But when I look back to when I was growing up, you know, we didn't go to the theater; we went to the movies, and only for entertainment's sake. We moved to Juneau, Alaska, when I was in the fifth grade, so I must have been ten or eleven. There was a movie theater there that played a different movie every Saturday because the population in Juneau was so small. So, if you went, there was always something different playing and we saw whatever was there, which meant we would all go

I THINK THAT THE TRICK OF ACTING IS TO BE ALIVE ON CAMERA, AND I THINK WHEN PEOPLE SEE THAT, THEY FEEL THE SCENE

and see something like *The Aristocats*. But I also saw *Minnie and Moskowitz* there, you know, [John] Cassavetes' film, when I was ten, and I saw *One Day in the Life of Ivan Denisovich*. So, I saw a wide range of films there. I think it was the first time I became aware of film as a medium, you know, as a form of communication rather than just a form of entertainment. So, I think that whoever was programming that movie theater …(*laughs*).

HHM: (*laughs*) Made a huge impact on your life.

JM: Yeah, they really did.

HHM: Nowadays, what makes a good script or an interesting project for you?

JM: Well, what makes an interesting project is a good script. For me, a strong sense of language is really important. I look for compelling and human stories. I look for stories that make sense emotionally, that seem to reflect something real. Even fantasy needs to have a real human dilemma and a real meaning. It is all about reflection of the human condition.

HHM: You have delivered several critically acclaimed performances throughout your career. What has been your most radical performance?

JM: I don't know. It's funny because I don't think anything I have done has been particularly radical. I want to be real. I don't want anyone watching it to feel they are watching something that isn't real. So, in that sense, it shouldn't startle you. I want a performance to bring you closer to yourself and to your own understanding of something. I think that the trick of acting is to be alive on camera, and I think when people see that, they feel the scene.

HHM: I remember a scene in *Magnolia* where you have a meltdown in the middle of the pharmacy that stayed with me. That movie deals with pain on so many levels …

JM: Oh, yes.

HHM: Why is pain important for an artist?

JM: I think it is important for everyone, and it's important to recognize that everybody has a degree of discomfort, pain, or unhappiness. The idea that any of these emotions are singular to you is a false one. I think that what artists are trying to do is to tap into whatever we share emotionally, and whatever is universal, and to always be folding that into their work—to try to find a way to reflect the notion that everybody has a degree of suffering.

HHM: Another role that had a big impact on me was your part in *The Big Lebowski* …

JM: Oh! (*laughs*).

HHM: (*laughs*) A powerful confrontation with female empowerment. Why were you interested in that particular project?

JM: It was a beautiful script. It was beautifully written and so precisely constructed. The Coen brothers are really great filmmakers—their scripts are amazing linguistically. All their language is so specific, and so filled with character. It is easy. You just do what they write. My character was inspired by somebody they had met—a German performance artist. It was very specific, obviously, to them, and I remember being in New York in the eighties when performance art was happening all over the place, and there were so many people I knew who kind of lived in that life, and performed in that way. So, it was just a welcome thing to do …

HHM: Were you interested in performance art back then?

JM: Yes, performance is interesting. I like to watch it, but I don't know if I want to do it … But I like art and anything that is compelling and creates a feeling. I think what I don't like is people talking about art (*laughs*). You know, telling people what it is or means … Am I not supposed to sense what it is? One of the fascinating things about performance art is that you go and have an immediate reaction to it. That was also important while playing that role; it was nice to play a character who had an outsized sense of herself and her art, and, as you said, was confident. Here, you had someone who talked about her art and lived in this big world, but you never knew what her art was. I think that sometimes, in film, people become very literal about art—you see someone painting or sculpting, and that sort of takes the magic of it away.

HHM: I find the correlation between visual art and the moving image very interesting. How do you think art influences film?

JM: It's funny because I was just thinking about that today. I think there certainly is a correlation, especially in terms of composition. You know, film is a visual medium, and that's kind of an interesting thing when it comes to film and television because television is about language, since there is less of a visual sense to it, whereas film is incredibly visual. How you compose a shot and how you tell a story are reliant on how well versed you are in the visual medium. I think that a lot of great filmmakers are interested in art and spend a lot of time studying it and looking at compositions, and looking at how our eye moves over a frame. I always say that the director's job is not to be an acting coach, but rather to direct the audience's eye through a film. Directors are telling you where to look and what to see; they are directing the audience, and they do it visually. In that sense, I think there is a strong correlation to visual art.

HHM: In all of film history, whom do you wish could have directed you?

JM: Wow, that is an interesting question … I have never thought about that. I was really lucky with Robert Altman. It was a crazy accident of birth to have been born at a time when I could work with Bob Altman because I think he was one of the premier filmmakers of our time. Maybe Billy Wilder, because I think he had a warmth about him and a humanity that is really compelling—an empathy that is really interesting.

HHM: Someone once told me that it is important for an artist to work from a place of having no sense of consequence. What role do chance and accidents play, if any, while performing?

JM: A tremendous amount. There is a part of me that does a huge amount of preparation. I know the material really well, I do the research I need to do, but then, when I am actually on a set, it has to go away, and I have to act from a place of unconsciousness. I can't determine what I am going to do, so I have to wait. For me, the idea is that I am prepared and know the material enough just to allow something to happen to me on camera. There are times when I am working on a film, and often, after finishing a scene, I don't remember what I have done. I experience a sort of blackout because you just want to let it happen to you, and sometimes, when that happens, you just don't remember.

HHM: So interesting … I once read that a flood of adrenaline induces short-term memory loss. So, in that sense, where does Julianne Moore end and the unidentifiable voice of a character begin?

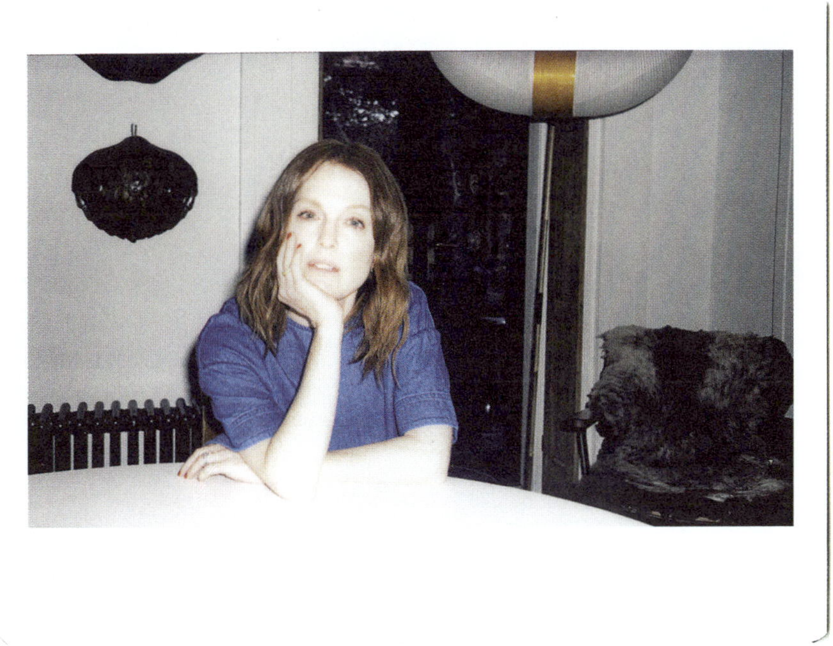

JM: I think all art is related to the artist, and I think that is why we do it. We are doing it as a reflection of ourselves and as a way to connect with other human beings. So, you are taking something that is the utmost personal thing to you and throwing it out there into the world for other humans to consume, absorb, or connect to. So, there isn't a conscious place where I begin or end while I am working. I bring my person to that other person—that character—through me. I am necessarily very involved in the creation of that character because it is my physical body. I may not intellectually be able to tell you where I do it from, and a painter or a writer might not be able to either, but it is all done through this sieve of the self, somehow.

HHM: In your opinion, what role does an actor play in society?

JM: OK, here is something: How do we know if somebody is a good or bad actor? If you haven't been trained or have knowledge about acting, you might not know. As an audience member, if you suddenly respond to somebody, you wouldn't immediately know why you responded. We think something is bad or we consider someone a bad actor when they are missing the human element—that thing that makes you go, "Wait a minute! That is a real person! Wait, no, that is not a real person, that is an actor and that is a story, and they are pretending but this seems so real!" So, actors in society sometimes become avatars for people within their own hopes and desires and interests.

HHM: A reflection.

ART IS ALWAYS A REFLECTION OF WHAT IS HAPPENING IN CULTURE, POLITICS, AND THE WORLD. WE ARE NOT FORTUNE-TELLERS. WE ARE ALWAYS REFLECTORS

JM: Yes. People are going to project ideas and feelings onto them … and they are not always right, because obviously, there is a separation between what people project and what they project is about them, not about you. So, I think it is very important for actors to be clear about who they are, where they are standing, and what the job is. Because a lot of the attention that happens is around our jobs, it's not based on us.

HHM: Do you think politics and film are intertwined?

JM: Oh, absolutely. I always say—when talking about movies "leading the way"—that they are not. Art is always a reflection of what is happening in culture, politics, and the world. We are not fortune-tellers. We are always reflectors. There is always a seed of something happening somewhere in the world or in culture for an artist to pick up on and amplify. So, yes, we are there as cultural reflectors, I suppose.

I LIKE FILM BECAUSE YOU CAN COMMUNICATE MEANING BY COMPOSING SOMETHING, BY THE WAY YOU COLOR IT OR HOW YOU MOVE THE CAMERA—ALL OF THOSE THINGS ARE INTERESTING TO ME

HHM: I can see how the human condition is a big subject for you and your work, and find it very interesting that you continuously talk about how "behavior is not character" but is mutable and changes from place to place.

JM: Well, I think you learn that when you move around a lot. If you've ever only lived in one town where everyone speaks the same language and has the same ethnic makeup, and you have lived there for a long time, you would see that people behave in a similar fashion—their speech is similar, the way they dress might be similar, etc. There would be some variations, but you'd notice what that culture and community consists of. How they move, how they dance, how they talk ... But then you go somewhere else and everything is utterly different—the way people speak, the way they dress, the way they behave, and even the weather is different. Once again, you'll also notice there are similarities in our humanness that remain intact. There are universal things that have to do with being a human being that don't have to do with behavior. So, it is important to say that the way someone speaks, walks, dresses, or gestures can be related to culture, community, national identity, and so on, but that is not always who that person is. Instead, it is what they identify with based on how they live. You have to look through that to figure out who they are. Everything we do is a signifier in one way or another, but we have to be really careful not to say, "Ah! This person is a stiff person." Well, no … Maybe their culture is restrictive. You have to look beyond all the things that seem to define us.

HHM: What is your concept of beauty?

JM: Things that feel close, real, and human are the things I think are most beautiful.

HHM: I find so much beauty in the way many of the films you've been involved in were shot. Is that the basis for how you choose some of your film projects?

JM: I think the reason I have been in many films that have been beautifully shot and beautifully composed is because of the people I chose to work with—the people who are lensing things, specifically placing meaning in a frame. This is why I like film, because you can communicate meaning by composing something, by the way you color it or how you move a camera—all of those things are interesting to me. I think about a film like *Call Me by Your Name* and the director [Luca Guadagnino], you know,

JULIANNE MOORE

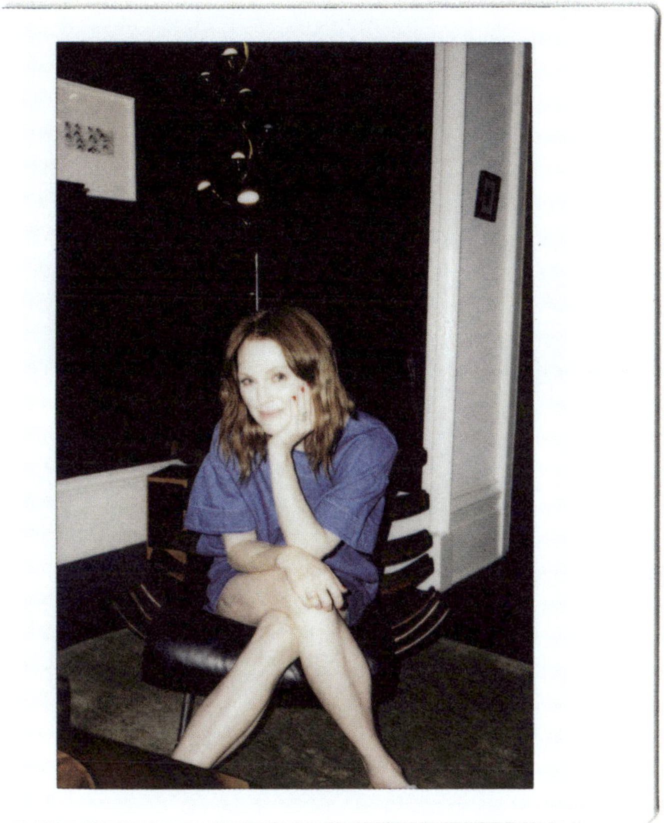

he is wonderful with composition, color, and framing, but what he does best and really kind of blows people away with is that he embosses it with so much humanity and fleshiness. You see people's skin, the food they eat, and the clothes they wear—all these things matter to him. Everything human and earthly really matters to him, and that to me is beautiful. It doesn't feel distant; it feels close.

HHM: What are your thoughts on the rise of the artist as celebrity?

JM: I think they are different things. A celebrity is someone who is well known, and they don't have to be well known for doing anything. An artist is somebody who is always trying to say something about the human condition.

HHM: What inspires you the most?

JM: Great writing. I find that incredibly inspiring. My friend Deborah Eisenberg asked me to do an audio recording of one of her stories, and she is such a spectacular writer. I kept thinking, "How does she do that?" I was so touched by her insights and so moved by her work and kept thinking, "Look at things more carefully, really examine them, think about them, and try to explore them the way she does."

HHM: Do you have any recurring dreams?

JM: Not anymore. I think I had them when I was a child—all those scary things happening. But I am always interested in how many dreams I have and how cinematic they are. I think everybody's dreams are fairly cinematic.

HHM: What are your thoughts on the big film festivals like Cannes?

JM: I love them. For me, it is an opportunity to run into a lot of my peers and colleagues and to maybe meet people that I want to meet, or meet actors from other countries that I don't have the opportunity to meet very often. You know, to be in Berlin or to be in Cannes or to be in Venice and see filmmakers and people interested in film … I also like watching the movies. I saw a Polish movie called *Cold War* that was at Cannes and it was just exquisite, and then to be able to turn around, see the filmmaker and cast right behind you, and applaud them and be able to say congratulations at the premiere of the film, I mean, what an opportunity! That is what I love about film festivals.

HHM: What is the most honest thing you can say about yourself?

JM: I am persistent.

IN

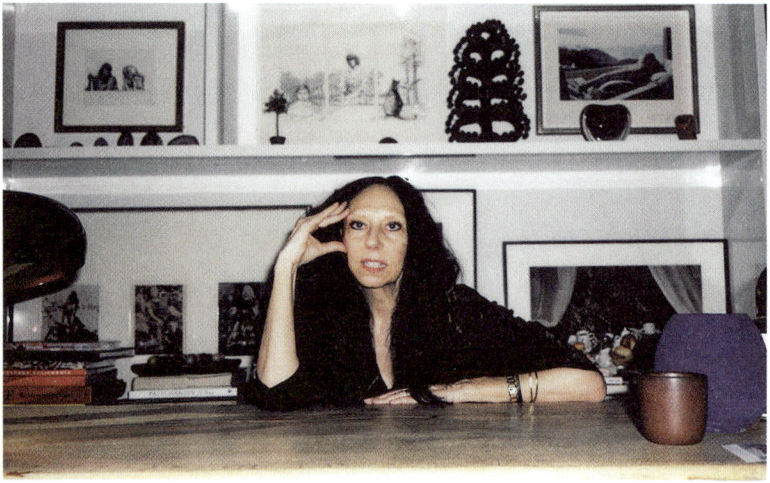

INEZ VAN LAMSWEERDE

NEW YORK, 2019

E

Z

Inez van Lamsweerde, one half of the photography duo Inez and Vinoodh, has a seemingly endless capacity to explore new visual territory. In the early 1990s, they were among the first practitioners to show the possibilities of digital-imaging technology as a creative and meaningful medium. They developed a signature style of visual seduction paired with provocative narratives, which infused new ideas into photography. Since the early 1990s, they have created groundbreaking editorials. Their approach is seen in campaigns and films for fashion houses, and they have also expanded into the world of film and video, directing innovative music videos.

I met Inez (and Vinoodh briefly) at their 1970s-inspired loft in NoLIta, filled with flowers, art, and furniture they designed themselves. Inez came across as a warm, outspoken, and intellectual artist who has no fear of expressing herself through art and in real life. The works of both artists feed off each other for inspiration and thus blur the boundaries between art and fashion. It is hard to open any fashion book these days without encountering an image created by them, yet they inhabit a creative place entirely of their own, which is rare in the often closed-off, cut-throat world of fashion.

HUGO HUERTA MARIN:
There is an interesting symbiotic relationship between the photographer and the muse. Do you have a specific subject whom you want to photograph over and over again?

INEZ VAN LAMSWEERDE:
Well, you know the thing that is kind of inherent to the fashion world is that everyone is always looking for "the new": the new face, the new girl. But when I am interested in someone's face, I immediately become interested

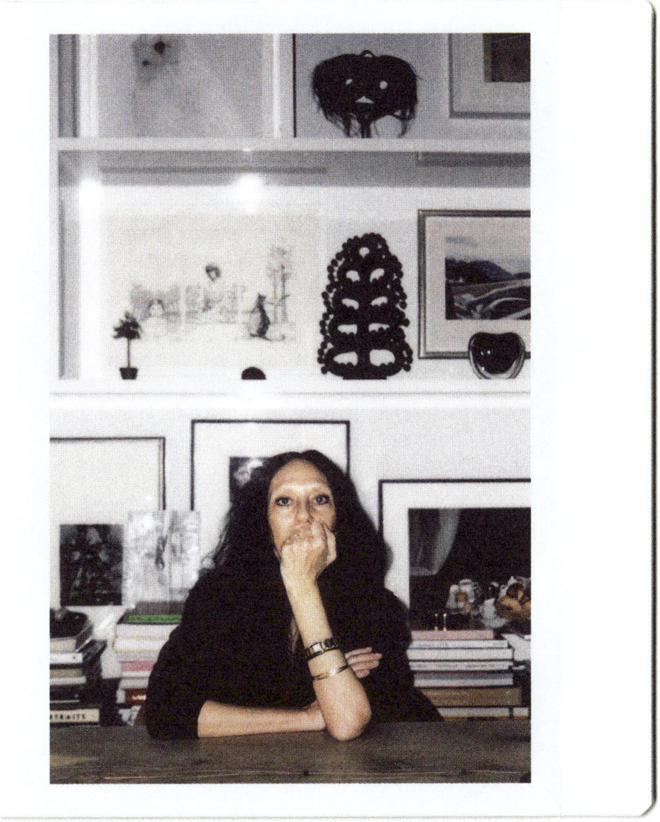

BEAUTY AND ITS OPPOSITE —THE GROTESQUE. I THINK THOSE TWO THINGS ARE CONSTANTLY AT PLAY

in their personality. Then when we work together and it happens to be a great experience, I tend to keep on photographing them over and over again. Actually, that is one thing that fills me with joy, you know: the fact that I am still photographing the same women whom I photographed in 1999, and who are still fascinating to me. I still want to "own them" by taking their pictures, so I have a lot of muses because I like the idea that you are growing up together.

HHM: Is there something like a "Dutch school" or a "Dutch eye" for photography?

IVL: I think there is. There are two types. One is very composed and kind of based on the old Dutch masters' way of looking at things —it doesn't have a lot of depth, and the perspective is quite short, you know, there is a certain flatness to it, but there is definitely a composed side. I feel there is a whole area in photography that has this kind of staged photography idea, which is very Dutch. Then there is another side that is extremely documentary-based or photojournalism-based. So, I think that as far as Dutch influences go, they both influence me a lot. You just grow up spending a lot of time looking at Rembrandt, [Johannes] Vermeer, [Peter Paul] Rubens, and all those incredible works form your ideas about how to compose something. At some point, I had to "unlearn" it in order to broaden the work into other areas. My first reaction is still to treat everything in that way, but then I have to consciously say, "OK, don't always shoot everyone from the front." You know, my first instinct is to always have everything aligned, everything symmetrical, and everything facing forward and flat. So, I have to remind myself to look at other angles and other perspectives.

HHM: What role does beauty play in your work?

IVL: I think it is the main subject; beauty and its opposite—the grotesque. I think those two things are constantly at play. Sometimes, it goes more toward one or the other, but when I look at our work over the last thirty years, there is always a balance in it, and it has never changed.

HHM: Yes, it seems that there is a particular interest in the grotesque in many of your images, and also a duality: beautiful and grotesque, punk and high fashion, man and woman, perfection and imperfection ...

IVL: Yes, to me, that is the bottom line: the confusion between the two. What I find interesting is not knowing or not being able to put your finger on why you are drawn to something or why you think something is breathtaking when it has all the characteristics of being unattractive. But then, the sum of everything is what makes you want to keep looking. I could say that there is perfection in imperfection. That may be why I admire the work of Ellsworth Kelly so much, because he plays with that same idea in an abstract way, searching for where perfection and imperfection meet.

HHM: Could you ever make a work about something you truly disdain?

IVL: I don't think I would want to do that. There could be a work that maybe has a small political undertone in that respect. Still, at this moment, it's more the idea of repulsion that is at play, because when you are talking about disdain, I can't think of anything else but our president [Donald Trump], and I don't think I would like to grant him the extra thought.

HHM: I couldn't agree more ... If we talk about the concept of horror embedded in beauty, there is one image in particular that comes to my mind: *Me Kissing Vinoodh (Eternally)*, where your body is covered in red paint, looking as if it's been flayed. It goes hand in hand with the idea that the grotesque in Western contemporary art is inherently associated with the feminine.

IVL: Yes, I can see that.

HHM: It feels as though artists are deploying monstrous bodies to empower the marginalized or to play with taboos and conventions.

THE FEMALE FIGURE HAS BEEN CELEBRATED IN EVERY POSSIBLE WAY THROUGHOUT ART HISTORY, AND MEN HAVE ONLY BEEN DEPICTED AS THEMSELVES IN PORTRAITS. I FIND IT KIND OF FASCINATING

IVL: Yes, I agree with you. I think it is interesting that you said that because I feel that men are completely underrepresented in art. There is an overwhelming number of male artists, but the representation of the male figure is nowhere …

HHM: In what way?

IVL: I mean, I am talking through my relatively shallow understanding of everything that is going on in the art world, but before now, I can't really recall any artists who have talked about "maleness." The female figure has been celebrated in every possible way throughout art history, and men have only been depicted as themselves in portraits. I find it kind of fascinating.

HHM: Absolutely. And even when male artists have portrayed themselves, it has often been as women: Andy Warhol, Mike Kelley, Robert Mapplethorpe, Marcel Duchamp as Rrose Sélavy …

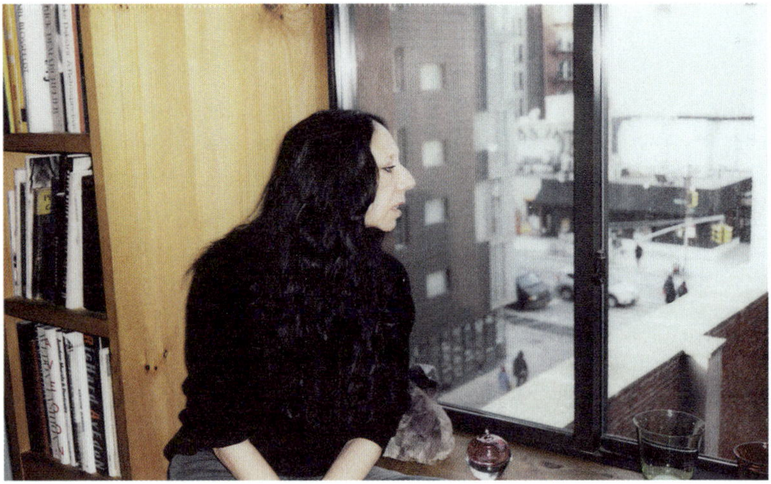

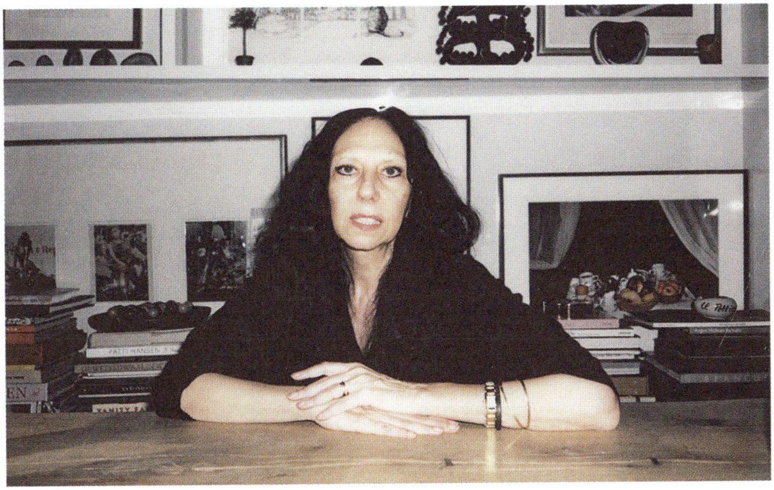

IVL: Exactly. I think it does say something about our society. I guess there is maybe less complexity when it comes to men, I don't know … But I feel there is definitely something that is still undiscovered.

HHM: Would you say female artists are more inward-looking?

IVL: I think so. I think there are definitely exceptions on both sides, but I would say there is a certain macho behavior in the male artist world, and it actually works for them—it really does. Some of the work that comes out of that is magnificent and exciting, but it is something that women aren't interested in—they don't need to yell really loudly. Women have a subtle and delicate way of looking at life, and being more inward is definitely inherent within the female way of looking at art, or practicing it.

HHM: In that sense, one of the things I wanted to ask you is about the way in which you portray sexuality now compared to the way you portrayed it twenty years ago. How has it changed?

IVL: That is interesting. I think that when I started out, I was a young person looking at all that and perhaps trying to be subversive. Now, when I look at some of my past work, I think, "Well, I would never make that now, because I know much more about what it means to be a woman." You know, when you are starting out, you are kind of finding it all out, and you don't really know what everything means because you haven't really lived that long or you haven't experienced everything, or you haven't heard so much about other people's lives. In the last ten years, I have been much more interested in there not being genders, rather than focusing on the allure of one gender or another. I am much more interested in the human than male or female, or the complications between them, or the attraction between them. I think there is something about it that is too one-dimensional … I guess it is the idea of in-betweenness that interests me the most, but it might change. I don't know … It could go the other way again.

HHM: It brought to my attention the series of portraits of you wearing a beard. How did you get to that concept?

IVL: The picture of me with the beard was for the cover of *The Gentlewoman*. I thought exactly about that duality that you were talking about: male, female; grotesque, beautiful. So, I thought about how to work with that within myself, how to express it. How to talk about the fact that I don't care whether I am a man or a woman, and that is how I got to the beard. I think the fact that it's all summed up in one person is exciting. It's kind of the way to be, I believe.

HHM: What differences are there between working on intellectually interesting images that are not very commercial, and vice versa?

IVL: When my husband [Vinoodh Matadin] and I work in a commercial setting, you know, for a commission, it really depends … Some brands work within a very commercial frame-work, and we know exactly what they are looking for. There is something about giving the best

I LOVE SOCIAL MEDIA AND LOVE WHAT IT HAS DONE FOR PHOTOGRAPHY. I THINK IT'S AMAZING THAT EVERYONE IS A PHOTOGRAPHER NOW. IT IS AN OUTLET FOR IMAGES

you can in that situation that for us is freeing, because there are so many parameters and compromises that it feels good to still make an image you like. Sometimes we don't like what we are making, but the client does, and that's great. But then there are other times when you are in the same situation, and you actually make something incredible, because, you know, when you work in the fashion industry, 60 or 70 percent of the time, there is compromise. You have to be able to work within limits.

There are also other times when we either make our own private work, or we have complete freedom from a commercial client or for a magazine or whatever it is, which leads to a whole other type of work. Sometimes we make something that is very extreme, and then a commercial client comes along who wants the same thing, so there are different situations to work with. But it is wonderful when someone is brave enough to say, "Go right ahead," and it is possible to change the landscape a little bit. It is not all about showing the product in one specific way. For instance, we just recently launched a new campaign with [artistic director] Virgil Abloh for Louis Vuitton, which, at the moment, is breaking all the records of most-watched videos on the internet for them, and it hardly has a product in it. It is a short video of a baby playing with Play-Doh. The video plays with the feeling and idea of infancy, boyhood, and adolescence. It was a beautiful project where we were able to work freely.

HHM: Technology has taken photography to a whole different scale. How do you think social media has changed photography?

IVL: I love social media and love what it has done for photography. I think it's amazing that everyone is a photographer now. It is an outlet for images. I love the dialogue; I love the reaction, and I get inspiration from it. I think it can be challenging on many different levels … There are a lot of things to compare yourself to nowadays, which can be a little tricky, especially if you are a teenager, I believe. But for myself, where I am at the moment, I find it wonderful and entertaining.

HHM: With all of this exposure, do you think a photograph is less valuable today than it was twenty years ago?

IVL: No, not for me. I think that a breathtaking photograph shot by someone who isn't a professional photographer is just as valuable as one made by Irving Penn or Jeff Wall. I wouldn't see the difference. I mean, perhaps one problem is that sometimes—mainly with young photographers—you can find someone and see one work that is incredible, but then the rest of the work isn't. Someone like that might still be at an early stage and has to develop a technique, but gets overwhelmed with attention or requests, and gets stuck into one trick that people seem to like. But I think the value of photography has always been questioned. Actually, I think photography is still a bit of a step-child in the art world.

HHM: What were some of the things that influenced you to become a fashion photographer?

IVL: Well, my mother was a fashion journalist. She started in the fifties, reporting for a Dutch paper, and she would go to the shows in Paris every season and bring back French *Vogue*. So, I grew up looking at French *Vogue* throughout the seventies and eighties, and that helped form my ideas about femininity, style, photography, color, and composition. I think that is where my interest in photography came from. Then, when I graduated from high school, I thought I was going be a fashion designer, but once I was studying, I noticed that I was taking pictures all the time instead of making outfits, and so I switched to art school for photography, and that is how the whole thing started.

HHM: What are your thoughts on the rise of the artist as a celebrity?

IVL: I think it is great. Why not?

HHM: Where do you go to be alone?

IVL: I am literally never alone.

HHM: At what point in your career did you feel that you were a successful artist? Was there one image that shifted everything?

IVL: Yes—*Me Kissing Vinoodh (Passionately)*. I think that image really summed up everything that my work was about. It shows something eternal about the internal emotions of love, loss, and fear.

HHM: What inspires you the most?

IVL: Humans … And human faces.

HHM: What is the most honest thing you can say about yourself?

IVL: I have a lot of patience for people, but zero patience for machines.

CH

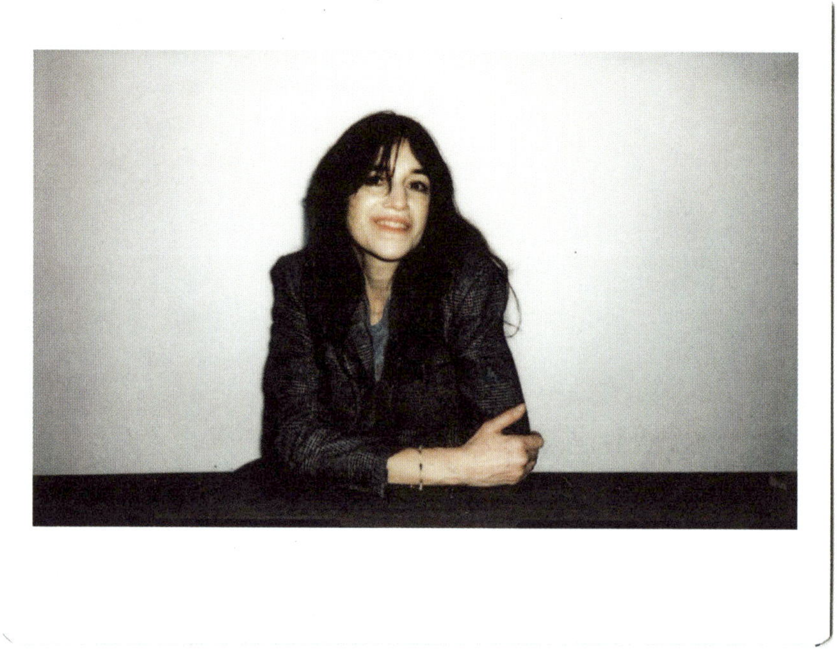

T

CHARLOTTE GAINSBOURG

NEW YORK, 2020

AR
LO
TE

Charlotte Gainsbourg is an English-French actor and singer-songwriter. After making her musical debut with her father—French pop star Serge Gainsbourg—with the song "Lemon Incest" at the age of twelve, Charlotte completed her debut album at fifteen. Since then, her list of musical collaborators has included Beck, Jarvis Cocker, and the French music duo Air. Charlotte has also appeared in a variety of films, including those directed by Lars von Trier, leading her to commercial and critical success.

Charlotte's performances lend refinement to the most distressing situations. Her characters have never been "ordinary." From the age of fifteen, when she won a César award for Most Promising Actress for her starring role in *L'Effrontée* (*An Impudent Girl*), to her award-winning turn at Cannes as the sadomasochistic grieving mother in *Antichrist*, there always seems to be an interesting tension in Charlotte, a bent toward gentleness with the sense that any minute, things may go the other way. Charlotte is not afraid to explore tragedy or the human condition in real depth and complexity, yet she maintains a rare quality, a certain purity, that makes her character a cult figure for the arts.

HUGO HUERTA MARIN:
Let me start off by talking about music.

CHARLOTTE GAINSBOURG:
Sure.

HHM: I read that you wrote the songs for your latest album *Rest*.

CG: Oh, yes.

HHM: I have the impression that sometimes lyrics represent not the writer speaking, but the language of performing. Where does Charlotte Gainsbourg end and the shapeless voice of a character begin?

CG: Well, there is no real formula for when the work starts or when it ends. The thing is, I like collaborating with other artists. I love being able to rely on someone else's judgment and taste. Because I'm not one of those singers who can just take a guitar, compose a tune, and perform, I need a sound, and I need someone behind that sound. I need someone to be in control, and afterward, I can give my creative input. But, when I write lyrics, I work on my own … I don't feel that I am very much in control of any process, so I'm always amazed when something good comes out; it comes in little bits, and it's all these little bits and pieces I have to put together to make new music.

HHM: Have you found that your relationship with music has changed over time?

CG: Completely. I mean, I was twelve when I started out, and I had no idea what I was doing. At that time, I made a very controversial song with my father [Serge Gainsbourg] called "Lemon Incest," which, back then, was very shocking to certain people. It wasn't shocking for me—I was just working with him. Then, when I was fifteen, my father wrote an album for me [*Charlotte for Ever*], and I think I was more interested at that point, but I wasn't really starting a career. When I was nineteen, my father died, and I thought: "Well, now this is over. Music is over for me without him." It took me twenty years to go back to music. I was thirty-five when I recorded *5:55* with Air …

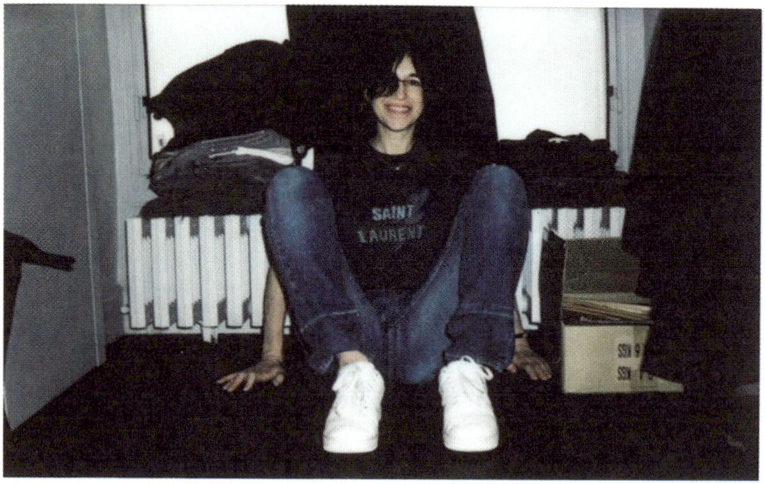
SAINT
LAURENT

It was a big deal for me to go back into the studio with all the ghosts, the old impressions, and the memories, but once I started working, I didn't want to stop.

HHM: I was once told that you can do anything you want as long as you are a great performer. You can repeat a word over and over again, just as long as you're a fantastic performer. Do you think performance has become as much of a statement as songs?

CG: I think so, but it's difficult when you don't have the voice of a great singer, or when you haven't written the lyrics, and you're not a dancer, you know? It is very hard to feel that you have to give something on stage, and it's actually easy to feel that there is no meaning in doing it. So, it's still quite difficult to feel that I am a performer because I am not … I am just being myself on stage, and sometimes it's a little challenging to have enough confidence. You can write songs with no confidence, you can make an entire album with no confidence, but you can't go onstage without confidence. It is part of the show to believe in yourself.

HHM: Is there an engrossing intersection between music and fashion?

CG: I don't know… Perhaps if you are Beyoncé and fashion is part of the show. I mean, the light, the dancers, the stage, the whole thing is huge, and fashion plays a part in it, but in my case … It's just the way I see myself and the way I want people to see me. For the last show, it was important for me to be in jeans and a T-shirt because that is who I am, that is what I wanted to show.

I NEVER THOUGHT THAT I WAS A REAL ARTIST, AND I THINK THAT COMES FROM MY FAMILY BECAUSE WE WERE ALWAYS A LITTLE EMBARRASSED TO CALL OURSELVES ARTISTS. WE ALWAYS UNDERPLAYED IT

HHM: Perhaps fashion is not the right word …

CG: A style.

HHM: I can think of Iggy Pop wearing nothing but a pair of leather pants and making a statement, Sid Vicious wearing a padlock necklace, PJ Harvey's makeup … There are a few moments when the language of a culture was shifted by clothes and music. Do you believe that music can still be that subversive?

CG: Yes, of course. I mean, rappers … hip hop, all that music. There is a whole industry behind all of that, and fashion is completely embedded in music nowadays—you're right—but I can't really relate to it, because I'm not making a statement with the clothes that I decide to wear. It's part of my skin … For instance, my last album was about my sister [Kate Barry], who died, and it was very intimate. I wanted the show to reflect that same intimacy, and I wanted to feel like myself as much as I could.

HHM: How does that freedom affect your work?

CG: Well, the thing is, I'll never be an incredible singer, like an opera singer. I don't have a method while performing like some artists do—almost like wearing a mask. So, I have to trust in accidents; otherwise, there is nothing left to propose, and that's the beauty in it. Especially today, where everything is made perfect and polished by a computer … I just feel there's not much life in that.

HHM: Do you have the same approach when it comes to acting?

CG: I feel that as an actor, you are not an artist. Actors interpret. I mean, you are part of a group, yes, you make films, so there's an artistic understanding of the whole thing, but you are not performing as an artist. As an actor, I feel that I am part of an artistic work, but that's it.

HHM: The label is too loaded?

CG: Yeah, I never thought that I was a real artist, and I think that comes from my family because we were always a little embarrassed to call ourselves artists. We always underplayed it.

HHM: It seems that you are unafraid of examining the dark side of human nature through your work. In that sense, do you think pain is important for an artist?

CG: More and more, I believe so. One of the things my father used to say is that it's not interesting to talk about the blue sky, what's interesting is to look at the dark sky, the lightning, the chaos … I feel that way as an actor because most of the films I've done have induced pain; it has always been part of the process, and I find it interesting to put myself in those positions, to go into those weird grounds of masochism … I mean, I know that I'm a masochist, and I'm not ashamed to say that there is some pleasure in pain. I experienced that a lot while working with Lars von Trier. It felt like part of the journey, and I am sure he understood that part of me.

HHM: So, do you think it's a matter of nature to choose certain types of roles?

CG: What do you mean by nature?

HHM: Well … Do you know the fable of the scorpion that stings the frog that helps him cross the river?

CG: No. I don't think so.

HHM: A scorpion asks a frog to carry him across the river. The frog hesitates, afraid of being stung, but the scorpion says that if he did that, they would both drown … Halfway across the river, the scorpion stings the frog, drowning them both. The frog asks, "Why did you sting me?" and the scorpion replies, "It's in my nature."

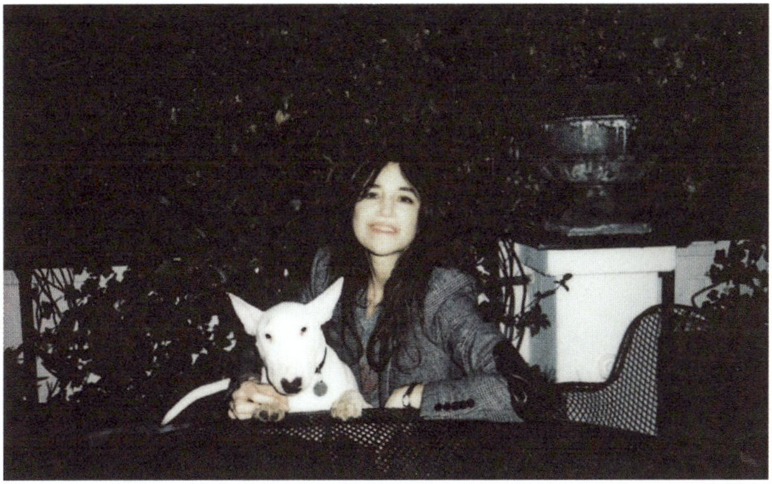

THE BEAUTY STANDARDS TODAY ARE REALLY UNINTERESTING TO ME, AND I HOPE THAT WE CAN GO BACK TO SOMETHING A LITTLE MORE EDGY, SOMETHING MORE ORIGINAL

CG: Ha! Yeah, that's interesting … I think so.

HHM: I also have the impression that von Trier derives an impish sort of pleasure from exposing the actors he works with …

CG: I mean, I think Lars wasn't interested in my acting, he was more interested in the performance, and it was one of the most interesting works that I have been able to perform because there was no barrier. He wanted to see a real person in the film, and very often, he would cut a scene and say: "I don't believe you, I don't believe what you just said," and he was always right. He just wanted the truth … So, I tried different mechanisms and ways of making it happen. I think that is why I don't like seeing myself on-screen. I'm very hard on myself and can always recognize when I'm not being truthful while acting.

HHM: I once read that you prefer brutality because softness bores you. What has been your most radical performance?

CG: Oh, for sure the films I did with Lars. I've done three films with him, all very different, but to me, *Antichrist* was the most revealing. The whole thing was very raw. *Melancholia* was terrifying but less brutal, and then on *Nymphomaniac* we had fun in a weird way—it was so extreme, and the sex scenes were so extreme, that we had to laugh about a lot of stuff—but *Antichrist* was extremely brutal, and there was something that was completely exhilarating about it all.
I remember I got used to screaming and taking my clothes off and crying. Then after shooting, I would suddenly go back to real life, and it was very disturbing. It was a shock for me not to be able to scream out in the forest (*laughs*).

HHM: These are all very graphic projects in which beauty is embedded in horror.

CG: Oh, yes.

HHM: What is your concept of beauty?

CG: I don't really have a concept but … You know, I sometimes draw, and I find it revealing that if I try too hard, the drawing becomes really boring. There is suddenly no emotion in it; it just becomes a nice drawing. But as soon as there is emotion involved, or as soon you include something a little more extreme …

HHM: A subversive twist?

CG: Yes. But you also need to know when to stop, and that can be tricky. If you use too much energy, it becomes artificial. I think it's the same when it comes to singing. I remember when I was recording the last album, I always wanted to go back to the studio and get the singing right, but it was never good enough. In the end, we used the very first takes I had done a year earlier because they had something. They were imperfect but they had something …

HHM: The ground where beauty and the grotesque collide.

CG: Completely. I don't relate to beauty through perfection. I feel that ugliness and imperfection are components of beauty. You know, I have a seventeen-year-old daughter, and she is very much influenced by all these actresses and singers that look so physically perfect. They all look alike: they have little noses, big boobs, and a kind of perfection that I find absolutely boring … The beauty standards today are really uninteresting to me, and I hope that we can go back to something a little more edgy, something more original.

HHM: Francis Bacon said that the job of the artist is to deepen the mystery.

CG: Exactly. Something you can't understand. Mystery goes much further and is so much more interesting.

HHM: It is interesting to push things further, but I believe most people are scared of what will happen if they go too far. When it comes to your work, how far is too far?

CG: I think the limit is when your life gets too involved. I've realized that when the work becomes too personal, I'm not on the right track. For instance, when I was filming

EVERYTHING IS CONDEMNED TODAY, AND I FIND IT TERRIFYING. NOT IN REAL LIFE, BUT FROM AN ARTISTIC POINT OF VIEW

Antichrist, I remember there was a point where I felt we were not doing the film anymore. It was like being part of a porn film …

HHM: In what way?

CG: There was one scene where Willem Dafoe was replaced by a porn actor, and Lars asked if I could share the screen with him—obviously, the camera wasn't filming his face, but Lars needed my face in the same shot, so I said OK. The take started, and it was just becoming a porn film for me because Willem wasn't there anymore … it was really strange. In the end, I told Lars I couldn't do it any longer … It just took me out of the film.

HHM: Then I read that for the X-rated scenes of *Nymphomaniac* he melded the bodies of the actors and porn actors together …

CG: Yeah. And then he put my face on top (*laughs*).

HHM: (*laughs*) That sounds avant-garde.

CG: It was.

THE FACT THAT I'M ALWAYS UNSATISFIED IS PERHAPS WHAT GIVES ME AN APPETITE

HHM: Is sex a major aspect of your work?

CG: I think sex is a major aspect of every work, even if it doesn't talk about sex directly. I mean, it might not have anything to do with sex, rather it might have to do with sexuality, with attraction, with disgust. You can relate to sex in any kind of way, and I find it really interesting.

HHM: Sexuality always has a metaphorical dimension.

CG: Completely. Every perversion, every dangerous conversation is worth talking about, because that's what makes us human. Today with all these movements like #MeToo, I mean, they are great because women's voices are being heard, and nobody can force you to do anything you don't want to do, but at the same time, everybody is afraid now … Afraid to talk about sex, to put their hand somewhere else, or to whistle at a woman on the street. Everything is condemned today, and I find it terrifying. Not in real life, but from an artistic point of view … It's scary because there is not much going on. We don't have much to say if every form of seduction is removed. In the past, people were reacting, shaking things up, and that was great.

HHM: To provoke?

CG: I think that is what my father did all his life, and I feel it is quite necessary. To react to something. To be shocked … Everything now is so politically incorrect. It's just so boring.

HHM: In this regard, what is your position on pornography?

CG: That's difficult because I've seen maybe three porn films in my life. They were quite well done—you know, they were still films … But nowadays, I can't really say what pornography is about. I mean, young people are growing up with the internet and with free porn, and all these images that are just so ugly. Before, porn films had something more … You know, ding dong (*laughs*).

HHM: (*laughs*) A plot.

CG: There was a story. Now, everything is so fast. No one has hair—which I find revolting—but I know that for this new generation, it's normal … But perhaps I am just talking about porn films, and maybe pornography is something different … I don't know. It's a concept too big to put in a few words.

HHM: What are your thoughts on the rise of the artist as celebrity?

CG: I have the impression that celebrity doesn't last very long. It has nothing artistic in it, and the whole concept is just a bit fake. But at the same time, it wouldn't be very honest to say that, as an artist, you are not seeking celebrity sometimes. I mean, when you do a film, when you put out a record, you are looking to be acknowledged by the largest amount of people possible, and in that way, celebrity is involved, but I don't think they coexist very well.

HHM: At what point in your career did you feel that you were a successful artist?

CG: I always had doubts. When I was young, I was very uncomfortable with the idea of being well known—it didn't mean anything to me, and I think I sort of grew up with that idea. At the same time, I have the impression that if I was ever satisfied, the next step I take, I'd fall, so it's quite unsatisfying on the whole.

HHM: Do you worry about being overexposed?

CG: No, because I can do films and I can do music, and I feel that I can always step back. I am exposed in different areas, so I don't ever really worry about that.

HHM: What inspires you the most?

CG: I think emotion. I was looking into a [Andrei] Tarkovsky film the other day called *Ivan's Childhood.* The whole sum of it deals deeply with emotion. The images are so beautiful, and that carries an emotion in itself. It's so powerful.

HHM: What was the first record you ever bought?

CG: Bob Dylan's "Lay, Lady, Lay," but it was just a single, I didn't buy the whole record.

HHM: What is the most honest thing you can say about yourself?

CG: The most honest thing I can say is that I wish I could love myself more. I wish I had more sympathy for myself. But in fact, I like saying that I don't like myself because I feel that I am being truthful … No, I don't have the face I wish I had, I don't have the talent I wish I had … But the fact that I'm always unsatisfied is perhaps what gives me an appetite.

TWI

GS

FKA

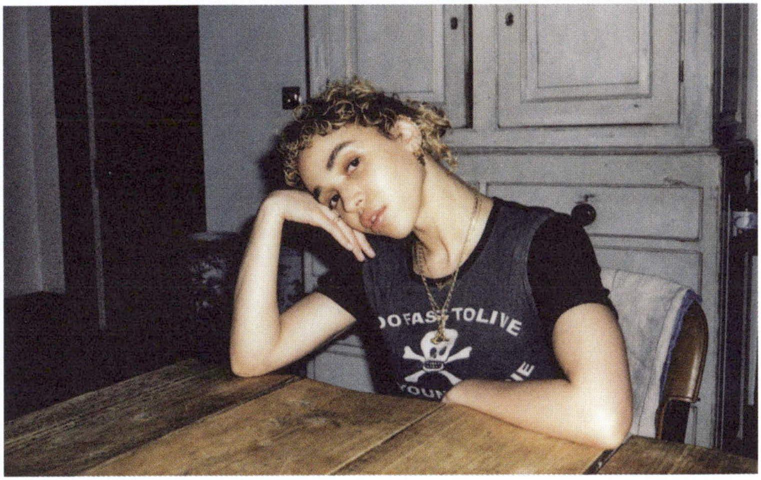

FKA TWIGS

LONDON, 2020

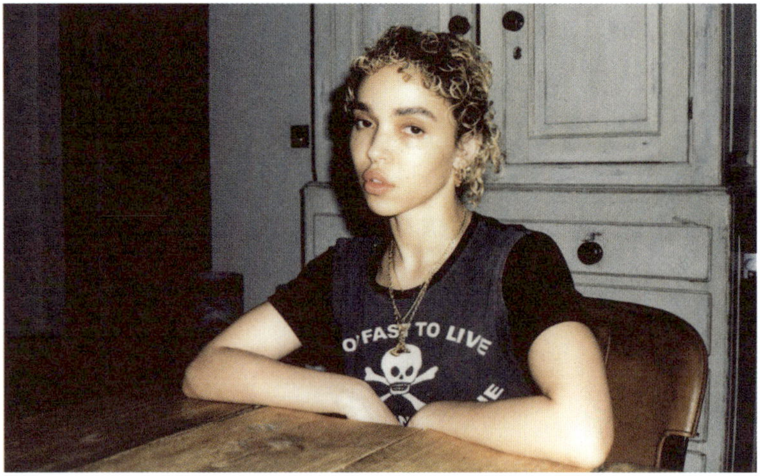
FAST TO LIVE

FKA twigs is an English singer, songwriter, dancer, and producer. With a monastic devotion to her work, including three EPs, a Mercury Prize, a Brit Award-nominated debut album, and her latest release *MAGDALENE*, FKA twigs has established herself as one of the most innovative artists of her generation. She is a pre-eminent innovator and a fearless proponent of the avant-garde whose discography defies the staid categorization of genre.

When we first talked, twigs and I discussed music, dance, race, and the responsibility that comes with being part of a minority in the spotlight … a commonplace for her. What makes twigs' work unique is a subversive twist, an uncanny ambiguity that traps us in a very complex system of references. She has chosen to use her own body in order to expose the trace, stain, or imprint on the artist's body in response to political, economical, and social phenomena. Twigs keeps raising questions through creation, while living her art literally and courageously in her own skin.

HUGO HUERTA MARIN:
Let's start out by talking a little bit about music.

FKA TWIGS:
Yeah, let's do it.

HHM: In the collapsing of biblical stories there are three Marys that are merged into a single figure: Mary of Bethany, Mary the Magdalene, and Mary the prostitute, and perhaps no figure in history is as controversial as Mary Magdalene.

FT: Yeah.

HHM: Why did you choose Magdalene as an inspiration for your album?

THERE ARE MANY WOMEN THROUGHOUT HISTORY WHO HAVE EMBODIED FEMALE EMPOWERMENT [...] WE DON'T KNOW A LOT ABOUT THEM OR HOW MUCH THEY TRULY IMPACTED OUR SOCIETY

FT: It kind of happened by accident, if I'm honest with you. When I first started writing, I was actually quite fascinated by Lilith—she was Adam's first wife—and I started using a lot of different swords while practicing wushu, and I called my sword Lilith. So, I started to get into her story and the different myths around her. Lilith was a very strong, defined, and proud woman, and I thought that I was foreseeing a connection between us, but at that time I was feeling much more fragile and vulnerable than how Lilith presents. Then one day I had a really inspiring conversation with a friend of mine called Christi [Meshell], who makes amazing perfumes and works with oils and herbs. We spoke about Mary Magdalene and I genuinely found a connection with her in a very natural way—you know, the fact that she is represented as always living under the shadow of Jesus.
I think there were points in my life where I was living under the shadow of men, whether lovers, friends, or mentors, so that's something that I clearly relate to. But Mary Magdalene was very much Jesus' equal. I believe she was a big

part of his story and she founded a lot of his journeys and missions. And in many ways, she was what we now call a doctor, in the way she blended her skills to practice the art of healing. She knew a lot about herbs, about oils—she blended all of her knowledge together—and I was just really inspired by her. I was thinking a lot about men and the idea of the Mary complex—which is basically when men see a woman as either a whore, a prostitute, the scarlet woman, the temptress, or a virgin, the innocent, maternal, caring woman who obeys men. I became quite fascinated with that concept as well. My mother's middle name is also Mary, so there just happened to be all these Marys around me. And then, I wrote a song called "Mary Magdalene" … and for me it's some of the most powerful writing on the album.

HHM: There is certainly a constant element of contradiction and paradox around Mary Magdalene's myth. Even her hair is a symbol of charity and redemption, but it also hints at her profession's presumed immodesty. Do you think these characters highlight female empowerment?

FT: Of course. I mean, Mary Magdalene's hair has a big part in the story. Mary took spikenard—a very expensive oil—and poured it on Jesus' feet. She wiped the excess oil off with her hair, using it like a mop, and I have always thought that this is such a powerful image. Of course, there are many women throughout history who have embodied female empowerment; it's just unfortunate that we don't know that much about them, because it's been easy for the patriarchy to suppress those stories. Years later we're left filling in the gaps; we don't know a lot about them or how much they truly impacted our society.

HHM: What is the starting point for a concept of an album before you move toward its realization?

FT: Well, I've always believed it's important for things to come from the inside out, and not from the outside in. It is as I said at the beginning of the conversation: Just because I liked Lilith didn't mean that I would write songs about her or that she would inspire my work. On the other hand, Mary Magdalene was a concept that came in a natural and organic way. I wasn't looking for anything; she just started appearing in my life in different ways. I guess when I'm writing I don't necessarily think about the end goal. It just starts to appear.

HHM: For instance, do you name a song after it is completed, or does the title develop during the process?

FT: It just develops. I'm always quite hesitant when talking about process, because it just sort of happens. I don't really have a specific way of working—there is no secret, no mystical, magical way I do my work. I can't explain it, but it's simple and honest.

HHM: It shapes itself.

FT: Exactly, it shapes itself, and that is why it's hard for me to talk about, because I'm afraid I might sound pretentious, and often when people ask me about process it is almost like …

I'M ALWAYS QUITE HESITANT WHEN TALKING ABOUT PROCESS, BECAUSE IT JUST SORT OF HAPPENS. I DON'T REALLY HAVE A SPECIFIC WAY OF WORKING—THERE IS NO SECRET, NO MYSTICAL, MAGICAL WAY I DO MY WORK. I CAN'T EXPLAIN IT, BUT IT'S SIMPLE AND HONEST

you can see the disappointment in their eyes. But it's very basic: I just enjoy making songs. I enjoy dancing. I enjoy beautiful sounds, and I really like putting all of those things together.

HHM: Sometimes art is not a mirror held up to reality, but a hammer with which to shape it. Do you think musicians and songwriters are the consciousness or the unconscious of the time?

FT: I don't know. I think that if you're making honest work, it will naturally speak of the times.

HHM: There are recurring themes in your work that seem to link carnal desire and emotional pain. What role does pain play in your work?

FKA TWIGS

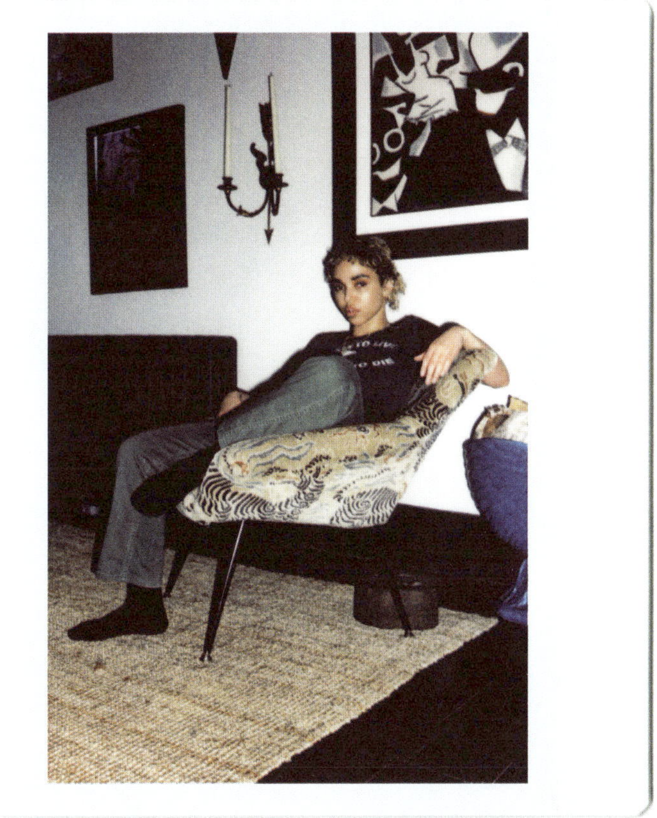

I DON'T FIND IT UNCOMFORTABLE TO EXPLORE THINGS THAT DON'T FEEL GOOD

FT: Yeah, pain and trauma play a big part in my work. Again, it's hard to pinpoint it, but I feel comfortable exploring it: It's not something I feel the need to shy away from. I don't find it uncomfortable to explore things that don't feel good, and there is often something quite intense about that.

HHM: Do you think pain is important for an artist?

FT: I think truth is important for an artist. If the artist treats the work as pain, then sure; if an artist treats the work as happiness, sure. I just think that if you put down what you feel, someone, somewhere in the world is going to resonate with it.

HHM: Do you think it is possible to separate art from its creator?

FT: Yeah. Definitely.

HHM: Do you find that there is a difference between writing a poem and a song, between words that are to be read silently and those that are to be sung?

FT: I think it's easier to write music. I do write poetry sometimes, and I have one good poem; the rest are pretty average. My success rate with writing songs is higher. I'll probably just stick to that (*laughs*). So far I have been writing one good poem every three years, so it might take me a while to collect a few.

HHM: There seems to be a very strong interest in the relation between the body and your music project.

FT: Yeah.

HHM: And the kind of awareness that your art brings is very much a visceral one. Do you think that certain things can be said with words, and others with movements?

FT: Yes. I mean, I just love moving my body. It inspires me so much and I think that as an artist I am understanding how important that is over and over again. I am just starting to understand that the relationship with my body is vital to the rest of my work. I used to deny it, but I am starting to accept it now.

HHM: You have used a wide range of dance styles, from pole dancing to voguing, wushu, and krumping. Which kind of corporeal method speaks to you best?

FT: That's difficult. I love them all. And I just like being around people who do them. I have not vogued in a while, though, and it's not because I don't love it: It's because I'm not spending that much time in New York. When

I'm in New York I love hanging out with my friends who vogue, and I completely immerse myself in that world, because it is so authentic. I find that when I am not in New York and I try to do it, it feels forced. I tend to do things depending on where I am in the world … I just love learning and being involved in culture, and so I sacrifice the time to do it, because time is the most precious thing—the one thing we are all running out of. I love that conscious sacrifice to learn something. I find that so sexy … To be around something because you enjoy it, that is beautiful.

HHM: How did you first discover the ball scene?

FT: In a weird way. I started voguing when I was about twelve, and I used to make my own voguing routines. I only had a couple of videos, but I didn't really know what I was watching. One of my uncles used to vogue, so he would teach me some voguing moves. But I didn't know what it was, you know, I was a kid—I just knew it was a dance, a style, but I didn't really understand the roots of it. Then, when I was making my album in New York around 2012, I was hanging out with Arca and Shayne [Oliver] from Hood by Air, and I think maybe Arca was the one that took me to Escuelita for the first time, and I completely fell in love with it. There, I met a dancer called Derek Prodigy, who offered to teach me how to vogue, and they just took me under their wing straight away. I wasn't a well-known singer back then, I was just a girl from London, and they just … I don't know, I liked them, and they liked me, and I went on to meet some amazing people.

So, I started training with Derek Prodigy and then with Alex Mugler, and it took me a really long time to find out what style was mine, and to be honest with you, voguing is something I'm still not very good at. I would say that I feel insecure, and the reason I feel insecure is because I'm not in New York enough. To me voguing is not just a dance class, it's not just practicing at home; to me it is matching with someone in the ballroom and really understanding what that scene is. I think that is why I love being in New York so much, because I just feel the most authentic when I am there and doing it. So, I don't know, I just like to try and find …

HHM: The soul of things?

FT: Exactly, the soul. I mean, I love wushu and I haven't been to China yet, but I learned from people that are really legit within the wushu community. My first teacher, Master Hu, choreographed the Chinese Olympics and was in films with Bruce Lee—you can't get more legit than that—so, I don't know, I just like to immerse myself in culture, even if that sounds a bit naive.

HHM: I think it's true. I am not a big fan of electronic music, but whenever I go to Berlin and visit the Berghain and experience the core of electronic music, it just sort of permeates your spirit …

FT: Definitely.

HHM: So, voguing uses corporeal language as a formal structure, and has always been a form of resistance.

I THINK THAT PEOPLE WHO AREN'T THEMSELVES A MINORITY—WHO DO NOT FIND THEMSELVES IN A SECTOR OF SOCIETY THAT IS OPPRESSED OR MISUNDERSTOOD—CAN BE PROBLEMATIC WHEN THEY ONLY EXPERIENCE MINORITIES THROUGH ENTERTAINMENT AND SPORTS

FT: Yeah.

HHM: And it had a huge comeback in recent years. Do you think that it will bring to light other issues, like it did back then? Or will it put on blast how little things have changed for trans women of color or queer people of color, specifically?

FT: I think it is a really difficult subject to comment on … Because even if voguing is part of queer culture, I feel that people outside that community are seeing only one side of it, the performative side. Voguing is painful but it's a very beautiful side of that culture, so I don't know if voguing is directly helping the gay, trans, or queer community … What about when voguers go home? What about where that trans woman is living? What about where the people within the community are working? Are they safe? You know, somebody that's not part of the community can't really understand these things by merely watching someone voguing. To be honest with you, I feel the same way about the Black community, in terms of how non-Black people often experience Black people only through entertainment, through dance, music, or sports. It is almost patronizing and uninformed just to engage with one side of a culture … My point is that it is a double-edged sword. I would say that I'm an ally to the queer community, or would like to think of myself as such, but it's hard to talk about specific issues that I am not a direct part of. I guess I can speak as a minority, as a woman of color … So, let's put it like this: I think that people who aren't themselves a minority—who do not find themselves in a sector of society that is oppressed or misunderstood—can be problematic when they only experience minorities through entertainment and sports. I just feel those things are not painting a true picture.

HHM: Absolutely. It reminds me of the talk I had with artist Carrie Mae Weems, where she said that nowadays there is a kind of shift in the thinking of culture, but the thinking isn't complex, it's reactionary. Sort of including Black or brown people in cultural projects … But the question is more, can we get you in? Rather than: What is the structure of your contribution?

FT: First of all, Carrie Mae Weems is my favorite artist. Let's reference the work of Carrie Mae

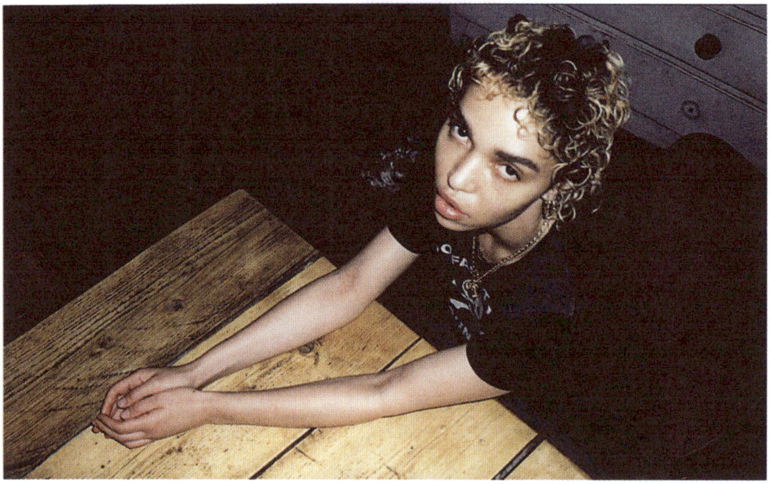

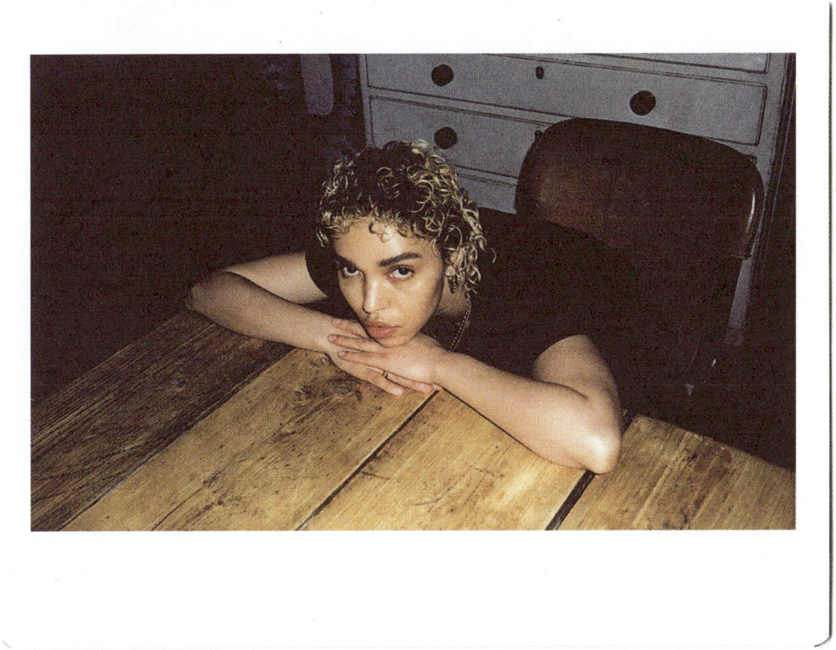

Weems—this is a very, very private conversation that I have had with myself many times.

HHM: OK.

FT: I went to see Carrie Mae Weems' work at Tate a couple of years ago, and she had an exhibition where there were different pictures of Black people with a title underneath—"cook," or "house," or "field"—and there was a picture of a lighter-skinned Black woman in a beautiful Marilyn Monroe satin dress surrounded by white men, and underneath the picture it said "accomplice," and that image hit me so hard, so, so hard ... I got very emotional and I had to really take a step back and think of what that meant to me. I mean, as a dark-skinned woman, I can say that to get where I am now hasn't been easy. My stepdad sat me down at a very young age—I was seven or eight—and he said to me: "Because of the color of your skin, you are gonna have to work twice as hard as the white girl next to you, and if you wanna win, you have to be twice as good as the white girl next to you." And as I get older and people ask me: "Twigs, you are such a good dancer, how are you so good?" the truth is that I know I am good because I'm insecure ... because I knew that—especially when I was younger—I had to be twice as good to get out of my situation from a working-class family. You know, I grew up on benefits, I grew up with the government providing money for food, for my college education. I grew up rich in love, but poor financially. We were really poor at times, and for me to get out of that position, I had to train harder ... Twice as hard. Even now, at my age, inside I still feel that I am constantly in survival mode, and honestly, sometimes it's

SOMETIMES THERE WERE SITUATIONS WHERE I FOUND MYSELF BEING … EXOTIC, AND IT FELT VERY UNCOMFORTABLE, AND IT HAS TAKEN ME A LONG TIME TO UNRAVEL THAT

exhausting. But don't get it twisted, I know that I am lucky, and I know that all I ever wanted in life was to have a stable roof above my head, and now I am lucky that I have one. My point is that I need to stay focused and know where I am standing, and when I saw that Carrie Mae Weems' photograph it was kind of a reminder, because I don't want to be that, I don't want to be an accomplice to anything problematic, and I have to think about that all the time, about what I'm doing, because I know where I come from, and I know my roots and I know how hard I had to work … I don't know exactly what it means, but I do know that that picture is always in the back of my mind.

HHM: I understand.

FT: Sometimes, I don't feel right in situations or at certain dinner parties. I don't engage anymore, but when I first started being a girl in the music scene, sometimes there were situations where I found myself being … exotic, and it felt very uncomfortable, and it has taken me a long time to unravel that. There is a certain collective consciousness that works to unravel things that are really deep and traumatic and complicated for other people. At other levels, people are giving amazing talks or writing political essays on these matters, helping me understand why as a Black woman I sometimes just feel so uncomfortable … and I am still figuring it out. Like I said, I don't have the answers, but I know that when Carrie used the word "accomplice" on that picture, it hit me …

HHM: I've found myself many times being the only brown person in the room, at a dinner party or art event, and it kind of works out in your favor in a twisted double-edged knife way … Being the exotic in the room can give you a certain opportunity, but the one thing I learned from Carrie is that it is what you do with that opportunity what matters …

FT: Oh yes.

HHM: This leads me to my next question. If we go back to music, there have been moments in history when the language of a culture was shifted by music, the Black movement in America, the early sixties during the Vietnam war, the punk movement … Do you believe that music still has the potential to be that revolutionary?

FT: A hundred percent. I think art does that. Not just music, but all art. I think culture is always led by the arts: Even people who don't engage in it, or people who believe they don't engage in it, are subconsciously driven by the work that

ARTISTS EXPRESS HOW PEOPLE ARE FEELING, WHETHER IT BE WITH A SONG, A VIDEO, OR A PAINTING. AND IT'S KIND OF: WHICH CAME FIRST, THE CHICKEN OR THE EGG? IT'S A CONSTANT RESPONSE TO THE WORLD, BUT IT'S ALSO LEADING THE WORLD

artists are making. Artists express how people are feeling, whether it be with a song, a video, or a painting. And it's kind of: Which came first, the chicken or the egg? It's a constant response to the world, but it's also leading the world. It is a revolving dance between arts, culture, and what is happening socially.

HHM: What is your concept of beauty?

FT: I do pole dancing, and often, at the beginning, you think that the beauty is in the big tricks—the splits, the upside-downs, the spins, and all these complicated moves—but as I've learned more, I've discovered the beauty in the transitions that lead you to the big moves. The things that aren't supposed to be beautiful. This also applies to life. For instance, you might think that the most beautiful thing in life is buying a house, but it's not … it's the transition to get there, the years of hard work to get there, you know? Maybe the most beautiful thing is to give birth, but actually the beauty is in what happened in those years before you get there. It's not always in the big things in life, or the big statements in work, or the big moves in dance … Sometimes beauty can be found in the awkwardness of the transition you go through to get to that point.

HHM: What type of recognition do you value most?

FT: I don't know. I am mostly weird about recognition, but I love the relationship between student and teacher, or student and mentor. That is my favorite recognition, when a teacher says that I've gotten better, or I've done good.

HHM: And how does that relationship change when you become a mentor for other people, for instance, for your dancers?

FT: Like on tour?

HHM: Yes. I'm thinking the work of someone like Pina Bausch … Pina Bausch's pieces are her dancers, but each dancer is Pina Bausch.

FT: To be honest with you, I feel I learn from them. We share our knowledge. On my last tour I had four dancers, LaTonya [Swann], Frankie [Freeman], VJ [Vea], and Andrew [Perez], and they were the four elements. We learned from each other. Maybe when I was younger, I used to be more like a mother figure to everybody, but I can't do that anymore: I need to be more of an equal to feel that we are all in it together. Obviously I know that this is my project, and I recognize that it's mine to shape as I like, but once we are on stage, I like it to be more equal. I don't want to have a hierarchy; I want to give everyone that space to create, to do their own thing on stage, to have moments that feel completely theirs.

HHM: Do you have any recurring dreams?

FT: My dreams are quite dark, and I definitely dream a lot about murders.

HHM: What inspires you the most?

FT: Falling in and out of love.

HHM: What was the first record you ever bought?

FT: It was a Prince album.

HHM: What is the most honest thing you can say about yourself?

FT: I am still learning.

U

M

A

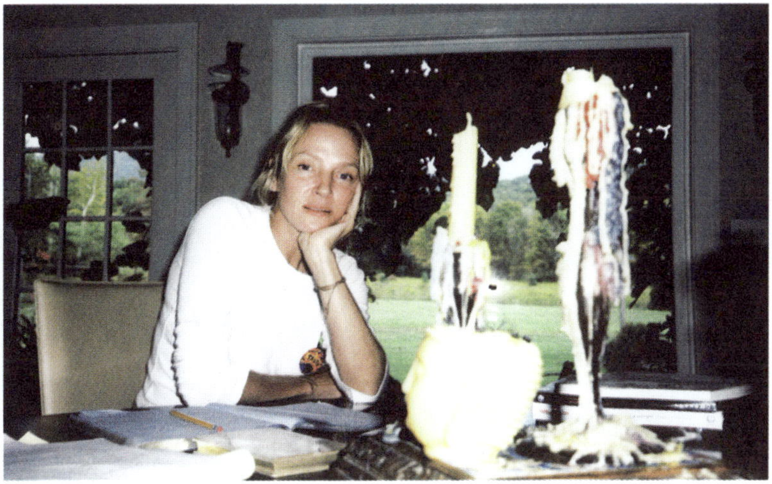

UMA THURMAN

NEW YORK, 2020

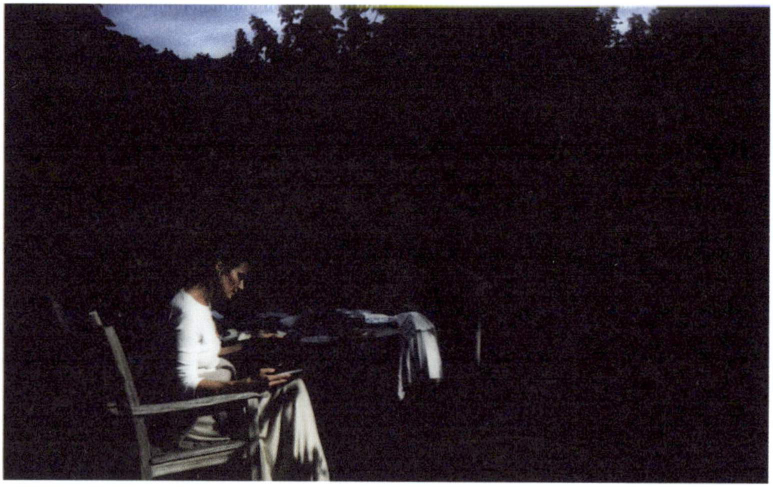

Uma Thurman is an American actor and philanthropist. She rose to international prominence with her performance as Mia Wallace in Quentin Tarantino's 1994 film *Pulp Fiction*, for which she was nominated for an Academy Award, BAFTA, and Golden Globe. She reunited with the director to play the main role in *Kill Bill: Volumes 1* and *2*, which brought her two additional Golden Globe nominations. Established as a leading Hollywood actor, Uma Thurman earned a Golden Globe for *Hysterical Blindness*, which she produced and starred in.

I first met Uma backstage at the Hudson Theatre while she made her Broadway debut in *The Parisian Woman*. We managed to take some portraits inside the theater which captured that moment. The second time I met with her was a completely different experience. We met at her house in Woodstock in upstate New York. We had a sharp, enlightening conversation while Uma was sitting on top of a giant rock in her garden, wearing a long, white skirt. Lissom goddess; forceful, high-voltage presence on film: In person, Uma is exactly that. Uma Thurman is a force of nature.

HUGO HUERTA-MARIN:
What is more important for art, the idea, or the execution?

UMA THURMAN:
Both, equally. The ideas and their execution. An idea can seem abominable but be executed in a way that exposes some sort of profound truth, humanizing and shifting the whole concept. Similarly, a beautiful idea can be poorly executed, making it irrelevant, so I think they are inextricably linked.

HHM: I read that you trained in three styles of kung fu and sword fighting for your role in *Kill Bill* and that you had to deliver an "animal scream" as Mrs. H for *Nymphomaniac*. Where does the process of creating a character begin for you?

UT: It always begins with the script—finding in it the metaphor of the struggle of the character. And then sometimes, I draw from life, from people I've seen and known who will trigger me to react to a piece of material in a particular way. So, it's a combination of the metaphor in the writing and of observations, both of the internal, personal kind and of other people.

HHM: How do you bring humanity to characters like these?

UT: Well, I wouldn't know how not to bring it, is a better way for me to answer. I don't know how to leave humanity behind; I don't have a choice.

HHM: When it comes to extreme roles like the one of Mrs. H, is it sometimes like preparing a theater scene for a movie? How do you get to that place when you are on set?

UT: Well, I mean, it really depends on the writing. But, for instance, I prepared the *Nymphomaniac* sequence of Mrs. H since it is a monologue …

HHM: In my opinion, that performance alone conquered an entire movie in such little time.

IT'S INTERESTING SOMETIMES TO PLAY A CHARACTER WHO MIGHT BE DELUDED INTO BELIEVING THEY ARE INVULNERABLE, BUT THE WHOLE ASPECT OF WHAT MAKES US HUMAN IS THAT WE ARE ALL VULNERABLE

UT: No one really speaks to her, no one really answers her; she has a seven-page conversation at people, but it's really with herself. She answers her own questions, she poses new ideas, she contradicts them, she goes back, she tells a story … So that scene is an example that I prepared as a seven-page monologue.

HHM: I have the impression that one ambition of performers, perhaps even in life as well as their craft, is to become less afraid. Do you think vulnerability plays an important role in performance?

UT: I think vulnerability is always present and is part of humanity. No character is truly invulnerable. It's interesting sometimes to play a character who might be deluded into believing they are invulnerable, but the whole aspect of what makes us human is that we are all vulnerable; we are all mortal, regardless of our convictions that there is some greater truth, which is being vulnerable, like a fly on a leaf.

UMA THURMAN

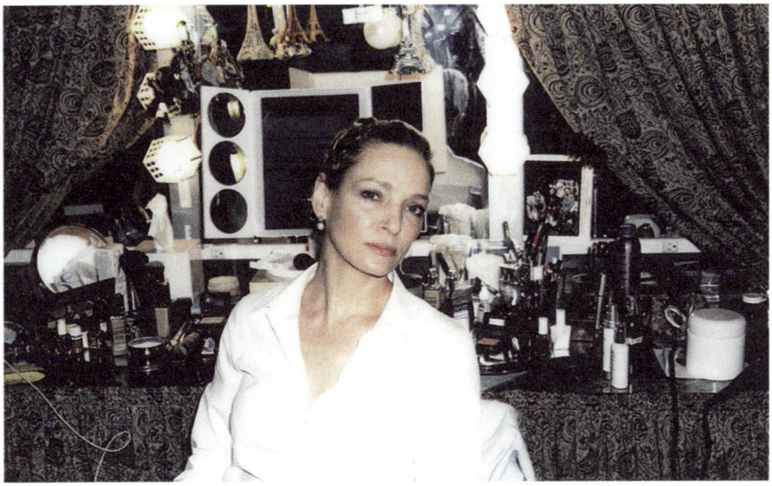

HHM: I believe shame could be placed in the same territory.

UT: I think that's true.

HHM: What is interesting for me about the concept of shame is that it breaks down the wall between the performer and the audience.

UT: I think that watching characters wrestle with, or experience, or process their own shame which is typically a very private experience—creates a deep connection between people. Comedians can access it in a way that makes it appear more public, but I think dramatic work is more about the sharing of the secret, which is universal—so it is actually not a secret—but the shame is the part that tries to hide it.

HHM: Do you ever experience shame as a performer?

UT: Only if I am not connecting to the material. I feel shame if I somehow can't find something that is true, or if I find there to be some kind of conflict or flaw for myself with the material that means I can't deliver it honestly, and I have to perform it or finesse it in some way that is inauthentic. That is shameful.

HHM: Do you think is important for an actor to be exposed to chance or accidents?

UT: I think that chance and accidents are real, and they happen when you perform. I think that being super-present and truthful means you

I FEEL SHAME IF I SOMEHOW CAN'T FIND SOMETHING THAT IS TRUE, OR IF I FIND THERE IS SOME KIND OF CONFLICT OR FLAW FOR MYSELF WITH THE MATERIAL THAT MEANS I CAN'T DELIVER IT HONESTLY

have to be available for any fluke, and that is part of what is exhilarating, particularly about live performance.

HHM: Sometimes a fluke or a flaw is what makes something special.

UT: Yeah.

HHM: What is your concept of beauty?

UT: I think beauty is in alignment with a deeper sense of truth that you can share. That is the most beautiful transformative energy to work with.

HHM: And when it comes to filmmaking, do you think art influences film? Or what fuels films these days?

UT: I don't know. I think that when something is illuminating or beautiful it becomes art, and at other times it's just entertainment, but when it's well done, it's almost art again, so I guess art, like beauty, is in the eye of the beholder.

HHM: Do you think there is a correlation between art and how filmmakers portray beauty?

UT: Simply put, great directors are visual artists. So, it's not surprising that a director's work is very much a conversation with all forms of visual art. I've worked with many directors who are avid scholars of the visual arts, like James Ivory, for instance. His style involves working off of classical painters like Titian, or great classical writing. He is a great scholar of art and a great artist; a very special director.

HHM: Do you think filmmakers help create an image of an actor in a lasting way?

UT: I think that great directors are doing exactly that.

HHM: In all of film history, who do you wish could have directed you?

UT: Ingmar Bergman.

HHM: It is interesting to see how great art is generally made during an empire in decline …

UT: Yes.

HHM: And the conversation we're having in culture right now is about resistance, but it's also about larger battles —women's rights, Black lives, Latino lives, trans lives …

UT: And I know it's an enormous source of pain.

HHM: What role does an actor play in society?

UT: I mean, being an actor is not about yourself, it's about discovering other things, other people, and other cultures, and the richness that my work has brought to my life is immeasurable. So, I guess actors play whatever role they play in theater or art. It is impossible for me to describe a specific societal role. Acting has just been part of the path of my life, not an artificial choice, you know. It was just one step after the next.

HHM: What are your thoughts on the rise of the artist as celebrity?

UT: I really think celebrity is its own animal. I have never been particularly interested in celebrity for its own sake, but I see that some people have taken celebrity and turned it into its own art form. I just personally don't relate to it. It's never been my point of interest.

HHM: At what point in your career did you feel that you were a successful artist?

UT: I don't know, maybe in the last few years. I think going over to the theater has been a really great challenge for me, and has stretched me enormously.

HHM: Do you worry about being overexposed?

UT: No, not anymore. I haven't been giving interviews or communicating about stuff for a long time … I used to, but I put a stop to it.

HHM: What inspires you the most?

UT: I think writing. Not actually writing myself as much as reading the writing of others, so I guess reading.

HHM: What was the first record you ever bought?

UT: A Blondie album.

HHM: What are your thoughts on the big film festivals like Cannes?

UT: I think they are fascinating, and can be kind of crazy, but these festivals are crucial to support and to promote film. I've truly enjoyed how they've exposed me to the world of cinema in a way that you just don't find anywhere else. I think they are quite extraordinary.

HHM: What is the most honest thing you can say about yourself?

UT: That I don't particularly like to talk about myself (*laughs*).

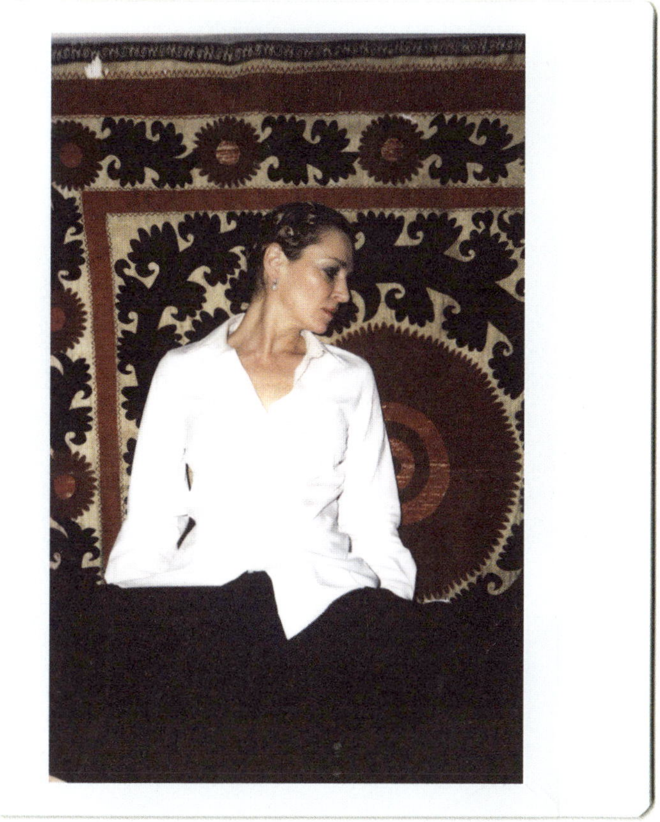

IS

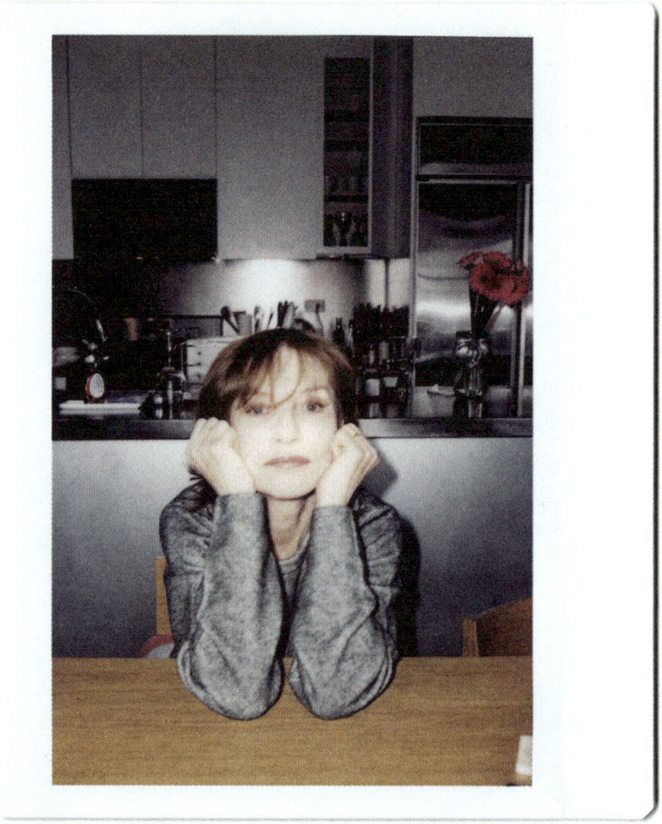

AB

EL

ISABELLE HUPPERT
NEW YORK, 2019

LE

Isabelle Huppert is a French actor. She studied Russian at the National Institute for Oriental Languages and Civilizations in Paris while also enrolled in drama classes at the National School for Theater Arts and the National Academy of Dramatic Arts. In 2005, Isabelle was awarded a Special Lion for Overall Work by the Venice Film Festival, where she had previously won two Best Actress awards. In addition to having twice earned the Best Actress award at Cannes, she has served as host, jury member, and jury president of the festival. Her performance in *Elle* also earned her a Best Actress award at the Golden Globes, and an Oscar nomination.

I met Isabelle in New York while she was rehearsing for the play *The Mother*. Inside her apartment, we talked about film, beauty, and performance while she did her own makeup. She effortlessly plays with her own image while seeming to detach herself from it, making each of her performances thoroughly captivating. Her fearless performances are the stuff of legend, and perhaps no international star has challenged the traditional rules of female behavior in film more fiercely than Isabelle Huppert.

HUGO HUERTA MARIN:
Was there one specific moment when cinema captured your attention? Perhaps a movie that stayed with you?

ISABELLE HUPPERT:
Yes, I remember it was a Russian movie called *The Cranes Are Flying*. In French, the title is *Quand passent les cicognes* and in Russian, *Летят Журавли*. It was by a Russian director named [Mikhail] Kalatozov, and it starred a great Russian actress named Tatiana Samoilova. It won the Palme d'Or at Cannes in 1958, I believe, and it was about World War II. I saw it on television when I was a little girl, and I think it was the first movie that really struck me.

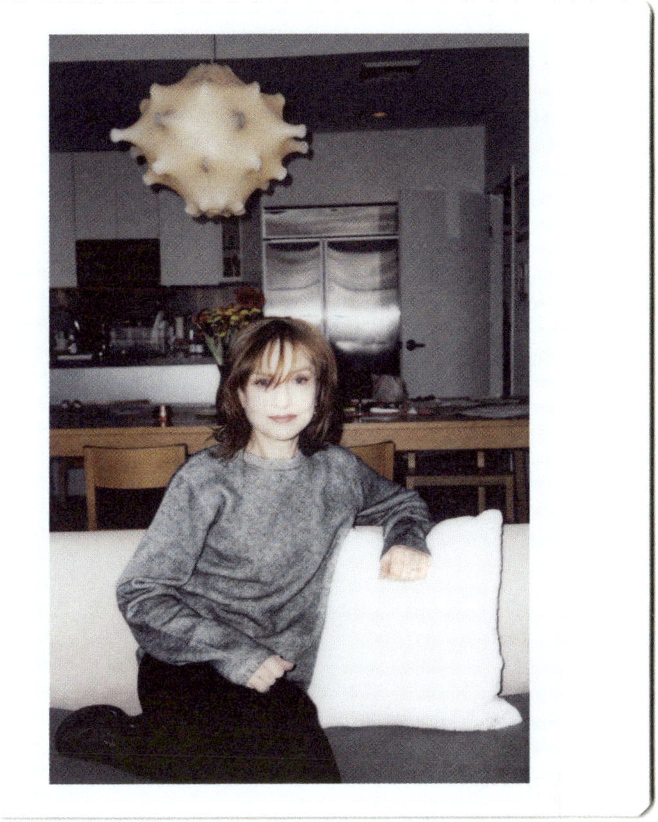

HHM: I am interested to know more about some of your influences, as I believe most of the roles you choose to play are in really unusual movies like *Loulou*, *The Piano Teacher*, or *Elle*. These are all brutal films …

IH: Yes.

HHM: We don't see movies like that very often, and it seems that you are unafraid to examine the dark side of human nature. How do you choose your roles?

IH: Well, I just chose them naturally. They are just great roles, and I don't know — I read scripts, and I don't think a lot before doing them. My interest in the role has less to do with the role itself, and more to do with working with a certain type of director. I mean, if it wasn't for Michael Haneke directing *The Piano Teacher*, I am not sure I would have done it. I also don't see the bad in these roles, only the good. I only see the different shades of human nature — the ambiguities and complexities — and I think cinema is the ideal medium to express these ambiguities.

HHM: Art brings that which is hidden to the surface.

IH: That is right.

HHM: Do you think these roles highlight women's empowerment?

IH: In the sense that you bring attention to these women, and specifically, to these characters.

There is something that ties them to one another in the sense that they're all survivors, not necessarily winners, which I think is probably closer to reality. But it doesn't necessarily highlight their power as women or as being a caricature of men's power. These roles highlight their fragilities, their weaknesses, and they certainly place women at the center, and that is enough for me to call it "women's empowerment" in a way.

HHM: What is the process of creating the aesthetics for such complex characters?

IH: Well, you know, that comes with any character you are playing. The aesthetic is always an important component. You have to create a character, and that means creating something that is far from you, but close to you at the same time, and that is the whole challenge. When you play a role, obviously, you wear a mask, but you are behind the mask, so it is tricky because I think the character has to always come across with something that belongs to you; otherwise, you lose any proximity to the role. But it is a nice little game to play—how to create a character and, at the same time, make it your own. As easy as it sounds.

HHM: What about the corporeal language you use while performing? Do you think about it in advance?

IH: Corporeal language is something else. I think each role commands its own corporeal language, from the top of your head to the soles of your feet. It contributes to creating a character.

For instance, I didn't walk the same way in *Elle* as I did in *The Piano Teacher*. The shoes are a central part of creating a character for me. When I am asked: "Where do you find the role?" I always say, "In my shoes." It is sort of a joke, because whether you walk with flat shoes or high heels, they command the way you walk, and that determines your view of the world.

HHM: It seems there is an interest in the baroque and the grotesque in some of your films. Do you think that the concept of attraction and repulsion can get along?

IH: Well, it depends on what you call attraction, and it depends on what you call repulsion. Repulsion can be attractive for certain people, and attraction can be repulsive for others. There is not a certain definition.

HHM: Horror has been embedded in beauty throughout the history of art.

IH: Absolutely.

HHM: It is an interesting subject. I read an essay recently on how the grotesque in Western art is often associated with the feminine. Of course, it is not just "owned" by female artists, but it is also interesting to see how queer artists have played in this terrain as well. It feels as though artists are deploying this to empower the marginalized, or to play with taboos and shift the parameters of morals and conventions.

IH: But I don't think it necessarily belongs to women or queer artists. I mean, over the centuries, if you take [Hieronymus] Bosch, for example, he knew how to illustrate the grotesque in a masterful way.

HHM: Right. But if you think of Western contemporary art, artists like Cindy Sherman or Marilyn Minter ... It feels as if these monstrous bodies are a response to societal standards, which goes back to my question about women's empowerment.

IH: Yes. In the case of an artist like Cindy Sherman, she crosses these borders as you just said, and she also explores the limits of the gender. What does it mean to be a man? What does it mean to be a woman? And to push that as far as Cindy does is extraordinary.

HHM: I remember the series she made of dismembered plastic dolls in a variety of violent scenarios. Horror rather than eroticism ...

IH: Exactly.

HHM: Your acting career has crossed many of these borders as well, dealing with concepts of shame and eroticism in a very provocative and profound way.

IH: There is an interesting line in *Elle*, where my character says, "Shame is certainly not an emotion that should prevent us from doing anything."

HHM: So, she is above the notion of shame.

IH: Yes. My character is being confronted by her friend in the office, who just found out that her husband was sleeping with another woman—who happens to be me—but, of course, she doesn't know that, and so my character comes up with this line about shame … Shame might be a concept that, most of the time, is dependent on someone else, but at the same time, it is such a complex subject because there are so many situations where you can feel ashamed, and that is not easy. It is a subject too big to be put into words …

HHM: What about the concept of shame as a performer?

IH: As a performer, you don't have any shame because you make things into metaphors in order to give shape to whatever it is you are playing. As a performer, shame doesn't exist. I have never felt ashamed while acting. In real life, there are so many situations that can make you feel ashamed or humiliated. But it is interesting because when you are acting, the border can be very thin, you know; if you step aside, you might find yourself on the wrong side. But if it is rightly done and properly perceived, I believe it is protective: Nothing can really reach you.

HHM: It seems that humor is a key element in your work.

IH: Yes, indeed, that is for sure.

HHM: How do you locate the irony in a project that might otherwise seem dark?

I DON'T THINK EMOTION COMES FROM SENTIMENTALISM OR PATHOS. IT COMES FROM SOMETHING ELSE, IT COMES FROM A CERTAIN KIND OF COLDNESS, AND THAT IS WHEN EMOTION IS POSSIBLE

IH: I think you can find irony everywhere. I am doing a play right now called *The Mother* by a French playwright named Florian Zeller, and it's very dark. It is about an ill mother going mad because she feels lonely, but, in fact, the play is supposed to be a black comedy. In general, I can say that over the past few years, I have been highlighting the humor in my roles. I think that in all great literature, theater, or any kind of expression, comedy is close to tragedy; they always come together.

HHM: An infallible combination.

IH: Yes. And it also creates distance. It helps to take away any attempts at sentimentalism and pathos in the role, and that is the key. I don't think emotion comes from sentimentalism or pathos. It comes from something else, it comes from a certain kind of coldness, and that is when emotion is possible.

HHM: What role do chance or accidents play while performing?

CINEMA IS THE ART OF … WE HAVE A WORD IN FRENCH, "L'IMPONDÉRABLE," MEANING THE ART OF THE UNKNOWN AND UNANTICIPATED

IH: Oh, a central role, because cinema is all about accidents and chance. Cinema is the art of … we have a word in French, *l'impondérable*, meaning the art of the unknown and unanticipated. It is the art of something that literally springs up without our expecting it, and most of all, it is art about the moment.

HHM: In your opinion, what role does an actor play in society?

IH: Oh, I don't know. I have no answer to that question because I don't consider that I play a role for society. I just play a role for myself. I see acting as something that goes on between me and myself, and that is enough. On the other hand, I guess a little story between you and yourself is, in the end, a story between you and others, because you are the others in a way.

HHM: A reflection.

IH: In a way, yes.

HHM: In all of film history, whom would you have liked to have directed you?

IH: Alfred Hitchcock.

HHM: I can see that … Hitchcock's oeuvre is filled with various cultural references, where each narrative is multilayered. In that sense, how do you think visual art influences film?

IH: That is a difficult question because I am not a director myself. As an actress, I tend to follow rhythm and music instinctively. Acting is not about aesthetics and visuals; it is all about rhythm and, therefore, music. I think aesthetics is something that belongs to the director.

HHM: And as an actress, who do you think owns the performance at the end?

IH: It might belong to the audience. I think a film is a different experience for each person. Everyone creates a different perception of a film, and that is exactly the strength of a great film. Now, because of the roles I tend to choose — which are often at the center of the story — I am able to create my own film within the director's film. The director does a movie, the script does a movie, and the actor does a movie; the final product is a reunion of these imaginary processes.

HHM: What is your concept of beauty?

IH: Well, I could tell you that beauty has something to do with being natural, but I am not quite sure that is the case because when it comes to acting and performing, beauty also has to do with being artificial, you know? So, I wouldn't necessarily be opposed to being artificial; I wouldn't say that natural is beautiful and artificial is not. The artificial is also part of performing and is a part of any kind of expression, not only in films but in painting, in the arts ... There is beauty in the artificial.

HHM: What are your thoughts on the rise of the artist as a celebrity?

IH: Well, the concept of celebrity is so different nowadays than it used to be. First, because there used to be fewer people on the earth and, therefore, fewer people involved, and, of course, with social media and everything, the concept of celebrity has changed drastically. For me, celebrity doesn't mean having to be exposed all the time.

HHM: At what point in your career did you feel that you were a successful actress?

IH: I don't think you ever feel that, because it is such an abstract concept in a way. Sometimes, yes, you are acknowledged and recognized, but it is so relative, and the awareness of that has to be there all the time; otherwise, I think you are in bad shape as an actress.

HHM: What is the most honest thing you can say about yourself?

IH: I am a nice person.

ISABELLE HUPPERT

JE

N

JENNY HOLZER

HOOSICK, NEW YORK, 2020

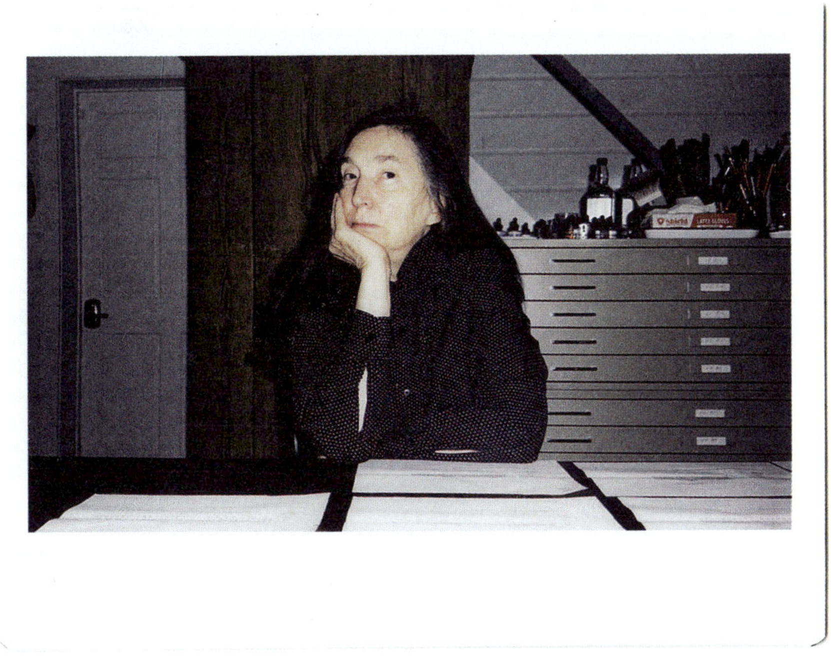

NY

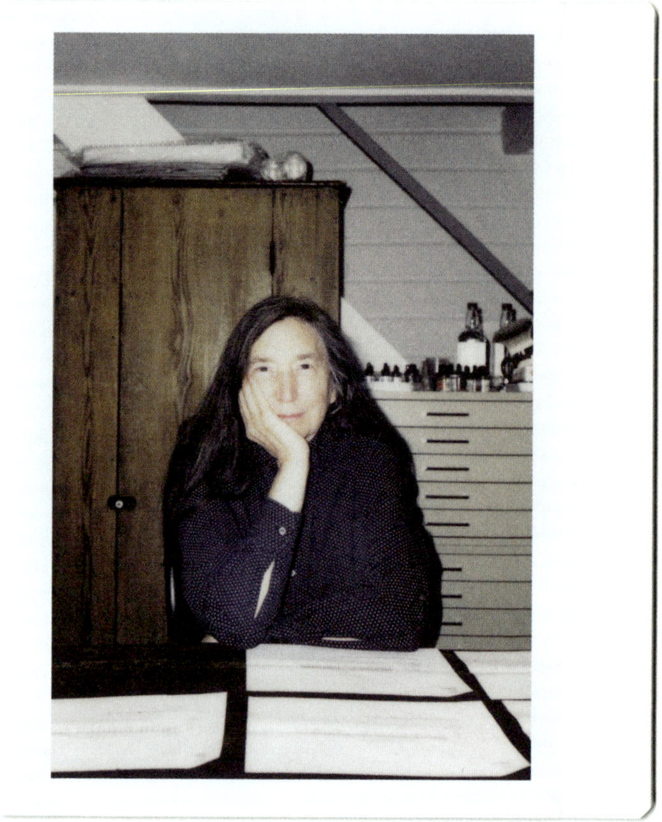

For more than forty years, artist Jenny Holzer has presented her astringent ideas, arguments, and sorrows in public places and at international exhibitions. Her medium, whether on a T-shirt, a plaque, or an LED sign, is writing, and the public dimension is integral to the delivery of her work. Throughout her career, Jenny has received several awards, including the Golden Lion at the Venice Biennale, the World Economic Forum's Crystal Award, and the Barnard Medal of Distinction.

A three-and-a-half hour drive from New York City led me to Hoosick, where I met with Jenny on a warm and quiet summer afternoon. We walked around her property until we found a pleasant spot to begin our conversation. For decades, Jenny has projected phrases on to surfaces such as mountains, ocean waves, and rocks. Going outside is her biggest inspiration, so meeting her in this natural context was a privilege for me. Starting in the 1970s with the New York City posters, and continuing through her recent light projections on to landscape and architecture, her practice has challenged ignorance and violence with humor, kindness, and courage. The reigning art world star Jenny Holzer occupies a territory in art that is entirely her own.

HUGO HUERTA MARIN:
Let's start by talking about the strong relationship between the language and the materials that you use in your work: large-scale projections, LED displays, T-shirts, bronze plaques, stone benches, offset posters, and condoms, to name a few. How do you decide which specific material to go for?

JENNY HOLZER:
Work often starts with the content. I like content—preferably difficult or at least on-point subject matter. Sometimes the text

will arrive and it will demand a particular medium. Other times there is a text that is very flexible—even promiscuous—that can live almost anywhere, from a poster to a shirt to a stone bench. The more serious texts seem especially suitable for stone, and when I want to present a high volume of material, an electronic sign with a big brain is a happy home.

HHM: Do some texts suit stone because engraving words in stone is associated with permanency or immortality?

JH: Or mortality.

HHM: Right.

JH: I appreciate how different media, different materials, inflect the content, and even change the way you read.

HHM: In what way?

JH: People might read stone with their hands. I've noticed that people trace letters with their fingers—while of course using their eyes and brain. An electronic display's fleeting, flashing presentation is quite distinct.

HHM: In this context, what role does space play in your work?

JH: I love being an installation artist. I do better when I attempt the whole surroundings. That's preferable to making one object that's to be everything. I adore impressive environments. I like to make the floor drop out from under me and everyone else. I color the air all around—and there needs be meaning in the surroundings.

HHM: I can see that. I've always thought that one of your pieces would be fantastic for Tate Modern's Turbine Hall.

JH: Yeah, I need an invitation though. It's preferable not to break in (*laughs*).

HHM: (*laughs*) What are the differences between making a work for a huge and public space like Times Square or the World Trade Center and making a work to be installed within a museum or a gallery context?

JH: There's some overlap between outdoor public spaces and museums, but people at art museums tend to be thinking about art proper, and people on the street think about lunch, love, money, movies … So there are different opportunities and challenges. It takes some doing to catch people's attention in the street without being cheap and sensationalist. It can be a luxury to have the relative peace and quiet of a museum with an audience made up at least partly of experts who might love art the same way you do.

HHM: How does the language change between one viewer and the other?

JH: I try to make language accessible more often than not, because I want the content to land. That said, in a museum I might present more content than I would in the street because I can expect people's attention spans to be longer indoors. The night-time light projections can have a poetic language, because people may be quieter after dark and more inclined to attend and linger.

HHM: Fantastic. And what would be the difference between making commissioned work and making work driven by your own impetus? How fluid is that back-and-forth, and how does it change the work?

JH: There can be more freedom in self-initiated projects, like the one beside us—which is dripping a bunch of watercolors on Mueller Report documents. I can't quite imagine the Medici who would want this (*laughs*), but I need to see the result. This will become a big grid—I'll probably have about fifty watercolors within it—so there will be a lot of drizzling.

I don't accept commissions unless I'll have enough freedom to make what seems appropriate for the space and the time. Otherwise there's no point.

HHM: Is there more tension while executing commissions?

JH: Well, there's more and different attention. When the clients are good I learn things, and I welcome that interaction. I tend to be bleak, dark, negative, dot dot dot. When I worked for the Silverstein family at 7 WTC they were determined to be optimistic, not to pretend that what happened didn't happen but to look ahead and stay constructive. That was interesting and welcome, if a little unfamiliar to me.

HHM: One of the things that came to my attention was the work you've done on memorial gardens like the Black Garden of Nordhorn or the Erlauf Peace Monument. When did you first become interested in the concept of memory?

JH: When I was young, I went to a cemetery in my grandparents' hometown—high on a river bank—and there was a stone bench inscribed with a poem, selected by the poet's widow to mark his grave. That caught me, because people could pause, look at the broad river, and think of a man and his expression.

Because I tend toward bleakness, people began to invite me to make memorials. I had largely stopped writing my own text then, so sometimes I'd use the writing of those who were to be memorialized. Perhaps these people had been murdered or died in some unnecessary way. It was a whole new experience, and a liberating one, to rely on the text of many others.

HHM: It seems that your work sympathizes with victims.

JH: Let's say I want to keep good people, with their virtues and their utterances, with us.

HHM: To put it better, is spirituality assumed in your work?

JH: Hopefully feeling is. I have a repressed spirituality (*laughs*). I am not religious in any conventional sense, but I am all for applying appropriate feeling that might make for sanity and better behavior.

HHM: So where does Jenny Holzer end and the formless and indefinable voice begin?

JH: Oh, I'd like to keep myself as far from the voice as possible, because, among other things, it's freeing, if unhealthy, to be disassociated from it. It's not an accident that I was an anonymous street artist. When I was a young woman, anonymity let me produce relatively unselfconsciously, and perhaps gave me a bigger voice than I would have had if my work were signed Jenny Holzer—a twenty-something-year-old female artist whom no one had heard of. That signature would have turned the volume down, that was an address for nowhere.

HHM: I also think it's no coincidence that many people think some of your work was done by a man.

JH: Absolutely.

HHM: Do you think it is because people associate the male voice with authority?

JH: Sure. When I was writing first the *Truisms* and then the *Inflammatory Essays*, I explored many different subjects, wrote from multiple points of view, and probably inhabited two, three, or four sexes, and some in between too. If you want to understand people's motivations, it's good to indwell as best as you can. Unless they're a murderer, then it's best not to follow through (*laughs*).

HHM: (*laughs*) The *Truisms* are perhaps some of my favorite works of art ever made. Can you share the genesis behind them?

JH: I'm impatient and an attention deficit sufferer, but I wanted to contribute in some way. I wanted to find much content to consider, and to represent this content in a way that would be accessible, available to people. The *Truisms* started when I distilled a grand reading list. I have always liked clichés so I suppose it's only logical that I went to *Truisms* as a form.

HHM: Our view of history is gradually changing. Do you think we should be skeptical about absolute truths?

JH: Well, skepticism about and disgust for strategic lying is pragmatic and healthy right now. I'm thinking about President Trump. Too much relativism can be dangerous, because there are things that are criminal—cruel neglect and

JENNY HOLZER

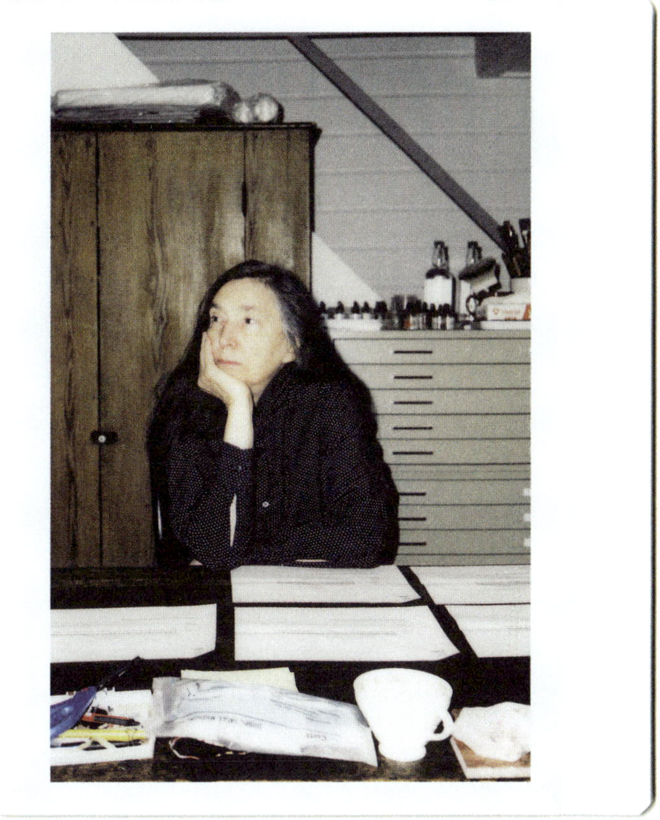

mass murder, for example. That said, I don't want the will or the stories of any one person to be imposed on all others, as if that were the only way to think or operate. That can be dirty and can have serious consequences.

HHM: What is your relationship to writing like?

JH: Troubled. Reluctant and frightened, resentful, slow … a lot of sad words like those. That's the reason it was a tremendous relief to start making memorials with others' texts, to go to poems for projection, to greatly improve on what I could do solo and to present more than I could generate myself. I'm honored to show text by people who are real writers. Once in a while, as recently for trucks with electronic displays, it's been possible to compose blasts like "COVID-19 PRESIDENT" or "COVID-19 ECONOMY." That kind of writing I can muster, to steal what's now and flash it.

HHM: Do you find there is a difference between writing words that are to be shown and those that are not?

JH: I mostly don't retain notes. Someone with very good intentions once gave me a number of beautiful diaries to fill in, and in the end I gave them to a poet friend after they sat empty for ten or fifteen years. I desire to be anonymous and largely invisible, so perhaps that influences what I show and what I don't, what I keep and what I won't.

HHM: It seems that you are unafraid to examine the dark side of human nature—murder, sexual violence, the abuse of power, war, deprivation. Is it your intention to raise awareness of these difficult themes?

JH: I hope, however unrealistic it may be at times, to cut the number of incidences of rape, murder, abuse, neglect, starvation, and so on. That's the dream. I had an unusual childhood so I have first-hand experience with rough stuff; it's part of my deal. I'm sure the cruel exists, and you know there is more evidence for it daily.

HHM: Do you consider yourself a political artist?

JH: I'm an artist, and a person who is political; I make some separation here. I do not represent that art is as straightforward and immediately effective as voting or doing community work, and I don't think art always can or should be pragmatic and utilitarian. At times, however, art can fuse a dreadful or wonderful reality with dreadful or wonderful representation so that people realize and feel what is, and then act.

HHM: Sometimes art can be a tool for social change.

JH: Yes. Let's just say Goya was a great artist and no fool.

HHM: Do you think pain is important for an artist?

JH: It can be inspirational and realistic, and potentially empathy-producing, but it can make people horrible, it can go either way. Here's to art that celebrates! I am a Matisse fan, I'm all over his *Joy of Life*. I don't have a real formula for the transcendence that may come from joy or from suffering, as in Rothko's work.

HHM: But also sometimes horror is embedded in beauty throughout your oeuvre. What is your concept of beauty?

JH: Here is a thin answer, but one I think is accurate: Beauty can come in any number of forms and expressions, from the absolutely desperate to the grotesque to the lovely and the lucid. I like all flavors.

HHM: Do you agree with Marcel Duchamp's claim that the audience does half of the work? What is your position on the interaction of the viewer and the artwork?

JH: Well, when you are lucky the audience does half the work! And I would never argue with Duchamp. I would lose (*laughs*). But I read that he stole the infamous urinal from a woman. Can you imagine? It's quite a story. Look up Baroness Elsa von Freytag-Loringhoven. Her life could change your life. Her writing was fantastic. Notice where she moved, see her friends, notice her end.

HHM: How did that happen?

JH: It is a very interesting story and seemingly true. This is a research project for you. I think you'll be delighted by the baroness. She died partly mad and in poverty, you know that tale. She was avant-garde to the extreme.

HHM: We know that kind of story. It is …

JH: It's traditional.

HHM: Yes. Do you think things have changed for female artists over the past decades?

JH: Sure. You know, a lot of things are better, but the pace is too slow. More women are able to work, are encouraged, make a little more money, and show more often. But just like it is for civil rights in this country, it's ridiculously wrong for females in the arts, and at large. There are stutter steps, two moves forward, one back, or one forward, three back. I never thought it would still be this stupid when I was this age.

HHM: What are your thoughts on the rise of the artist as celebrity?

JH: I saw something in *ARTnews* about a talent agency taking on artists, and that gave me the creeps a little, at least with regard to overprivileged white boy artists. Perhaps there is a reason though; of course it's nice when artists can practice what they love and not need a couple other jobs. One wonderful thing about working in Europe is there's respect and provision for art as an occupation, a preoccupation, and a paying profession.

HHM: At what point in your career did you feel you were a successful artist?

JH: When I had enough *Truisms* to alphabetize them. Then I thought there was hope for having plenty of something to offer people.

HHM: Do you worry about being overexposed?

JH: I worry about not being a good enough artist. If one looks at art history, it's terrifying! Plenty of artists are wonderfully and infinitely gifted, and that sets a standard that's approximately or utterly impossible to meet. But it's good to try. I'm working on a show of work by Louise Bourgeois. The proximity is soul-destroying but utterly inspirational (*laughs*). I'm the curator, sort of, and as such I'm learning more about what she achieved. I'm seeing how a beautiful, nimble mind, a dose of agony, a wicked sense of play, insomnia, and a great hand can conspire to yield the consistently astonishing.

HHM: What inspires you the most?

JH: Brushing up against artists like Bourgeois, going outside, not seeing any humans, that's good. Watching the moon.

HHM: Do you have any recurring dreams?

JH: I mostly repress my dreams. That is part of my suppression regimen. Once in a while something will break through.

HHM: What was the first record you ever bought?

JH: I only remember it was a 45. But I recall my parents having Tennessee Ernie Ford's song about coal miners, which for some reason I would play compulsively: "You load sixteen tons, what do you get? / Another day older and deeper in debt. / Saint Peter don't you call me 'cause I can't go, / I owe my soul to the company store."

HHM: (*laughs*) I love it. What are your thoughts on the big, international blockbusters, like documenta or the Venice Biennale?

JH: I haven't attended recently, so I am not current and shouldn't opine, but I recall being happy and alarmed to be invited way back when. Going to a documenta in the early eighties was a crash-course in art education and an all-purpose eye-opener. I was terrified to represent the United States in Venice. That was difficult because I did shows at Dia, the Guggenheim New York, and Venice in a compressed couple of years. I had a baby in that time, the baby almost didn't make it, my relationships were askew …

I was a hippie in my teens and early twenties—this after my mother impressed on me that I had to be a good girl. The difference, this dissonance between hippie and good girl, with variations on the theme later, and being the first—semi-dissident—female to represent the U.S. in Venice, was alarming.

HHM: What is the most honest thing you can say about yourself?

JH: I don't think I can tell you the truth (*laughs*).

DE

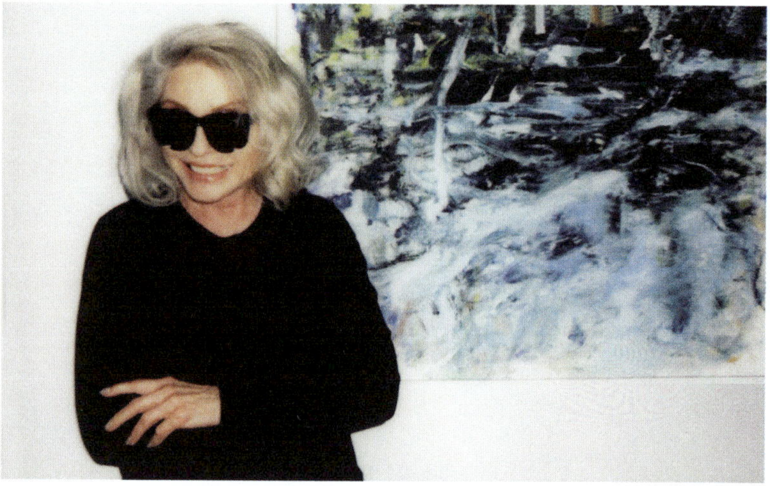

BB

DEBBIE HARRY

NEW YORK, 2021

IE

The name Debbie Harry evokes many images: seminal rock 'n' roll figure, songstress, incandescent front woman, actor, and fashion icon. As a vibrant global force and a shaper of pop culture, Debbie's chart-topping success, fearless spirit, and rare longevity led to an induction into the Rock & Roll Hall of Fame for Blondie in 2006. With Blondie, undeniably one of the most influential bands of our time, she and co-founder Chris Stein brought together the worlds of rock, punk, disco, and reggae.

The first thing that's striking about talking to Debbie is how soft and melodic her voice is. It contains the hush and clarity of confession, yet it embodies the daring woman who has sold more than 50 million albums worldwide and created acclaimed solo projects. Debbie has also engaged in a successful acting career, with over thirty film and television roles to her credit. From an irreverent Lower East Side punk goddess to a bona fide international ambassador of New York cool, Debbie Harry will forever be synonymous with that punk spirit that lives somewhere in all of us.

HUGO HUERTA MARIN:
I believe that the thing that makes art interesting is when an artist has incredible pain or incredible rage …

DEBBIE HARRY:
Well, it certainly is a very poignant way of expressing oneself, and I also think that it creates an understanding of the balance between, you know, joy and pain, or comfort and discomfort, and that it is a vital source of energy in art. In any art really.

HHM: Back in the prime days of the punk movement, I have the impression that the New York bands were much more into their pain, while the English bands were more into their rage.

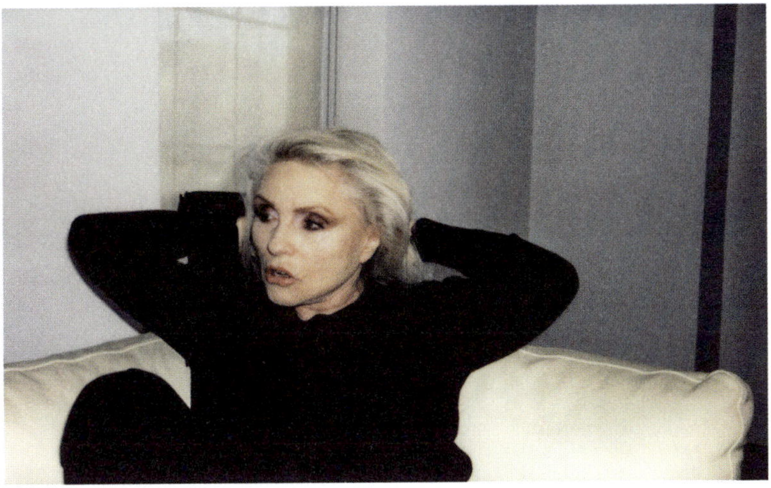

DH: Well, I guess that is actually true, but I also think that a lot of the punk scene in the UK had to do with the Irish tradition. There was a lot of rage there, you know, the North versus the South, for instance, and that has been an ongoing thing for many years.

HHM: The punk era wasn't really about just one musical style, but the bands had the same kind of philosophy. Glam rock was about decadence: platform shoes and boys in eye makeup, David Bowie and androgyny. But I believe punk was more about resistance or rebellion.

DH: It was also about chaos and deconstruction—deconstructing musical ideas. There was a lot of satire around: making fun of customs, the rules of adulthood, and what had been considered "proper behavior" maybe ten years before. There was also a big sexual component to it, which became very apparent. It was no longer just about good old boys talking about their lives on the road and picking up dirty women and so on. It became a much more comprehensive view of social mores, or morals, or whatever you want to call them.

HHM: That is interesting, and it goes hand in hand with the idea that the grotesque in Western contemporary art is inherently associated with the feminine and with Queer art …
I believe that's what attracted everybody to Andy Warhol's Factory. All of sorts of marginalized lifestyles and identities. It was like a sideshow—

IT WAS NO LONGER JUST ABOUT GOOD OLD BOYS TALKING ABOUT THEIR LIVES ON THE ROAD AND PICKING UP DIRTY WOMEN AND SO ON. IT BECAME A MUCH MORE COMPREHENSIVE VIEW OF SOCIAL MORES

come look at the freaks! And all the uptown jet-setters would come down and look.

DH: Yes, I think there is a great tradition in the arts to have a swing of the pendulum. And then that becomes the counterculture. It's a way of energizing a society, and it also has to do with up-and-coming artists. It's a very magical function and an energizing force. That is why people flock to it, you know, because it gives them a sense of purpose, or a sense of life. And sometimes it's good and interesting and exciting work. I don't know if it's the case for all of society, but it's true certainly for people who want to have a little bit more edge in their lives, and then it is eventually incorporated into the rest of society and it becomes accepted. It does take a while for things to be part of the generally accepted way of life, or style, or art, or music, or whatever it is, and I guess that is the beauty of it.

HHM: The scene that happened around CBGB and Max's Kansas City, when the Factory was in full swing, was really what anybody who dreamt of coming to New York or being in the art world or the music scene was thinking about at the time. How do you think these places molded New York as we see it today?

DH: Well, it gave people a sort of ownership or belonging, a sense of identity and strength. I experienced that very early on in the years of Blondie when we would play at CBGB, and CBGB was not a popular place to go in the early seventies. We would have a very small audience of maybe twenty or twenty-five people who became our regular following. It was funny how when we became more well-known and our audience got bigger and bigger, the original people that followed us were very upset, because they had felt ownership and they were losing it.

HHM: You can feel nostalgic when you walk down the Bowery and see that CBGB is now a John Varvatos store ... Do you think there's a sense of continuity with the New York underground culture nowadays?

DH: Well, I think so. New York has always taken a certain position. However, I think some things have been smoothed over, banned in a way.

HHM: I agree, even in fashion, particularly if we think about it during the punk era, which I guess goes back to what you were saying about ownership and identity. Black leather, latex, padlock necklaces, T-shirts with real chicken bones on them … It is interesting to think about fashion as a political tool.

DH: Oh my God, if you look down through history, it is very clear and political, especially in the UK … Think about it in simple terms, the redcoats. There are all kinds of references and subcultures, like the Mods versus the Rockers, for instance. They were political statements and also segments and levels in society. It is certainly interesting to think about identity through codes.

HHM: Thinking about signifiers, there was also a loathsome motif that many bands used: the swastika. Playing around with the ultimate taboo, it's interesting to read in interviews with some punk bands of the time that the use of it wasn't political, or even racial, but sexual. Dee Dee Ramone once said he was fascinated by Nazi symbols.

DH: Did you know that he grew up in Germany? His family was in the military, so it was a big influence on him.

HHM: Exactly. I think it has to do more with deconstructing ideas as you said before, and the power of fashion and music to confront. There are a few moments in history when the language of a culture was shifted by clothes and music. Do you think music can still be that revolutionary?

ART AND COMMERCE DON'T MIX, BUT THEY PUSH THINGS, THEY MAKE THE STANDARDS CHANGE

DH: I don't really know. Technology has taken it over and created a sort of level playing field in terms of communication. I can't predict where that will go.

HHM: Certainly music is no longer a boys' club. How do you think things have changed for women in the industry in the past few decades?

DH: It has become accepted and proved their worth, and whenever something becomes worth a few dollars, I mean it's over, there is no question about it. Art and commerce don't mix, but they push things, they make the standards change. Perhaps that relates back to what we were saying earlier about the synergy between something that is ugly and something that is beautiful. The commercial forces that operate music are destructive to art, but art can't live without them.

HHM: Art is a reflection of society and it gives us an understanding of how people live. Do you think contemporary music symbolizes the emptiness of a modern society?

DH: Well, no … In some ways it is a matter of taste, but somehow people can sense the difference between a song that was created through an algorithm and a song that was created through angst or anger or lust. There is great difference, and it is about instinct really, hormones, many things. You can follow a formula but it is not gonna get you anywhere. It needs to have something behind it.

HHM: I am wondering if this premise applies to performance. Do you think that accidents or chance are important while performing?

DH: Oh, absolutely! That's one of the things that you hear jazz musicians refer to and that I know from my experience with Blondie. That is the most exciting and the most special thing and one from which you really learn a lot. You know, when everybody goes off at the same time and everybody loses their place or some kind of craziness comes into the atmosphere and then you come out on the other side. It's a sensation that in a way is like an electric shock, or when you bump your elbow and hit that nerve … For me that's the really special kind of magic that can happen while performing. It doesn't always happen, unfortunately, but I, for one, find real inspiration in it.
For many years, what we were doing was never recorded or taped or filmed, or anything like that. We would just do it and it would go out, and I always wondered about that. I felt it, and I don't know, sometimes I regretted the fact that it wasn't recorded, but on the other hand, I thought it was sort of better that it just went out and became the source of a field of energy …

HHM: It makes total sense. I am also curious to know whether sex plays an important component in performing, or in music for that matter.

DH: I think it is all about sex. The only thing that isn't about sex is politics. Everything else in the world is about sex: what you listen to, what you read, where you live, who you are with.

HHM: Have you found that your relationship with music has changed over time?

DH: My core and how I feel music have not changed. I think I will always be that way, thankfully. Of course my professional maturation as an entertainer and a singer has certainly grown, or deteriorated, however you want to look at it. I am not as much of a child as I was, but I think the purity and the childishness of my understanding of music remains the same.

HHM: Your cultural dominance includes not only music, but performance, films, and working with visual artists. What is your relationship to art?

DH: I was inspired by it, and when I was at school I loved to study it. I think I had an ambition to be a painter or something like that, a natural instinct, you know.

HHM: The band even used the 1980 Warhol portrait for the jacket of *Blondie 4(0)*—which is such a powerful picture. How was your relationship to Warhol back then?

THE ONLY THING THAT ISN'T ABOUT SEX IS POLITICS. EVERYTHING ELSE IN THE WORLD IS ABOUT SEX: WHAT YOU LISTEN TO, WHAT YOU READ, WHERE YOU LIVE, WHO YOU ARE WITH

DH: Well, I think it has been very much exaggerated over the years, but I loved Andy and I appreciate his work. He was like a Renaissance man in the twentieth century, which was very cool, and I admired his bravery, considering that he was completely out at a time that pre-dated the fashion of being out. I wish I'd had a chance to get to know him better, but I think we were at the beginning of a very nice friendship, and so I was lucky to have known him at all really.

HHM: Do you think art has influenced your work?

DH: I was always fascinated with Surrealism, and I think I tried to incorporate it into some of the very early Blondie performances, like one time I did a performance holding a fish bowl (*laughs*). I think that having those foundations was very good for me. I guess it is always a search, you know, internal and external; that kind of exploration is really important for an artist.

HHM: What are your thoughts on the rise of the artist as celebrity?

DH: I don't know—I mean, everybody works very hard to make a living and to tell their story. I went to see an artist at the Guggenheim who worked anonymously for her entire life, and I can't imagine what that could be like, because art is about communication. But it happens; probably it happens more to women than to men, because women were not really part of the art world for so long.

HHM: At what point in your career do you feel you were a successful artist?

DH: I guess in the 1980s. But it has do with commercialism—it didn't really have to do with being a great artist or not, it just had to do with being part of a business. As a successful artist, I don't know if I am ever gonna be satisfied.

HHM: What was the first record you ever bought?

DH: *Afro Blue* by Cal Tjader.

HHM: What is the most honest thing you can say about yourself?

DH: I have a good sense of humor.

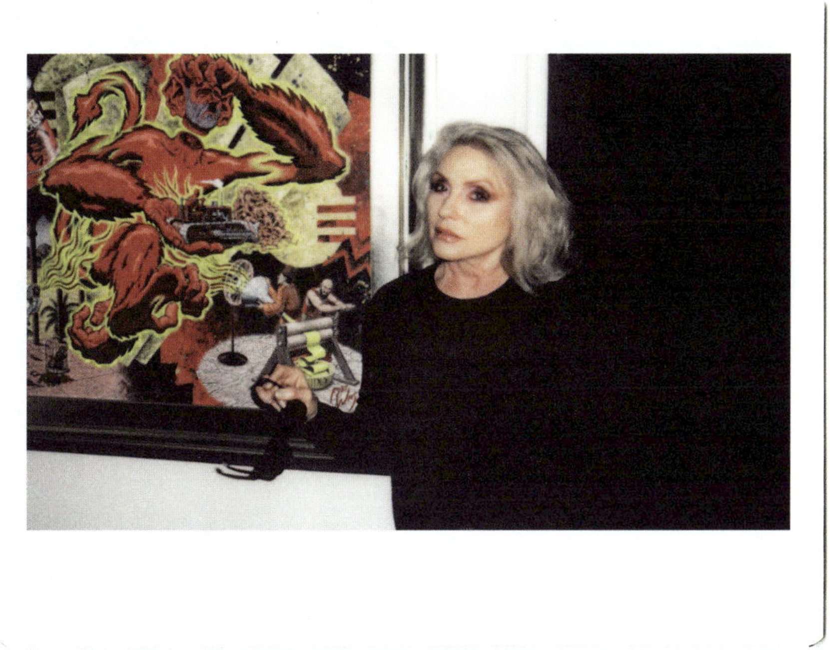

AG

N

È

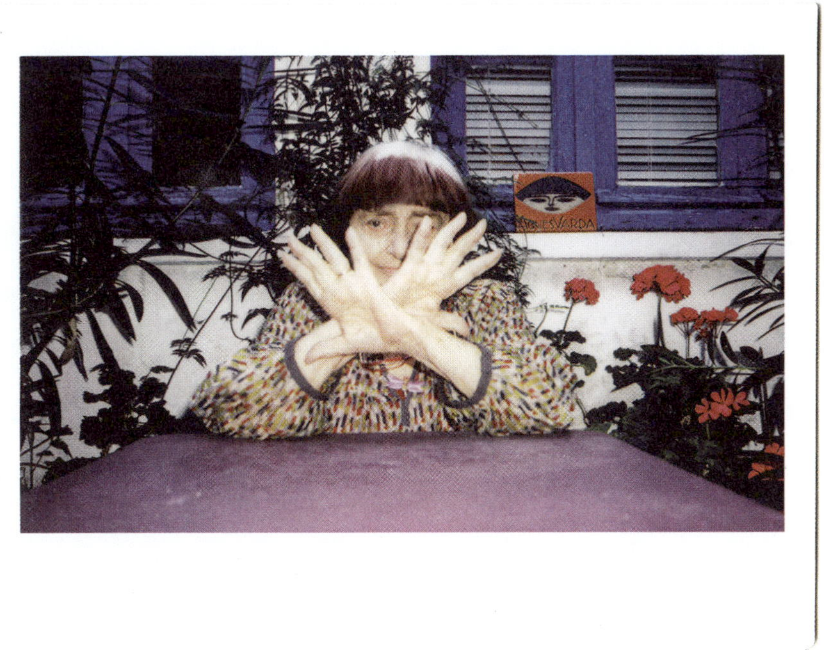

AGNÈS VARDA

PARIS, 2018

S

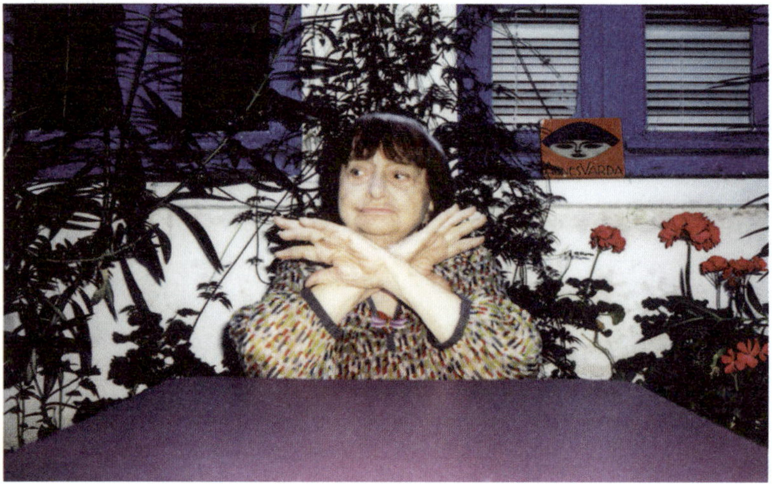

Agnès Varda made films for more than sixty years, focusing on documentaries in the latter part of her career. She received several awards for her work, including the Silver Bear at the Berlin Film Festival, the Golden Lion at Venice, the Palme d'Or d'Honneur at Cannes, the Grolsch People's Choice Documentary Award at Toronto, and an honorary Oscar.

The usual way to begin writing about Agnès is to note that she is the only woman associated with the French New Wave during the movement's peak. To me, her all-purple house on the Left Bank in Paris is the best place to start. Although she never usually met with anyone on Sundays, she invited me then because she thought it could be a peaceful time for us to talk about the past and the present. Her home was still and quiet, but contained colorful objects, plants, and playful cats, one of which napped next to us during this entire conversation. Agnès passed away in 2019, before this publication came to fruition. She left behind an astonishing body of work that consolidated her as one of the greatest directors in film history. I feel so lucky to have met her and captured her fantastic story. Farewell Agnès.

AGNÈS VARDA:
Have you seen the big orchid on the table?

HUGO HUERTA MARIN:
Yes.

AV: It is a beauty, no?

HHM: It certainly is … It's also a bit bizarre.

AV: Yes. It's bizarre and beautiful. I want to start our conversation like this: Hugo, we are together, sitting near a big, white orchid; it is bright, it is bizarre in its shape, and it is beautiful … as I believe every person in the

I HAVE ALWAYS BEEN SWIMMING IN BETWEEN FICTION AND REAL SITUATIONS THAT I WANT TO MAKE UNDERSTANDABLE, BEAUTIFUL, INTRIGUING TO THE WORLD, AND SHOW THAT ORDINARY PEOPLE ARE BEAUTIFUL

world to be. If you look at people, we all share the desire of finding beauty in one way or another, and in fact, you can find beauty in every single person. I have always been interested in ordinary people, the unknown and anonymous people I have met throughout my life. In your book, you are portraying well-known women, some famous, and some not so famous—like me (*laughs*). But it is a different concept than my documentaries, where I chose to meet, portray, and speak with, you know, workers, fishermen, peasants, people in the street, people in the fields. I have made some fiction films with actors—good actors—but very rarely, and it is not really my field.

HHM: Before we get into talking about films, can we start by talking about your life before becoming a movie director?

AV: Well, when I was a little girl, I was never much of a student. I didn't go to university, so I have no credentials in that sense. I learned everything by myself. I never passed any exams; instead, I would go and listen to interesting people talk, like the philosopher [Gaston] Bachelard, who made a big impression on me and got me thinking differently. I went to listen to surrealistic poets and painters talk, like the famous painter of my youth, who was the master, [Pablo] Picasso. These artists inspired me even more than films did because I wasn't exposed to cinema back then. In fact, people always ask me which films inspired me the most when I first started writing my first movie at twenty-five years old, but the reality is that I only knew four or five films. Back then, I knew very little about cinema and by chance, I needed very little money to make the movie. I managed to find the money, mostly from my mother and from my father, who had passed away and left me a small inheritance. The rest, well, everybody worked for free. It was possible to do that back in the fifties, you know, this was 1953 or '54. And the fishermen in the village were so happy to be a part of it, and were so understanding of the craziness of the project. I say craziness because to put two actors in the middle of real fishermen is a little bit crazy …

HHM: Fantastic.

AV: Yes. So, I have always been swimming in between fiction and real situations that I want to make understandable, beautiful, intriguing to the world, and show that ordinary people are beautiful. Just people talking to others about their love, work, and families.

HHM: How did you get the title of "grandmother of the French New Wave" at such a young age?

AV: Well, ever since I made my first film, *La Pointe courte*, in 1954, I have been called the grandmother of the New Wave. It's weird because when [Jean-Luc] Godard and [François] Truffaut … let's say "shocked" the world of cinema with Godard's *Breathless* and Truffaut's *400 Blows*, those movies became instantly important and successful, and some people at *Cahiers du Cinéma* also joined the club, which, ten years later, was named the "New Wave." So, I have always been put alongside the New Wave group, but the reality is that I was never part of it; nor was I a part of the *Cahiers du Cinéma* group, which was also very important because they wrote and discussed film all the time. They probably saw about a thousand films …

HHM: Did you belong to any specific club?

AV: No, nothing like that. I was already living in this house, and I didn't go to any clubs or meetings. I made my films in a very lonely way. Then I met Jacques Demy, and we lived here together. We had other friends, Chris Marker and Alain Resnais, who lived around here, and they were also free people, you know, they weren't part of any group either. We were called the Left Bank [Cinema Movement], but again, it was still one group of people labeling others.

HHM: Was filmmaking a utopian activity for you back then?

AV: Well, you are raising the question of utopia, but I don't see how utopia applies when making films. I just wanted cinema to be different and not only an adaptation of a book, a play, a real social drama, or a cultural phenomenon you might read about in the newspapers. I wanted cinema to come out of nowhere—from an unexpected place. I saw incredible changes in literature and in painting, but cinema was just repeating itself. Some artists were trying to be different in that way—in experimental ways. Filmmakers like [Jean] Epstein from Europe, or Maya Deren from the States.

HHM: Andy Warhol.

AV: Andy Warhol was a very important filmmaker because he made films that are difficult to watch because they are endless. Like the film showing the Empire State Building or the film about a man sleeping for five hours. But you know, they were statements. He dealt with time and duration, and he didn't care about pleasing people when making films.

HHM: There is also a lack of narrative in most of his films.

AV: Yes, and even though we might not want to watch his films every evening, he is still a very important artist because he deals with repetition and series, and since we are already in a world of series …

HHM: He was a pioneer above all things, I believe.

AV: A pioneer in many ways … When he took the cans of Campbell's soup and put them in piles in the way we see them at the supermarket, you know, he was taking and using the reality of the world to make art. To show that life is art and art is life.

HHM: Did he influence your work to some extent?

AV: He didn't because I started using reality earlier. But I respected him a lot, and I think he helped artists and filmmakers to get out of the norm and out of the chronology, psychology, and storyline of films.

HHM: Especially when the mind is always searching for a narrative …

AV: I think that's why he should be an important reference for all filmmakers.

HHM: How did you first meet?

AV: I met him with Jacques Demy. We went to his famous Factory in New York. The elevator opened, and you were immediately thrown into that world. His friends were always there, young men, singers, writers, you know, it was a world of art—a world of outsiders—and because he had seen my films and said he loved them, he invited us there. The reality is that I was trying to get his muse, Viva [Hoffman], to star in my '68 film called *Lions Love (… and Lies)*. So, I went to get Viva, and he became interested in the project. That is why he put an image of Viva and me on the first cover of *Interview* magazine.

HHM: And fifty years later, you are on that cover once again!

AV: It is fun because it means that even if we don't want to be part of history, we are.

HHM: Has making money changed the way you make films?

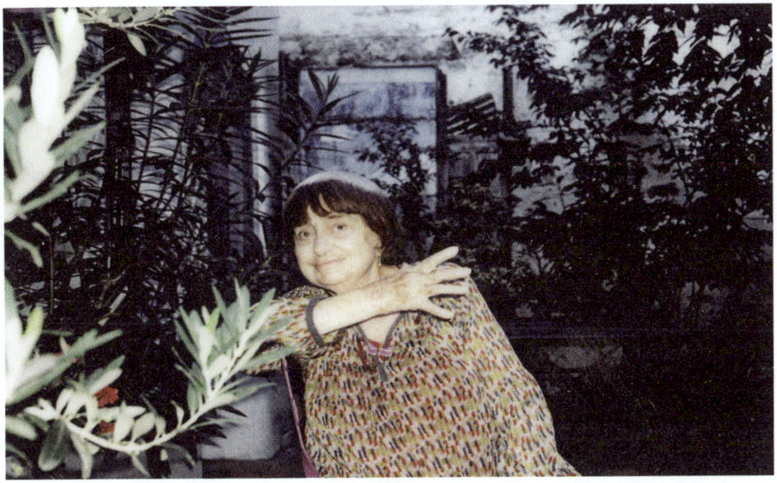

AV: My films never made money. Maybe one, maybe *Vagabond* made some, but I've only ever earned a minimal amount from each film. I'm seen mainly as an artist and photographer, and over time, I've been accepted as a filmmaker. I'd say I've even been appreciated and loved as an artistic filmmaker for not telling stories but experimenting with the different ways of structuring films. I'd use the tools, like close-ups, master shots, medium shots, low angles, and editing, my way. I'd do what I call *cinécriture*, which means cine writing, to try to find a style where I could capture the essence of people, not to please them, but for them to enter the film. As you know, the last film—a documentary—I made with the artist JR captured the essence of people. We had the pleasure of making a sociological work about unknown people in the countryside of France: peasants working in factories, people living in small villages, people making cottage cheese—good cheese—and had them talk about, you know, goats and about life. We had the pleasure of being free to question the world we live in with empathy, film the people, and bring our experience and friendship to the screen. What I would always do in my movies is work on one subject, but I would allow myself to go here and there … Sort of driving the film with my right hand, and with my left hand, taking pictures and making scenes that have nothing to do with that subject.

HHM: What role do accidents or chance play in your filmmaking?

AV: Well, a big one. I always give space to the unexpected. And that is why I enjoy being a filmmaker.

HHM: How do you choose the subjects of your films?

AV: My films are about people and history; they are a glimpse into people's problems and lives. People making little money, or sometimes no money at all. You know, when I filmed the shopkeepers in my street or the workers in a factory, I realized that these people wanted to express themselves and that they loved to be filmed. They loved it because it was a simple conversation rather than a TV show or a Q&A session. Instead, it was "Let's be together for a while." I consider what you are doing with this book to be the same. I'm not interested in giving you big answers about the "New Wave." That's a part of the history of cinema you can find in books and magazines. I'm interested in talking to other artists and other human beings. That's why I was happy to live with another artist and filmmaker, Jacques Demy. He made films differently from the others. Maybe you have seen *The Young Girls of Rochefort*, or *Donkey Skin*, or *The Umbrellas of Cherbourg*?

HHM: Catherine Deneuve's breakthrough movie.

AV: Yes. He made films outside of the mainstream, on the other side of the cinema that was making money. We never made blockbusters or films that gave us fame … But we managed to be a part of that fame, and of that history. Then, later in life, I took a different position.

HHM: A more artistic one. When did you decide to start making visual art?

I AM PROUD TO BE PART OF MOMA'S "MODERN WOMEN" CATALOGUE, BUT HONESTLY, I'D RATHER BE IN THE GENERAL CATALOGUE. WHY DO WE HAVE TO PLAY ONE GAME FOR MEN AND ANOTHER FOR WOMEN?

AV: That's right. After the 2000s, I started working as a visual artist. I was trying to change the relationship of the viewer and the artist. Instead of making films that could be seen on the big screen, I started to make films as installations. I made an installation about widows from the island of Noirmoutier in France, called *Les Veuves de Noirmoutier*, which included fourteen videos, but people would only hear one widow speaking. It was a juxtaposition of private and public, black-and-white and color, video and cinema, and trying to join them. I'm always trying to work with the tools that I have so that I can show a handful of emotions to the audience. Cinema and video are beautiful tools of communication, beautiful tools for understanding the world—not changing the world—but perhaps changing the point of view of the people watching films, watching art. As artists, we have to work from our point of view. What can we add to the realism of things? Reality is beautiful and ugly, you know? What we see every day in the news, in television, in advertisements; there are magazines that are full of ads selling cosmetics and clothes. Where is the content? Where are the real people? As artists, we have to bring this content and add something else to the world. So, I accepted this interview because it is an interesting project, and I like to sit with people I respect and be placed with a group of artists I love.

HHM: Which other female filmmakers do you feel connected to?

AV: Jane Campion is incredibly good ... I am old, I have holes in my memory (*laughs*). Oh, Chantal Akerman—an experimental and strong filmmaker.

HHM: In your opinion, how have things changed for women in the film industry over the last decades?

AV: Not much. You know, I don't mind being placed among female artists, and I am proud to be part of MoMA's *Modern Women* catalogue, but honestly, I'd rather be in the general catalogue. Why do we have to play one game for men and another for women? Society separates women from men all the time, and we have to fight to get the same salary for doing the same job. And in the film industry, why are there so few famous female directors?

HHM: Have you read Linda Nochlin´s essay "Why Have There Been No Great Women Artists?"

AV: What does it say?

HHM: Nochlin did not blame the capacities or lack of "greatness" of women artists, but the nature of social institutions.

AV: There are great women artists—I mean, Louise Bourgeois—and I can name many more, but I understand the point. There is a new Italian director called Alice Rohrwacher—she is original—and in America, they have a blockbuster film director, Kathryn Bigelow. There are also some very interesting artists who are not part of the mainstream. I don't want to repeat myself, but I think your book will help keep women artists on the map.

HHM: Thank you. I hope so too … Do you consider yourself a political artist?

AV: They called me a political filmmaker because I dealt with politics many times, mostly when I made the documentary *Black Panthers*. I was there during the Black Panthers' demonstrations, and I was there when they were protesting while Huey Newton was in jail. I also went to Cuba in '62. In a way, that was political because people didn't want to know what was happening in Cuba back then. I did a project in China in 1957, when the United Nations did not even recognize China. Can you believe that? They were giving recognition to Taiwan, but not the enormous world of China. I've also been involved in women's rights: how women are objectified, their salaries, and how they are treated overall. I have been a feminist all my life, and have been fighting for women's rights. You know, there was a march about climate change in Paris yesterday that my daughter [Rosalie Varda] went to. I remember going to all the demonstrations with her when she was young but now, she can't take her old mother into the streets for three hours. I simply can't do it. Perhaps later in my life (*laughs*).

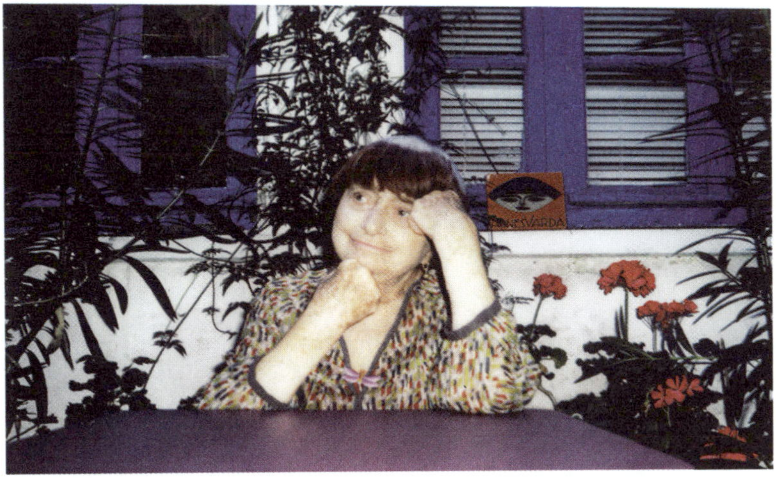

HHM: (*laughs*) Another political reference could be your film *The Gleaners and I*.

AV: Yes, and speaking of *The Gleaners*, there is something I use as a joke sometimes: potatoes are usually oval or round, but heart-shaped potatoes are special, and the peasants didn't want to sell them because they thought they were monstrous. It's interesting because I relate this to our society, where people who are considered to be out of the norm are treated differently and rejected. So, you know, everything is political: men, women, and even vegetables.

HHM: What is your concept of beauty?

AV: Everyday life is beautiful. Here is some advice I always like to give: Sit still in a café and look—look at the people and look at what is happening in front of you. If you have a frame, don't move from that frame. See what comes in and comes out. Learn from what comes into that frame like a cameraman or filmmaker. You will discover so much beauty from life just by sitting still in front of a frame.

HHM: What are your thoughts on the rise of the artist as a celebrity?

AV: It is subtle because when you are an artist, you want to be seen and known; you don't make art to put it in a drawer. It's the same for filmmakers, you know? We want to be known and appreciated. At some point, appreciation becomes important, so when more people know you, you become famous. It's normal that it ends in this way. Now, you can be known on different levels and for different reasons—because you make a lot of money, because you won a tennis competition, or because you are a decent artist—and that recognition is necessary. It feels good to be known on that level.

HHM: What inspires you the most?

AV: Sometimes reality, sometimes the work of other artists or filmmakers, and sometimes the pure surprise of inspiration. Unexpected thoughts inspire me.

HHM: What do you think about the big festivals like Cannes?

AV: We need festivals because they are the only places where films that are not commercial can be seen. So, we need to go to festivals to be noticed. But what comes with them? Costumes, celebrities, red carpets, prizes, and interviews. It's all part of the game. For cinema, prizes and awards help us survive. Festivals are windows for us.

HHM: What is the most honest thing you can say about yourself?

AV: Even though I am very old now, I remain curious, which is a privilege.

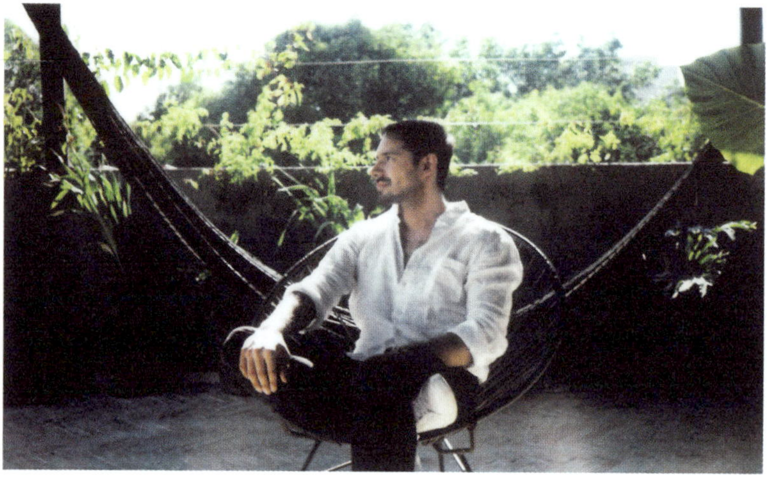

ABOUT THE AUTHOR

Hugo Huerta Marin is a Mexican-born multi-disciplinary artist and graphic designer whose work centers on gender and cultural identity. Since moving to New York in 2012, he has collaborated with cultural institutions in the United States and Mexico, including the Solomon R. Guggenheim Museum. In 2014, he joined the studio of the performance artist Marina Abramović as an art director, with whom he has collaborated internationally for venues across the globe including: the Royal Danish Library, Copenhagen; Sesc Pompeia, São Paulo; Moderna Museet, Stockholm; CAC Malaga, Malaga; The Art of Elysium, Los Angeles; Foundation Beyeler, Basel; and the Royal Academy of Arts, London. Hugo's solo exhibitions have been featured at The Hole Gallery in New York, Never Apart Gallery in Montreal and Casa Wabi and MUAC museum in Mexico City. He was also part of the 2019 Casa Nano art residency in Tokyo.

ACKNOWLEDGMENTS

I would like to thank everyone who made this book possible. Thanks to my editor Anna Godfrey for her extraordinary efforts and dedicated editing work. Genius! Thanks to Prestel and Holly La Due for bravery and believing in this project.

Thanks to my copy-editors Tereza Racekova and Martha Jay for the beauty of words. Thanks to Sonya Dyakova and her team for total graphic devotion. Perfection! I thank my agent Jon Michael Darga and Aevitas for careful and endless support throughout this journey.

A very special thanks to my family and friends for unconditional love and support.

Most of all I would like to thank the legendary artists who made this publication come to fruition. Despite being some of the greatest and most influential artists of our times, they agreed to open their homes, souls, and hearts when I asked them to. Thank you.

Special thanks to:
Giuliano Argenziano, Verónique Auriol, Tristan Breed, Nathalie Canguilhem, Angela Conant, Ciné Tamaris, Ian Costello, Christa Dallas, Todd Eckert, Sydney Fishman, Fondazione Prada, Gladstone Gallery, Tara Goldsmid, Anne Hermeline, Armando Huerta Sanchez, Armando Huerta Marin, Gabriela Huerta, Jo, Cathy Koutsavlis, Marc Kroop, Joaquim Lino, Thomas Manzi, Alicia Marin, Sofia Menasse, Connor Monahan, Diego Marroquín, Chiara Michieletto, Graehme Morphy, Emilia Muciño, Paola Origel, Suzannah Pettigrew, Tereza Racekova, Hector Robles, Julian Rosefeldt, Michael Stirton, Giulia Theodoli, Rosalie Varda, Verde Visconti, Harry Weller, and Billy Zhao.

Penguin Random House Verlagsgruppe GmbH
Neumarkter Str. 28, 81673 Munich

First published 2021

A CIP catalogue record for this book is available from the British Library.

Library of Congress Control Number: 2021017658

Editorial direction: Anna Godfrey
Copyediting: Martha Jay
Design: Atelier Dyakova
Production: Friederike Schirge
Separations: Reproline Mediateam, Munich
Printing and binding: DZS Grafik, d.o.o., Ljubljana
Paper: Amber Graphic
Printed in Slovenia

MIX
Paper from responsible sources
FSC® C106600

Verlagsgruppe Random House FSC® N001967
ISBN 978-3-7913-8748-2
www.prestel.com